Supporting Transfer Student Success

The Essential Role of College and University Libraries

Peggy L. Nuhn and Karen F. Kaufmann

LIBRARIES UNLIMITED®

An Imprint of ABC-CLIO, LLC

Santa Barbara, California • Denver, Colorado

Library of Congress Cataloging-in-Publication Data

Names: Nuhn, Peggy L., author. | Kaufmann, Karen F., author.
Title: Supporting transfer student success : the essential role of college and university libraries / Peggy L. Nuhn and Karen F. Kaufmann.
Description: Santa Barbara, California : Libraries Unlimited, [2021] | Includes bibliographical references and index.
Identifiers: LCCN 2020016791 (print) | LCCN 2020016792 (ebook) | ISBN 9781440873164 (paperback ; acid-free paper) | ISBN 9781440873171 (ebook)
Subjects: LCSH: Academic libraries—United States. | College students—United States—Transfer. | Libraries and students—United States. | Libraries and colleges—United States. | Information literacy—Study and teaching (Higher)—United States.
Classification: LCC Z675.U5 N84 2021 (print) | LCC Z675.U5 (ebook) | DDC 027.7—dc23
LC record available at https://lccn.loc.gov/2020016791
LC ebook record available at https://lccn.loc.gov/2020016792

ISBN: 978-1-4408-7316-4 (paperback)
      978-1-4408-7317-1 (ebook)

25 24 23 22 21   1 2 3 4 5

This book is also available as an eBook.

Libraries Unlimited
An Imprint of ABC-CLIO, LLC

ABC-CLIO, LLC
147 Castilian Drive
Santa Barbara, California 93117
www.abc-clio.com

This book is printed on acid-free paper ∞

Manufactured in the United States of America

Supporting Transfer Student Success

All of us are on a pathway of some sort as we wind our way through life. Some days, the path beckons bright with promise; other days, it twists, turns, and has potholes threatening to throw things badly out of alignment. This is true of the transfer student journey, and in the grand scheme of things, it is also true for each of us. In my personal and ongoing journey, I will be forever grateful to my mother, the most self-sacrificing person I will ever know, for a lifetime of encouragement and support of my goals in practical and meaningful ways, although she once mused, "You know, Peggy, no little girl ever says that when she grows up she wants to be a *librarian*." Thank you, Mom; **we** did this. Deep appreciation also goes to my husband for his unfailing love and support and to my son, my most favorite college student and millennial, for keeping me current, amused, and almost cool.

Having a good companion on a road trip is also a bonus. Many thanks to coauthor and friend Karen F. Kaufmann for sharing this journey.

—P.L.N.

Meandering is one of my favorite things to do. Writing a book is an experience of meandering with words and thoughts; with ideas and revisions; and conversations with my coauthor, colleague, and friend, Peggy Nuhn. It's altogether an experience that is both challenging and wonderful as an academic and a writer. I am grateful for the opportunity to share the words penned to the pages of this book and acknowledge that this is a collaborative work, as a coauthor working together with our publisher and supported by colleagues and family. I am truly blessed.

—K.F.K.

Contents

Foreword   ix

Introduction   xiii

Chapter 1   Transfer Students: Trends, Pathways, and
                Implications for Libraries   1

Chapter 2   Transfer Structures: Implications for Students   15

Chapter 3   Transfer Students: Challenges and Opportunities
                for Librarians   27

Chapter 4   Information Literacy Designed to Support Transfer
                Student Success   41

Chapter 5   Connecting the Library to Transfer Students   63

Chapter 6   Communication and Collaboration between
                College and University Librarians   91

Chapter 7   Connecting the Library to Support Virtual
                Transfer Students   105

Chapter 8   Niche Academic Library Initiatives That Support
                Transfer Student Success   121

Chapter 9   Textbook Affordability Initiatives That Support
                Transfer Student Success   131

Chapter 10 Holistically Supporting Transfer Student Success:
                The Essential Role of Libraries   151

Index   177

Foreword

As forward-thinking librarians, we care about finding the most effective and efficient ways to serve all our users. We feel compelled by marketing dogma to customize services based on the unique needs of each special audience whether it be gifted, at-risk, upper division, first-year, resident, transient, transfer, or any other category. This work by Nuhn and Kaufmann emerges from dedicated librarians who had a history of focusing on transfer student needs before transfer was trending.

These two librarians have a credible foundation for their experience, given that transfer students made up 51 percent of the 58,903 undergraduates enrolled at the University of Central Florida (UCF) in the fall 2018 semester.[1] This high percentage is a planned result of DirectConnect™ to UCF, a program that guarantees admission to eligible partner-college students. The university's official partners include six state colleges ranging geographically from Ocala to Palm Bay. Dr. Karen Kaufmann is a research and instruction librarian at Seminole State College of Florida (SSC), one of UCF's geographically closest DirectConnect partners. Peggy Nuhn is the UCF Connect Librarian resident on the SSC partner campus. Together, they investigate and summarize for readers their findings on the myriad transfer students' enrollment paths, needs, challenges, and stressors as well as implications and practical initiatives for academic libraries.

In addition to DirectConnect, UCF's Foundations of Excellence Transfer Initiative is another project designed to enhance transfer student success. The two-year self-study process, guided by the John N. Gardner Institute for Excellence in Undergraduate Education, helped raise awareness of transfer student issues. The study has evolved into an ongoing partnership called Transfer Alliance, which focuses on academic success, retention, and graduation. Because of these two programs, UCF received the 2018 Institutional Effectiveness Award for Students in Transition from the National Resource Center for the First Year Experience and Students in Transition.

One of Peggy Nuhn's first group projects at UCF was involvement in updating an online library orientation for students transferring from a Direct-Connect college to upper-division courses at UCF. Although the librarians were not in total control of format and content, supportive colleagues worked together to transform the simple PowerPoint orientation into a Canvas-based research-readiness quiz. The quiz is intended to reveal areas where students need help, and it does that well. Unfortunately, limited staffing only allows the quiz to serve as an introduction and invitation for students to engage with the library. Sufficient person-hours are just not available to address every individual student challenge. Undaunted by the limitations of this quiz, Peggy and colleague Min Tong did extensive literature reviews and surveys on how students actually do conduct research. Peggy's participation in these projects; her daily involvement with soon-to-transfer college students; and her desire to formalize more in-depth, online library instruction made her a perfect candidate to represent the libraries in the Foundations of Excellence Transfer Initiative.

On another front, Peggy's desire for a challenging research project that would delve into students' skills and gaps was about to be satisfied. The director of the library at Seminole State College asked Karen and Peggy to participate in *The Assessment Workshop Series* sponsored by the Northeast Florida Library and Information Network (NEFLIN). The nationally recognized faculty included Kristine Brancolini, Megan Oakleaf, Martha Kyrilidou, and Amanda Albert. In several sessions between November 2017 and June 2018, the two partner librarians, guided by experts, explored a collaborative research project on the alignment of information literacy instruction between SSC and UCF. They initially wanted to compare what is taught at the college and university in the first two years. Their research question grew, of course, to include a survey of all DirectConnect partners. The survey data analyzed in the assessment workshops informs the discussion in the following chapters. As Nuhn and Kaufmann both teach information literacy, this research was particularly meaningful, and Kaufmann's recent completion of a doctoral program investigating the relevance of information literacy nicely complemented their work.

In this endeavor of researching transfer students' needs, the authors' underlying driver is finding links to new roles for libraries. Is there an unmet need? Is there something we're not doing that we might add to our roster of services? What is the illusive essential role? This book explores many practical, theoretical, and inspirational answers to these questions through an impressively comprehensive literature review. I have no doubt readers will appreciate being so informed. Not intending to tip the authors' hands or reveal their findings prematurely, I do hope readers will enjoy, as much as I did, exploring and learning about transfer students' challenges, the uniqueness of various populations, the difference between andragogy and pedagogy, and the "no-excuses support" of one model institution.

In the course of fact-checking my own comments on UCF transfer student services, I came across a gallery of student-success graphics, mostly in the way of graduation celebrations. One black and gold UCF mortarboard was emblazoned with this quote, "The best things come to those who don't give up." No observation could be more appropriate for librarians like these authors and you readers who are pursuing ever-emerging, ever-enhanced student services. Thank you for your efforts.

Cynthia M. Kisby, Personnel Librarian
Former Head, UCF Connect Libraries
University of Central Florida

Note

1. University of Central Florida, Institutional Knowledge Management, accessed July 31, 2019, https://ikm.ucf.edu/facts-and-reports/interactive-facts/enrollment-2/.

Introduction

Recently, my colleague and coauthor, Karen Kaufmann, and I attended a conference on accelerating the academic success of transfer students, at which we were invited to provide a poster presentation. The conference had an impressive turnout, and speakers from several major institutions with large transfer student populations spoke during the program. Lively discussions on transfer student success, "transfer shock," and ways that student affairs professionals could better support transfer student success through a common course numbering system as well as waiving, or at least reducing, application fees ensued. The reality that transfer students comprise at least half (or more) of the student body at many institutions was expounded upon by representatives from some of the very institutions thus impacted. Articulation agreements, which simplify transfer from two-year colleges to state universities were discussed, and a panel of transfer students shared their respective experiences of the transfer process, which was, for us, the most enlightening portion of the day.

Interestingly, there was no mention of the role of libraries and librarians in supporting transfer student success. Our poster, which depicted the results from our original research on alignment and nonalignment in information literacy instruction between a large university and the university's feeder colleges, was the sole recognition of the role of academic libraries in transfer student success that day. There was nothing in the conference program regarding the significance of student information literacy in supporting the academic success of transfer students in *any* discipline or any mention of how libraries and librarians could work collaboratively to proactively support transfer student success. That struck us as such an unfortunate missed opportunity. The librarian colleagues who had attended this conference at our suggestion shared our disappointment at the absence of any discussion on the role of the academic library in transfer student success. After all, during the fall 2017 semester, the number of college and university transfer students numbered 1,431,269 nationally based on reports from 3,668 institutions of higher education (U.S. Department of Education, Higher Education Statistics).

Clearly, this is a significant and growing population. Karen and I knew from our literature reviews that librarians are beginning to share concerns about this unique population as well as undertake initiatives at some academic libraries to support the growing transfer student population in meaningful and creative ways. We also knew from our original research that coordination of instructional content on librarian-led information literacy between at least one major university (my employer) and its six partner colleges (one of which is Karen's employer) had not happened—and until our research—had never been a topic of significant discussion. The fact that our respective institutions are in Florida, the state that established the first legislatively mandated articulation policy in the United States, also factored into our interest and personal experience. State articulation policies facilitate transfer by providing a pathway for college students with a two-year Associate in Arts (AA) degree to earn a baccalaureate degree at a state university without imposing additional course requirements, thereby enabling AA-degreed students to transfer to the university as rising juniors. An enhanced articulation agreement, DirectConnect to UCF, is the foundation for the collaborative work between Karen and myself.

Thus, the focus of this book began to take shape with a renewed sense of purpose and urgency. How can libraries and librarians proactively reach students who will come to our campus after having attended another institution or will leave to complete their educational goals elsewhere? How do we reach out to them, and how do their needs differ from First Year Experience (FYE) or First Time in College (FTIC) or other student populations? How do we support transfer students academically and holistically, and how do we build librarian partnerships between our institutions, thereby enabling all of us to do more in a scalable, sustainable way? We hope to answer these questions and provide the inspiration and encouragement needed to develop new initiatives—whether on textbook affordability, in supporting growing numbers of online students, or in developing transfer-specific outreach—and to make these initiatives feasible and suited to *your* institution, *your* staffing, and *your* budget.

Make no mistake: transfer student success is a major topic in higher education. At the time of writing, a simple search of the Education Resources Information Center (ERIC) database (search terms: transfer students AND higher education OR college OR university) and limited to articles published between 2009 and 2019 yielded *nearly 4,000 articles* on some aspect of transfer student success. This included the costs associated with barriers to seamless transfer, policies, persistence, graduation rates, and much more. We must ensure that library services and librarian-led information literacy instruction are part of the scholarly conversation of transfer student success, as well as part of the solution, because supporting transfer student success isn't just the right thing to do: it's essential. Increasingly, institutional funding is performance based and relies on student metrics, some of which are affected by retention and graduation rates and may include graduation rates for our transfer student population.

Our role as academic librarians allows us a way to support institutional objectives related to performance funding, because information literacy provides a single set of multidisciplinary learning objectives that can prepare students for college success and timely graduation. For clarification, to be compliant with the language of the *ACRL Framework for Information Literacy for Higher Education*, we have replaced references to "library instruction" with "information literacy instruction." Use whichever term is preferred at your institution.

Our intent is for this book to be relatable to all instruction librarians, their administrators, and other campus decision-makers and to provide "real world" examples of what our colleagues are doing on campuses large and small, and why it's increasingly important for librarians to play a major role in supporting transfer student success. In some ways, perhaps this book is also a call to action. Because transfer students are not just coming to your campus, and to ours—they are already here—and they have unique needs, which we must understand in order to support their academic success, as well as the priorities of our respective institutions.

Reference

U.S. Department of Education, National Center for Education Statistics, Integrated Postsecondary Education Data System (IPEDS). Accessed March 31, 2019. https://nces.ed.gov/ipeds/trendgenerator/app/answer/2/4.

CHAPTER 1

Transfer Students: Trends, Pathways, and Implications for Libraries

It isn't enough to pick a path—you must go down it. By doing so, you see things you couldn't possibly see when you started out; you may not like what you see, some of it may be confusing, but at least you will have, as we like to say, "explored the neighborhood." The key point here is that even if you decide you're in the wrong place, there is still time to head toward the right place.

—Ed Catmull, computer scientist and
confounder of Pixar Animation Studios (2014)

The growing numbers of transfer students making up the student body at institutions of higher education have been on the radar of student affairs professionals for some time now. To that end, several national organizations serve to support, track, research, and share data relating to transfer students in higher education. The National Institute for the Study of Transfer Students (https://nists.org) was founded in 2001 to "improve the lives of transfer students" and "support professionals who directly serve transfer students, as well as those who create transfer policy and conduct transfer-related research" (https://nists.org). In addition, the National Student Clearinghouse Research Center (https://nscreasearchcenter.org) focuses on student educational pathways, including specific research on transfer student trends.

Admittedly, the role of librarians or library administrators in the transfer student experience, in terms of the functionality of the transfer process, or lack thereof, is outside our immediate scope. However, thanks to the concerted efforts of these organizations and other researchers, there is highly valuable information on changing patterns among our student populations, which should inform our information literacy instruction and library services. We can also learn how the transfer process contributes to student stress, which will inform us as we consider how transfer friendly our present library services, policies, or programs are, in addition to providing an impetus for developing new ones.

The following summarizes some of the stressors related to transfer, most of which connect to student finances at some point in the transfer experience.

- **Application fees** are generally modest; however, students may be paying to apply to more than one institution at a time or may transfer more than once, so these fees can add up.

- **Nonrefundable enrollment or tuition deposits** are frequently required to reserve the student's space in the incoming class; however, meeting the deposit deadline may mean the student is making that significant deposit before having complete information on how their existing credits will transfer (Ott and Cooper 2013).

- Probable **increases in tuition** from what the student is accustomed to, particularly because the per-credit-hour cost at a university may easily be double the per-credit-hour rate at community colleges.

- In the absence of **clear articulation agreements** (discussed in depth in chapter 2), there may be challenges regarding how **earned credits** will transfer, which may also affect student graduation rates

- Regardless of whether they are seeking on- or off-campus housing, transfer students report the experience of securing **housing** as "overwhelming and stress inducing" (Utter and DeAngelo 2015).

- There may be challenges on whether previously earned **credits will count toward requirements for the student's major** course of study at their new institution.

- **"Satisfactory Academic Progress,"** as defined by the U.S. Department of Education, requires a policy in place at each institution of higher education to ensure that students receiving federal financial aid meet minimum standards of progression throughout their academic program and must have both quantitative (credit hours earned) and qualitative (grade-point average) measures. The Federal Student Aid website advises students to verify the specifics of federal aid eligibility requirements of their particular institution, as follows: "Your school's policy will tell you:

- ○ what grade-point average (or equivalent standard) you need to maintain;
- ○ how quickly you need to be moving toward graduation (for instance, how many credits you should have successfully completed by the end of each year);
- ○ how an incomplete class, withdrawal, repeated class, change of major, or transfer of credits from another school affects your satisfactory academic progress;
- ○ how often your school will evaluate your progress;
- ○ what will happen if you fail to make satisfactory academic progress when your school evaluates you;
- ○ whether you are allowed to appeal your school's decision that you haven't made satisfactory
- ○ academic progress (reasons for appeal usually include the death of a member of your family, your illness or injury, or other special circumstances); and
- ○ how you can regain eligibility for federal student aid." (U.S. Department of Education 2019)

While a Satisfactory Academic Progress policy applies to all students, as noted in the U.S. Department of Education (2019) list, transfer students, in particular, may find that hours earned but not accepted upon transfer, or not accepted toward their major, could extend their time in school, thereby negatively affecting their continued student financial aid eligibility.

From reviewing these stressors, we can easily envision students who have made the hopeful choice to attend our institution without full knowledge of how their credits will be applied—therefore, without full knowledge of the cost of attending, or whether their federal financial aid will see them through to graduation. They may be scrambling for on-campus or near-to-campus housing; be unfamiliar with the area; and not know anyone on campus who can commiserate or, better yet, provide helpful suggestions. If they come to the library to use a computer and our first words are "You'll need to add money to your student ID in order to print," is it likely they will view us as an ally in meeting their educational goals, or as just another barrier?

Of course, for librarians, the very thought of being perceived as a barrier to students is abhorrent; however, it is essential to ask ourselves if we are addressing the needs of this student population. As a whole, academic libraries and librarians have been slow to adapt services and instruction to support transfer student success. Granted, navigating the transfer process has challenges; however, does this necessarily mean that the research and information needs of transfer students are different from those of any other student? Should we not expect a transfer student to be as prepared for academic research as a native student of the same class standing? To answer these questions, let us first explore the various transfer pathways.

Transfer Student Pathways and Descriptions

- Dual enrollment (also known as dual credit or concurrent enrollment)
- Vertical transfer
- Lateral transfer (also known as parallel or horizontal transfer)
- Reverse transfer
- Swirling transfer
- Double-dipping transfer
- Transient transfer

Dual Enrollment Transfer Students

Dual enrollment (also known as dual credit or concurrent enrollment) students are primarily high school students (in some cases, they may be middle-school-aged) simultaneously attending a secondary school (or being homeschooled) as well as attending college, with the intent of transferring those hours toward either an associate or a baccalaureate degree. They may be as young as 14 or 15 years of age and may have limited—if any—experience with library databases or other library resources. Either college instructors or high school teachers may teach classes for dual enrolled students, and classes may be offered online, at high schools, or at local college campuses. Specifics vary from state to state, but tuition and fees may be waived or reduced for dual-enrolled students. This pathway, once limited to academically advanced high school students, is now seen as a fast track for students to reduce the time to a degree and save money but may not be adequately preparing them. As one author opined, "Dual enrollment programs are not making students better prepared for the challenges of college; rather, these programs demand colleges and universities meet dual enrolled high school students at their current academic and maturity levels" (Thomson 2017).

Vertical Transfer Students

Vertical transfer students are primarily what we think of as the "traditional" community college-to-university students: the students who transfer to a university with an AA degree in hand; however, vertical transfers may also include students who transfer to a four-year institution *without* first having earned a two-year degree.

Given some of the potential demographic realities for community college students, finances may be a greater concern for vertical transfers. From our

Table 1.1   Student Enrollment Status and Employment

Student Enrollment Status	Employed Full Time	Employed Part Time
Full-time student	21%	41%
Part-time student	38%	34%

Source: American Association of Community Colleges. 2020, "Fast Facts." https://www.aacc.nche.edu/wp-content/uploads/2020/03/AACC_Fast_Facts_2020_Final.pdf

own, admittedly informal, research (asking for a simple show of hands during information literacy instruction classes over a span of multiple semesters), we learned that two-year college students are extremely likely to combine attending classes with outside employment. Frequently, these students hold down full-time jobs, and formal research supports our anecdotal findings.

According to Boone (2017), one of the greatest barriers to success among community college students is managing work-school balance. He referenced 2014 data compiled by the American Association of Community Colleges showing that **22 percent of students attending college full time worked full time**, and **40 percent of those students worked part time**. Of those attending college part time, 73 percent worked full or part time, which represents a significant challenge and barrier to completion. A review of 2015–2016 data on the American Association of Community Colleges website (https://aacc.nche.edu) shows little change in these figures (see table 1.1). Despite how important this source of income may be, the students' employment may or may not be sustainable after vertical transfer, whether due to simple logistics or the demands of more rigorous upper-division coursework.

The Aspen Institute and the Community College Research Center reported that students who enter a four-year institution through community colleges are much more likely than those who start at a four-year institution to be low-income or be the first in their family to attend college (Wyner et al. 2016). It is therefore reasonable to assume that financial pressures, as well as lack of familial understanding and informed support of the rigors of obtaining a baccalaureate degree, will carry forward as continuing stressors for many vertical transfer students.

Lateral Transfer Students

Lateral transfer students fall into two groups:

- Students who transfer from one two-year institution to another two-year institution.

- Students who transfer from one four-year institution to another four-year institution.

Bahr (2012) suggested that lateral transfer might be a strategic move on the part of students, possibly aligning with a period of exploration that declines when the student is close to earning the 60 credit hours typically required for an associate degree; however, considering this a "strategic" move does not mean this approach is efficient or effective.

Reverse Transfer Students

Reverse transfer students originally meant those students who *physically* transferred from a four-year college or university to a two-year college before obtaining a degree from the four-year institution. Recently, the concept of reverse transfer has evolved to include students who transfer *university-earned credits* from a four-year institution back to their prior two-year institution *and then retroactively receive an AA degree*. In fact, some community colleges are actively developing partnerships with universities to create formal programs for reverse transfer (Friedel and Wilson 2015).

The "Credit When It's Due" (CWID) initiative was launched in 2012 by the Funders Collaborative for CWID, comprising the Lumina Foundation, the Kresge Foundation, the Bill & Melinda Gates Foundation, USA Funds, the Helios Education Foundation, and Greater Texas Foundation. The purpose of CWID is to "significantly expand programs that award associate degrees to transfer students when the student completes the requirements for the associate degree while pursuing a bachelor's degree" (McCambly and Bragg 2016).

Swirling Transfer Students

The term "swirling" was first used by Alfredo de los Santos and Irene Wright (1990) in their research to describe the various paths taken by Maricopa Community Colleges to Arizona State University. It is defined as back-and-forth enrollment between two or more institutions. Twenty years later additional research by de los Santos and Sutton (2012) reported a continuation of the swirling path, noting, "It is not uncommon for students to enroll concurrently in both institutions or return to a community college for coursework after enrollment in a university" (p. 970). de los Santos and Sutton provided implications for swirling students, which include the need for institutions to focus intentionally on the needs of the students rather than the needs of the institution and advocated for developing a general education core that met the general education requirements of all public institutions in the state and that was automatically transferable (de los Santos and Sutton 2012, 980).

Double-Dipping Transfer Students

Double-dipping transfer students are similar to swirling students but generally defined as students concurrently attending two or more institutions (McCormick 2003). The primary takeaway here is, as the description implies, these students are not following a linear pattern.

Transient Transfer Students

Transient transfer students attend another institution with the intent of transferring those credits back to their home institution. One example would be that of a university student who returns home for the summer and enrolls in one or more summer classes at their hometown community college with the intent of transferring those credits back to their university.

Multiple Pathways: One Goal

It is fair to surmise that on any given campus at any given time there is a good-sized representation of transfer students, whether they arrived vertically, laterally, in reverse, swirling, or by way of their middle or high school. Their individual experiences will be as varied as their reasons for transferring and the pathways they selected for their educational journey.

The College Board Advocacy and Policy Center's 80-page report "The Promise of the Transfer Pathway: Opportunity and Challenge for Community College Students Seeking the Baccalaureate Degree" (Handel and Williams 2012) acknowledges that most students desirous of earning a baccalaureate degree may attend several community colleges before they transfer. The report also states that most community college students enroll part time and may "stop in" and "stop out," thereby completing only one or two courses in an academic year. Additionally, the authors (Handel and Williams 2012) note that despite the fact that the majority of students are not "traditional" vertical transfers, the vertical pathway represents the historical relationship between community colleges and four-year institutions, thereby remaining the most efficient, albeit the most rigorous, route to a baccalaureate degree for community college students (18). They (Handel and Williams 2012) therefore posit that efficiencies achieved in the vertical pathway will also aid students following other routes to obtaining their baccalaureate degree (Handel and Williams 2012, 18). (The complete 80-page report is referenced here and may be accessed through the Jack Kent Cooke Foundation website and through the ERIC database. There is also a 24-page summary report.)

For the purposes of this book, the vertical transfer pathway will be our primary example of transfer, with the understanding that a straight linear pathway is not taken by the majority of students. As noted earlier in this chapter, the vertical transfer pathway represents an important historical relationship between colleges and universities, and building upon those relationships is essential to communication, to building collaboration, and ultimately, to supporting the academic success of this student population.

Given these various and often nonlinear pathways, it is realistic to assume that some students may never have had the opportunity to attend an information literacy class before arriving and, up until their transfer, may even have obtained much of their research information solely from the internet. Although these students may now have access to more extensive and specialized library resources, they may be completely unaware of the existence or depth of these resources, let alone how to use them effectively. A recent case study noted that even when transfer students do receive library instruction at their former institutions, they may have trouble applying those skills at their new institution, especially for upper-level research assignments, and at present, many academic libraries do not offer specific instruction for transfer students (Roberts, Welsh, and Dudek 2019).

Implications for Library Services

Understanding that all student experiences are unique, we can nevertheless draw some reasonably solid conclusions about the transfer student population at any college or university, with implications for library services:

- Transfer students who came via the dual enrollment pathway may have no, or underdeveloped, information literacy skills and abilities.
- Transfer students may be cash-strapped and look to the library for assistance with textbook access.
- Transfer students may be combining employment with school or family commitments and may benefit from library services during extended evening or weekend operating hours.
- Transfer students—particularly community college transfers—may be the first member of their family to attend college based on statistical data, thereby lacking practical informed familial support of the academic rigors involved.
- Transfer students may initially lack a social support network on campus, a potential opportunity for libraries.
- Transfer students may feel like an outsider on their new campus, another potential opportunity for libraries.
- Transfer students, particularly community college to university transfers, may be unaware of the depth of library assistance available at a four-year institution, including major-specific resources, subject librarians, and access

to web-based bibliography management software, since the structure, support, and resources of a university library generally differ significantly from a college library.

- Transfer students who have had some information literacy instruction may not be able to apply that information to the resources in a new library.
- Transfer students may not know where to seek support at their new campus or be reluctant to ask; this may be particularly true of male students in general and can be exacerbated by culture (Peña and Rhoads 2019).
- Transfer students may feel underprepared or may suffer "transfer shock" when their first semester grades are lower than what they have been previously accustomed to.

We can better understand challenges for our transfer student population by considering that institutions identify incoming first time in college (FTIC) freshmen as a designated class (i.e., the Class of 2026), and as a cohort, they enjoy an immediate identity and automatic peers. They have opportunities to participate in a number of welcoming and orientation-type programs at which they may begin to develop a social network and often benefit from ongoing First Year Experience initiatives. Notice how one transfer student (Walker and Okpala 2017) expressed feelings of isolation and invisibility: ". . . because it's like you come in with your group of people when you first come in as a freshman. You know everybody that you came in with; you all go to almost the same classes. So as a transfer student you're just kind of, like, thrown in there. You know, thrown into the number" (Walker and Okpala 2017).

Transfer students may have had an orientation, or at least a campus tour, but perhaps our incorrect assumption has been that after a few weeks, they are fully assimilated, both academically and socially. However, as we can see, the challenges inherent in transferring are not immediately resolved. Certainly, there is a role for the library as a place of inclusion and support. We should also assume that transfer students are unfamiliar with the library services and sources at our particular institution in order to support them academically.

Transfer Student Enrollment Timelines and Implications

Finally, it is important not to overlook the impact of extended periods of student enrollment. The time between a student's initial enrollment in a postsecondary institution and graduation with a college degree is an important indicator of student success. Traditionally, this timeline has been two years for AA degrees and four years for baccalaureate degrees. This timeline is no longer proving to be the case, however, with all students on average taking a longer time frame and students attending more than one institution (i.e., transfer students), taking even more time to graduate. There are various reasons for this: the need for remedial classes; the lack of sufficient financial aid, meaning that more students hold jobs while enrolled, difficulties enrolling in required classes when needed, and the impact of students' changing majors (Shapiro et al. 2016).

Increasingly, funds obtained through performance-based metrics set institutional baseline budgets rather than using the performance metrics solely for "bonus" funding, and budgets for performance-based funding can be a significant amount of money. For the 2019–2020 fiscal year in Florida, performance-based funding awarded by the State University System Board of Governors totaled $560 million (McAuliffe 2019). This means that extended graduation rates have the potential to negatively affect institutional baseline funding, depending upon which particular performance metrics are being used as the measuring stick.

Academic libraries have never been a source of institutional revenue; with expensive database and journal subscriptions and other acquisitions, we fall much more firmly on the "expense" side of the ledger sheet. Therefore, strengthening our efforts to improve transfer student success has the potential to contribute directly to the bottom line of our respective institutions. Although libraries are often referred to as the "heart" of the campus, that term of endearment does not insulate us from the palpitations we feel over the impact of budget reductions and hiring freezes. Thus, by proactively supporting our transfer student population on a scale that is sustainable, whether in partnership with other institutional departments, such as the writing center or other student support services, or with libraries from neighboring or "feeder" colleges or partner/pathway universities, we have the potential to make an individual and institutional impact.

In *the Value of Academic Libraries* (2010), Megan Oakleaf pointed out that each academic library must determine the unique ways in which it contributes to the mission of their institution and use that information to guide their planning and decision-making. At present, graduation rates and student retention are major issues in higher education, and transfer students may impact those numbers as well. If your institutional effectiveness is gauged by performance-based metrics, then it is imperative to find ways for your library to support those institutional goals and do so in measurable ways.

Steven Bell (2008) noted that there are many reasons why students leave a college prior to graduation, but there is one factor students point to regularly: *people*. Students who enjoy relationships with other students, faculty members, advisors, and others are more likely to persist. Isolated students who fail to engage with peers, faculty, and others are at the highest risk of leaving. Thus, Bell posits, if administrators and staff can have an impact on retention, then logic would support that academic libraries and librarians could likewise positively influence student retention, in ways beyond a demonstrated positive relationship between library *expenditures* and retention.

Whether we engage in an information literacy instruction session and give students our contact information for additional after-class help as needed, send welcome emails to incoming students at the beginning of the term, host a transfer-specific activity early in the term, or have copies of the most in-demand textbooks, we are helping cement the student's relationship with our institution. This does make a difference.

Real World Scenario

Not long ago, a student needing assistance with her research paper approached one of the authors of this book, Peggy Nuhn. "After clarifying the student's topic, suggesting keywords, demonstrating a search and emailing an article or two to help her get started, I observed the student was thrilled to see how much was available, warmly expressed her appreciation and then confided that she had been reluctant to come to the library to ask for help. I looked at this intelligent and vibrant young woman, amazed that our bright, modern library seemed to her a foreboding place, or that speaking with a librarian was intimidating, and after thinking a moment, I responded, 'You are the reason we are all here. Yes, some days we may be a bit busy or seem rushed, but students are the reason for us to be here. Whether it is anyone in the library, an advisor, a faculty member or anyone else on this campus, when you have questions or need assistance, you must ask. And if their answer is unclear to you, you must tell them so and ask for clarification, or if that is not provided, you should ask for assistance from someone else.'"

Clearly, this young woman is not alone in a lack of awareness of how library resources can support her assignments as well as in her reluctance to reach out for librarian assistance. Thus, the responsibility to build relationships, which can support student persistence, lies with us. The importance of our doing so cannot be overestimated.

Practical Applications of Chapter 1

- Take it as a given that your institution both sends and receives transfer students.

- Accept that transfer students will be unfamiliar with your library's specific resources and may—or may not—have ever attended a librarian-led class in information literacy.

- Assume that the student will not fully appreciate the role of an academic librarian and reframe that as an opportunity to engage with them.

- Participate in any transfer initiative that may be in place, find out what your institution offers, and arrange to be included. It is easier to support an existing initiative than create one; it may also be easier to facilitate inclusion following departmental transitions and staffing changes. New people often bring and welcome new ideas.

- Prepare a transfer student–oriented library handout, and have copies available at the writing center, academic success center, and similar locations on your campus.

- Quick and easy outreach item: If you have neither time nor resources for a transfer-specific library handout, make labels of the friendly URL for your transfer student-specific LibGuide, and put them on the back of your business cards. Students will then know how to reach out to you and how to find online help. Distribute these at all transfer student orientations.

- Consider designating one or more librarians for transfer student outreach.

References

American Association of Community Colleges. 2020. "AACC Fast Facts 2020." https://www.aacc.nche.edu/wp-content/uploads/2020/03/AACC_Fast_Facts_2020_Final.pdf.

Bahr, Peter Riley. 2012. "Student Flow between Community Colleges: Investigating Lateral Transfer." *Research in Higher Education* 53(1): 94–121. doi:10.1007/s11162-011-9224-5. https://www.jstor.org/stable/41348999.

Bell, Steven. 2008. "Keeping Them Enrolled: How Academic Libraries Contribute to Student Retention." *Library Issues* 29(1): 1–4. https://www.researchgate.net/profile/Steven_Bell7/publication/264846192_Keeping_Them_Enrolled_How_Academic_Libraries_Contribute_to_Student_Retention/links/55aff34708ae11d31039a984.pdf.

Boone, Rick H. 2017. "Community College Student Perceptions of University Transfer Barriers." ProQuest Dissertations Publishing. https://search.proquest.com/docview/1896981231.

Catmull, Ed. 2014. *Creativity Inc.: Overcoming the Unseen Forces That Stand in the Way of True Inspiration.* New York: Random House.

de los Santos, Alfredo G., Jr., and Farah Sutton. 2012. "Swirling Students: Articulation between a Major Community College District and a State-Supported Research University." *Community College Journal of Research and Practice* 36(12): 967–81. Taylor & Francis Online. https://www.tandfonline.com/doi/full/10.1080/10668920903182641.

de los Santos, Alfredo G., Jr., and Irene Wright. 1990. "Maricopa's Swirling Students: Earning One-Third of Arizona State's Bachelor's Degrees." *Community, Technical, and Junior College Journal* 60(6): 32–34. https://eric.ed.gov/?id=EJ409048.

Friedel, Janice Nahra, and Sarah L. Wilson. 2015. "The New Reverse Transfer: A National Landscape." *Community College Journal of Research and Practice*

39(1): 70–86. http://www.tandfonline.com/doi/abs/10.1080/10668926.2014.882805.

Handel, Stephen J., and Ronald A. Williams. 2012. "The Promise of the Transfer Pathway: Opportunity and Challenge for Community College Students Seeking the Baccalaureate Degree." *College Board Advocacy & Policy Center*. https://eric.ed.gov/?id=ED541978.

McAuliffe, D. 2019. "Time for a Change? Rob Bradley's Ready to Overhaul Performance Funding for Universities." May 10. https://floridapolitics.com/archives/296092-lawmakers-overhaul-performance-funding.

McCambly, Heather N., and Debra D. Bragg. 2016. "Reforming Transfer to Meet the Needs of 'Post-Traditional' Transfer Students: Insights from Credit When It's Due." *Office of Community College Research and Leadership*. https://files.eric.ed.gov/fulltext/ED574589.pdf.

McCormick, Alexander C. 2003. "Swirling and Double-Dipping: New Patterns of Student Attendance and Their Implications for Higher Education." *New Directions for Higher Education* 2003(121): 13–24. https://onlinelibrary.wiley.com/doi/abs/10.1002/he.98.

National Institute for the Study of Transfer Students. https://nists.org.

Oakleaf, Megan. 2010. *The Value of Academic Libraries: A Comprehensive Research Review and Report*. Association of College and Research Libraries. www.acrl.ala.org/value.

Ott, Alexander P., and Bruce S. Cooper. 2013. "They're Transfer Students, Not Cash Cows." *Chronicle of Higher Education*. March 18. https://www.chronicle.com/article/Theyre-Transfer-Students-Not/137935.

Peña, Mauro Ivan, and Robert A. Rhoads. 2019. "The Role of Community College First-Year Experience Programs in Promoting Transfer among Latino Male Students." *Community College Journal of Research and Practice* 43(3): 186–200. Taylor & Francis Online. doi:10.1080/10668926.2018.1453393.

Roberts, Lindsay, Megan E. Welsh, and Brittany Dudek. 2019. "Instruction and Outreach for Transfer Students: A Colorado Case Study." *College & Research Libraries* 80(1): 94–122. https://crl.acrl.org/index.php/crl/article/view/16925/18608.

Shapiro, Doug, Afet Dundar, Phoebe Khasiala Wakhungu, Xin Yuan, Angel Nathan, and Youngsik Hwang. 2016. "Time to Degree: A National View of the Time Enrolled and Elapsed for Associate and Bachelor's Degree Earners." Signature Report No. 11. ERIC.

Thomson, Alec. 2017. "Dual Enrollment's Expansion: Cause for Concern." *NEA Higher Education Journal*. Summer. National Education Association. Accessed September 24, 2019. http://www.nea.org/assets/docs/2017S_Thomson.pdf.

U.S. Department of Education. 2019. "Staying Eligible." Federal Student Aid. Accessed September 11, 2019. https://studentaid.ed.gov/sa/eligibility/staying-eligible.

Utter, Mary, and Linda DeAngelo. 2015. "Lateral Transfer Students: The Role of Housing in Social Integration and Transition." *Journal of College and University Student Housing* 1(42): 178–93.

Walker, Kimberly Young, and Comfort Okpala. 2017. "Exploring Community College Students' Transfer Experiences and Perceptions and What They Believe Administration Can Do to Improve Their Experiences." *Journal of Continuing Higher Education* 65(1): 35–44. http://www.tandfonline.com /doi/abs/10.1080/07377363.2017.1274618.

Wyner, Joshua, K. C. Deane, Davis Jenkins, and John Fink. 2016. *The Transfer Playbook: Essential Practices for Two- and Four-Year Colleges.* The Aspen Institute, College Excellence Program and Community College Research Center, Columbia University. https://ccrc.tc.columbia.edu/media/k2/attach ments/transfer-playbook-essential-practices.pdf.

CHAPTER 2

Transfer Structures: Implications for Students

The task of the modern educator is not to cut down jungles, but to irrigate deserts.

—C. S. Lewis, author, educator, theologian

As librarians, our broad institutional role is to support student success regardless of the student's pathway. However, greater awareness of the challenges and implications within transfer structures, such as statewide and institutional agreements between community colleges and universities, can certainly be beneficial as we seek ways to reach students more effectively and design outreach and instruction, informed by the students' experience. Additionally, by committing to a deeper understanding of the issues and concerns of transfer students, we can provide valuable input on areas outside our immediate scope, through involvement in our faculty senate or campus-wide committees or initiatives.

Perhaps the most commonly held assumption about vertical transfer students (chapter 1) is that the majority of them will complete a two-year degree at their local community college, seamlessly transfer to a state university as a rising junior, and graduate with their baccalaureate degree within a couple of years. While the vertical pathway is the direction taken by a significant portion of the transfer student population, it may be surprising to learn that neither the numbers nor the scenario described here reflect the actual experience of the majority of transfer students. In fact, according to summary of a report released in 2016 by the Community College Research Center (CCRC), the Aspen Institute College Excellence Program, and the National Clearinghouse Research Center, "Only 14 percent of students starting in community colleges transfer to four-year schools and earn a bachelor's degree within six years of entry." This is despite studies indicating that 80 percent of new community college students do aspire to earn a bachelor's degree. The report went on to note that when individual states are ranked, even in states with higher success rates, *only one community college student in five will transfer and graduate within six years of enrolling at a university* (CCRC 2016, italics ours).

Those are sobering statistics, and indicate a significant disconnect between students' aspirations and their reality. Research supports a number of reasons for this extensive timeline for vertical transfer students as well as how these reasons influence student persistence toward degree completion. Some of the factors negatively affecting a student's progression to a degree are not within the realm of the college or university, such as the student's financial situation, their family responsibilities, or work obligations. For some students, enrolling in one or two classes per semester is a deliberate choice, allowing them to progress toward degree completion at a pace that balances classes with their other responsibilities, and we appreciate that. However, we do not want to overlook impediments to graduation, particularly when librarians or the institution can ameliorate them. Concerns that institutions can endeavor to address usually fall within two primary areas related to student persistence toward degree completion: supporting the student's **academic engagement** and facilitating the student's **social engagement** at our institution. Although student persistence and graduation rates relate to students' academic and social engagement, that relationship does not infer an easy solution is at hand. Vincent Tinto, a noted theorist on student retention and persistence, helps us better understand the importance of the student's perspective. Tinto states, "For years, our prevailing view of student retention has been shaped by theories that view student retention through the lens of institutional action and ask what institutions can do to retain their students. Students, however, do not seek to be retained. They seek to persist. The two perspectives, although necessarily related, are not the same. Their interests are different. While the institution's interest is to increase the proportion of their students who graduate from the institution, the student's interest is to complete a degree often without regard to the college or university in which it is earned. When viewed from the students' perspective, persistence is but one form of motivation. Students have to be persistent in their pursuit of their degrees and be willing to expend the effort to do so even when faced with challenges they sometimes encounter. Without motivation and the effort it engenders, persistence is unlikely—institutional action aside" (Tinto 2016).

Tinto (2016) recommends that institutions adopt the student perspective and focus not only on steps to retain their students but also to ensure that their students *want* (italics ours) to persist to completion. Tinto acknowledges that while student retention and student persistence are linked, in his words, "they do not lead to the same sort of conversations about institutional action" (Tinto 2016). Tinto advocates for supporting student persistence, which he says requires institutions to understand how student experiences shape the students' motivation to persist and what institutions can do to enhance the students' motivation (Tinto 2016).

Tinto also emphasizes the importance of holistic institutional change to support the needs of students, as opposed to an "add on" approach, which he colorfully refers to as "tinkering at the margins of institutional life" (Tinto 2008). Further, Tinto acknowledges that many experiences shape a student's motivation to persist in their educational goals, and not all are within the scope of institutions to influence. Of experiences the institution can influence, Tinto names three that he believes are central to student motivation: **students' self-efficacy, a student's sense of belonging**, and **students' perceived value of the curriculum** (Tinto 2016).

Tinto (2016) posits that self-efficacy or an individual's sense of being able to succeed is challenged, particularly as students encounter the increasing demands of college. He adds, "What matters for success . . . is not so much that students enter college believing in their capacity to succeed, as it is that *they come to believe they can as the result [of] their early experiences*" (Tinto 2016, italics ours). Tinto emphasized the importance of students receiving timely support in order to successfully manage difficulties in the academic and social demands of college—before those difficulties undermine the students' motivation to persist (Tinto 2016).

Community Colleges in Transition

Higher education is often in some state of transition. Within Florida, just the past decade or so has witnessed a major shift in nomenclature, as the majority of Florida's community colleges embraced "state college" rather than "community college" as their new identification, which acknowledges an expanded scope in offerings, including, for some, baccalaureate degree programs. Other colleges have taken a similar path, including Henry Ford College in Dearborn, Michigan (formerly Henry Ford Community College) and the former Seattle Community Colleges, now known as North Seattle College, South Seattle College, and Seattle Central College (Associated Press and KOMO Staff 2014).

In most cases these name changes were preceded by a shift in thinking, reflecting a new emphasis in increasing college enrollment as well as increasing access by offering selected baccalaureate degrees while continuing to offer two-year career focused Associate in Science (AS) or Associate in Applied Science (AAS) degrees. Although the majority of two-year institutions in the United States are presently retaining the "community college" name, there have been national shifts in adding baccalaureate degree programs to their offerings.

Often these additional baccalaureate degrees are in nursing or in fields of study that serve specific local economic needs. For example, as of the 2019 academic year, Ohio's Sinclair Community College (Dayton, Ohio) will offer two four-year degree programs: aviation technology/professional pilot and unmanned aerial systems. Both award a bachelor of applied science degree, and the college website states that both these programs of study "are designed to fulfill specific workforce demands in the Miami Valley region" ("Sinclair College Bachelor Degrees" 2019). According to an article on the Pew Charitable Trusts website, the Ohio Department of Education had to approve Sinclair's application to confer four-year degrees, and one requirement was that the degree was not already available at other in-state institutions (Povich 2018).

Community Colleges: A Brief Historical Overview

According to George B. Vaughan, president emeritus of Piedmont Virginia Community College, professor emeritus of higher education at North Carolina State University ("Dr. George B. Vaughan, Bio" 2019), and author of *The Community College in America: A Short History,* "the public community college in America today is a coat of many colors. Borrowing heavily from the public high school, the private junior college, and the four-year college and university, the community college not only possesses characteristics found in all of these, but at the same time maintains an identity of its own." Vaughan (1982) noted that several educational leaders of the last half of the nineteenth and early part of the 20th century, many of whom were influenced by the German university model, advocated for removing the first two years of higher education from the university environment and placing those two years in a separate institution.

According to Vaughan, these earlier ideas influenced William Rainey Harper (1856–1906), founder and first president of the University of Chicago. Harper (Vaughan 1982) established a junior college at the University of Chicago and successfully advocated for weak four-year colleges to drop the last two years of their curriculum and become junior colleges. Vaughan posits that even more significant for the development of public community colleges was Harper's influence in Joliet, Illinois, where two years were added to the high school program.

Joliet Junior College ("First Community College" 2019) acknowledges its roots as America's first public community college, begun as an experimental "postgraduate high school" in 1901, the result of a collaboration between J. Stanley Brown, superintendent of Joliet Township High School and William Rainey Harper. The college website (https://www.jjc.edu/about-jjc/history) states that Brown and Harper's innovation created a junior college, which academically paralleled the first two years of a four-year college or university, and was designed to accommodate students who desired to remain within the community, yet still pursue a college education.

Vaughan (1982) concludes by acknowledging that while today's community college is quite different from the junior college as envisioned by Harper, Harper is nevertheless still viewed by many as the "spiritual father" of the movement. Fittingly, and perhaps poignantly, Harper's humble birthplace, a log cabin on Main Street in New Concord, Ohio, still stands and sits directly across from the main entrance to Muskingum University (formerly Muskingum College), from which he graduated at age 14.

The American Association of Community Colleges (AACC) website lists its founding date as 1920—which is the year associated with the founding of the American Association of Junior Colleges (Zook 1921) and which transitioned to the American Association of Community and Junior Colleges in 1972. Reading the proceedings of the American Association of Junior Colleges' first annual conference, which took place in June 1920, just a few short years after Harper and Brown's experimental "postgraduate high school" and with the United States just out of the Great War, is both enlightening and even slightly prophetic.

George F. Zook (1885–1951), specialist in higher education, delivered the introductory statement opening the conference. Zook also served as editor of the manuscript of conference proceedings. In his introduction, Zook noted the growth of this new educational venture and stated that during the 10-year period from 1905–1906 to 1915–1916, there was an increase in attendance at colleges and universities of all kinds in the United States of about 50 percent.

Following Zook's introductory remarks, James M. Wood, president of Stephens Junior College, Columbia, Missouri, and conference chairman, seeks to define the role of junior colleges and, in so doing, takes a jab at traditional college curricula (Zook 1921). Wood states, "The legitimate field of the college is the period of later adolescence. From the ages of 16 to 20, the period of the great life decisions, boys and girls need closer personal contact with faculty members than is possible in the large universities. The college is at present occupying this field only partially because of the tradition that a student should enter school at the age of 6, and continue for 8 years in the elementary schools, 4 years in the secondary schools, and have reached the age of 18 before he can expect to enter college. By developing a four-year curriculum adapted to the interests and needs of later adolescence, the junior college will have become the pioneer college of the future. The task is a difficult one but very much worth while [sic]. Nor is its solution impossible. There is no great objection to granting the baccalaureate degree at the age of 20 provided it can be done without the loss of dignity on the part of the institution. Fortunately, the junior college has no dignity to lose; it may, therefore, with propriety assist the lower secondary schools in their efforts to save two years of a student's life. It may still assert that the human element is of more consequence than institutional pride" (Zook 1921).

Although Wood's proposal of a four-year junior college combining with and taking the place of what would now be the last two years of a high school curriculum, and then attaching the first two years of college, has not endured exactly as described; he was certainly a visionary. Wood's view of the (then) junior college becoming the "pioneer college of the future" is a concept that aligns rather well with our present path of dual enrollment, increasingly seen as a fast track for high school students to college graduation, or in Wood's words, a way to "save two years of a student's life" (Zook 1921).

Today, the American Association of Community Colleges represents nearly 1,200 two-year, associate degree–granting institutions and more than 12 million students (https://www.aacc.nche.edu/about-us/) Two-year colleges are widely considered to offer an affordable, accessible path for thousands of students; in fact, nearly half (49.2%) of all postsecondary students begin their college journey at a two-year institution (Glynn 2019), and yet, as noted earlier in this chapter, relatively few two-year college-to-university transfer students persist to graduation. The Jack Kent Cooke Foundation report (Glynn 2019) notes that failure to complete a bachelor's degree is not a measure of the student's academic ability as much as it is the result of insufficient financial resources, transfer advising, and limited course planning.

The Pell Institute report "Moving Beyond Access: College Success for Low-Income, First Generation Students" (Engle and Tinto 2008) acknowledges that two-year and for-profit institutions are major points of initial access to postsecondary education for low-income, first-generation students, observing that these students face a number of challenges to college success. These challenges include students being older and less likely to receive financial support from parents as well as a greater likelihood of having family and work obligations, perhaps limiting the student's full participation in the college experience. These obligations and the limitations they may impose can negatively affect student *engagement in academic and social experiences*, thereby affecting student persistence, referenced earlier in this chapter (Engle and Tinto 2008). The report goes on to state that low-income, first generation students are at greater risk of failure in postsecondary education and suggests this is as much the result of the experiences they have during college as it is attributable to the experiences they have prior to enrollment. Due to a lack of resources, low-income, first-generation students are more likely to live and work off campus and take classes part time while working a full-time job. Engle and Tinto (2008) observe that this thereby limits the time students can spend on campus. Therefore, activities promoting academic and social engagement, such as studying in groups, interactions with faculty and other students, participation in extra-curricular activities, and using support services may fall by the wayside (Engle and Tinto 2008).

Articulation Agreements

As mentioned in chapter 1, one of the largest transfer impediments occurs early in a student's experience and concerns how credit hours will transfer and whether the student will lose precious academic ground in the process. To remedy this, beginning in the mid-1970s, states began in earnest to develop articulation agreements, primarily between state universities and community colleges. These agreements facilitate entrance into a state university for the last two years of a baccalaureate degree program and were envisioned to smooth out some of the twists and turns in the community college to four-year institution pathway. At present, approximately two-thirds of the United States does have a statewide guaranteed transfer of an associate degree, meaning that students can transfer all the credits from their associate degree to a four-year institution and enter that four-year institution as a rising junior, without additional course requirements.

However, even with an established statewide articulation agreement, students may encounter some bumps in the road. For example, the State of Florida instituted a "2+2" articulation agreement in 1971. Presently there are 28 Florida public colleges, and many of them have established pathways or partnerships with Florida's 12 state universities, often based on geographic proximity between the institutions. While Florida AA-degreed students are guaranteed admission into a state university provided they meet requirements, including a cumulative GPA of at least 2.0, the Florida College System acknowledges that "this does not mean that every AA graduate will be admitted at the state university of his/her choice or into the upper division program of his/her choice. Application for admission to state universities (particularly into specific degree programs) can be a highly competitive process, so student performance in the AA program may be taken into consideration" ("Frequently Asked Questions" 2020).

Thus, Florida AA-degreed students who had hoped to transfer to a specific university, perhaps the one located closest to their home, may find that option is not available to them. Additionally, specific upper-division programs may have requirements exceeding the articulation agreement minimums. Other states have similar variations within their transfer and articulation agreements. For example, at the time of writing, the majority of states do not have a statewide reverse transfer mandate for public institutions; however, in a number of states *specific in-state institutions* do have agreements for reverse transfer (ECS 2020). The Education Commission of the States (ECS) (https://www.ecs.org/) maintains current information on the status of statewide articulation agreements and acknowledges states, such as California, with agreements between certain state systems, but without a statewide guaranteed transfer of an associate degree (ECS 2019). ECS also provides information on which states have common course numbering systems as well as those with a statewide reverse transfer policy. It is important to recognize that while some states may have common course numbering systems, which should make it easier to determine which courses will transfer, there still may be no "statewide guaranteed transfer of an associate degree." The term "statewide guaranteed transfer of an associate degree" is extremely important, because without the "guaranteed transfer" aspect to the agreement, students may be able to transfer a portion of their lower-division credits but may also be required to take additional types of courses upon transfer. This could result in an extended graduation timeline, which may in turn shorten students' federal financial aid timeline. This significantly adds to the stress of the transfer experience.

As librarians, we will of course depend upon the expertise of other academic departments to determine which credits transfer and which do not. Our purpose here is not to advocate for librarians to become experts on these policies but simply to heighten awareness of how our students are affected by these agreements; by variations between the states; and in some cases, by the complete lack of a statewide guarantee of transfer pathway.

To illustrate, consider the following: According to ECS data, presently only seven states: Colorado, Florida, Kansas, Louisiana, Missouri, Nevada, and Tennessee have **all** the following elements, designed to smooth the student transfer experience. ECS defines these elements of transfer and articulation as:

Statewide guarantee of transfer, meaning that AA-degreed students with a specific GPA (generally 2.0) will enter a four-year institution as a rising junior with no additional required coursework. Some states phrase this as "completion of all lower-division general education coursework" or similar wording.

Common course numbering systems, which facilitate the transfer of credits for equivalent courses.

Transferable core of lower-division courses. ECS defines this as "a set of general education courses agreed upon across all public postsecondary institutions. It must be fully transferable at all public institutions. Institutions may have different naming conventions; however, if that is the case, there is a crosswalk for institutions to use in the transfer process."

Statewide reverse transfer policy. As noted in chapter 1, some students do wish to apply their university credits back to their college for an AA degree. Students may find this detour from their planned route advantageous, given the overall low numbers of students who persist in obtaining a baccalaureate degree after transferring to the university prior to receiving an AA. Given the time and financial investment these students have already made, it seems reasonable for them to apply their university-earned credits back to their college for an AA degree. In fact, studies have indicated that associate's degree graduates earn a higher income, accumulate higher lifetime earnings, and are less likely to be unemployed than those who completed some college but do not hold an academic credential or individuals who hold a high school diploma as their sole academic credential. Thus, for many students the reverse transfer pathway makes sense, even if it represents the exit ramp of a student's postsecondary education, and in some early studies, the reverse transfer for an AA may in fact predict completion of a bachelor's degree within two years (Taylor and Giani 2019).

Many of the states without statewide articulation agreements do have institutional agreements. California is an example of a state without a statewide articulation agreement at this time but with a designated transfer pathway between the 23-campus California State University system and California's 115 state community colleges. According to Cal State's website (https://www2.calstate.edu/apply/transfer/Pages/ccc-associate-degree-for-transfer.aspx), an associate in art for transfer (AA-T) and an associate in science for transfer (AS-T), which are no more than 60 semester units or 90 quarter units, are fully transferable ("CCC-Associate Degree for Transfer" 2019).

These processes may still be confusing for students, however. As one researcher (Boone 2017) learned, in a state without a statewide articulation policy but with a specific institutional agreement, students attempting to transfer may still struggle with incorrect guidance, lack of orientation resulting in missed information, counselors who were too busy to help or give enough information, and an inability to enroll in needed classes. One transfer student (Boone 2017) described a counselor who did not agree with the student's decision to seek a specific university and advised them, "Are you sure you want to do this? Don't take that, don't take this." As a result, the student did not feel supported or respected by the counselor. Additionally, students in this same phenomenological study (Boone 2017) reported receiving contradictory advice as well as struggles with a lack of promised counselor follow-through. Students in the study acknowledged that it was their responsibility to meet requirements and follow a process, but without clear explanations, it was also easy for them to make a mistake (Boone 2017).

As librarians are often parallel to counselors in the campus organizational chart, we do understand what it is to be understaffed, and when that is the case, miscommunications more easily occur. While these student comments may not reflect the experience of the majority, they are certainly meaningful and give us important insights into the transfer process from the student's perspective. If as the result of a poor experience at this early juncture, the student comes to believe that he or she cannot succeed, based on Tinto's (2016) research on persistence, then the student is negatively affected.

Although not perfect, overall, statewide articulation agreements and defined institutional pathways are beneficial to students, particularly for those who wish to complete a baccalaureate degree, as Boatman and Soliz (2018) point out. They note that simply by outlining a pathway or a core set of courses for students, students may be more likely to see transfer as an actual possibility and begin to take steps in that direction, which they may not have previously considered. Boatman and Soliz (2018) posit that the existence of a pathway encourages students to consider transferring to a four-year institution, particularly if they are assured their courses will count toward graduation at their new institution. Thus, articulation agreements and defined institutional pathways may help to promote not only transfer but also promote BA-degree attainment (Boatman and Soliz 2018). This may be due to a number of factors, but an important one is academic momentum. Boatman and Soliz (2018) continue, "Academic momentum, or the speed at which students are able to complete their college coursework, is an important predictor of bachelor's degree completion. As the amount of time students spend successfully earning credits each term increases, the likelihood of graduation also increases."

So that we can maximize our impact and minimize misdirected efforts, our next chapter will explore in greater depth how our services and instruction can be most effective for students transferring both *with* and *without* an AA degree.

Practical Applications of Chapter 2

- If you are not already familiar with this, find out whether your state has a "statewide guarantee of transfer" in place. The Education Commission of the States website is a good resource (www.ecs.org) for this information. If you are in a "guarantee of transfer" state, your institution is likely serving a significant number of transfer students, indicating that library support of transfer student success is essential, and underscores the importance of building collaboration between librarian colleagues, particularly when there are existing institutional relationships as feeder colleges and transfer pathways.

- Does your institution have a designated department for transfer students? If so, make a connection and begin to investigate potential collaborative opportunities.

References

Associated Press and KOMO Staff. 2014. "3 Seattle Colleges Dropping 'Community' from Names." *KOMO News*. Accessed September 17, 2019. http://komonews.com/news/local/3-seattle-colleges-dropping-community-from-names.

Boatman, Angela, and Adela Soliz. 2018. "Statewide Transfer Policies and Community College Student Success." *Education Finance and Policy* 13(4): 449–83. doi: 10.1162/edfp_a_00233.

Boone, Rick H. 2017. "Community College Student Perceptions of University Transfer Barriers." ProQuest Dissertations Publishing. https://search.proquest.com/docview/1896981231.

"CCC-Associate Degree for Transfer." 2019. Accessed May 16, 2019. https://www2.calstate.edu/apply/transfer/Pages/ccc-associate-degree-for-transfer.aspx.

Community College Research Center (CCRC). 2016. "New Report Ranks States Based on Colleges' Performance in Helping Students Transfer to Four-Year Universities and Earn Bachelor's Degrees." Accessed September 17, 2019. https://ccrc.tc.columbia.edu/press-releases/new-report-ranks-states-on-colleges-performance-helping-students-transfer.html.

"Dr. George B. Vaughan, Bio." 2019. Virginia Community College System website. Accessed August 17, 2019. https://opd.vccs.edu/dr-george-b-vaughan-bio/.

Education Commission of the States (ECS). 2019. "Transfer and Articulation: Statewide Guaranteed Transfer of an Associate Degree, June 2018." Accessed September 26, 2019. http://ecs.force.com/mbdata/MBquest3RTA?Rep=TR1801.

Engle, J., and Vincent Tinto. 2008. "Moving Beyond Access: College Success for Low-Income, First Generation Students." The Pell Institute. https://files.eric.ed.gov/fulltext/ED504448.pdf.

"First Community College." Joliet Junior College website. Accessed August 11, 2019. https://www.jjc.edu/about-jjc/history.

"Frequently Asked Questions." 2020. The Florida College System website. Accessed April 19, 2020. http://www.fldoe.org/how-do-i/fl-colleges.stml.

Glynn, Jennifer. 2019. "Persistence: The Success of Students Who Transfer from Community Colleges to Selective Four-Year Institutions: Jack Kent Cooke Foundation." https://www.jkcf.org/wp-content/uploads/2019/01/Persistance-Jack-Kent-Cooke Foundation.pdf.

Povich, Elaine S. 2018. "More Community Colleges Are Offering Bachelor's Degrees—and Four-Year Universities Aren't Happy about It." Pew Trusts. Accessed September 17, 2019. https://www.pewtrusts.org/en/research-and-analysis/blogs/stateline/2018/04/26/more-community-colleges-are-offering-bachelors-degrees.

"Sinclair College Bachelor Degrees." 2019. Sinclair Community College website. Accessed August 11, 2019. https://www.sinclair.edu/academics/bachelors/.

Taylor, Jason L., and Matt Giani. 2019. "Modeling the Effect of the Reverse Credit Transfer Associate's Degree: Evidence from Two States." *The Review of Higher Education* 42(2): 427–55. doi:10.1353/rhe.2019.0002. https://search.proquest.com/docview/2164141873.

Tinto, Vincent. 2008. "Access without Support Is Not Opportunity." *Inside Higher Ed*. Accessed September 17, 2019. https://www.insidehighered.com/views/2008/06/09/access-without-support-not-opportunity.

Tinto, Vincent. 2016. "From Retention to Persistence." *Inside Higher Ed*. Accessed September 17, 2019. https://www.insidehighered.com/views/2016/09/26/how-improve-student-persistence-and-completion-essay.

Vaughan, George. 1982. *The Community College in America: A Short History*. American Association of Community and Junior Colleges. AACJC Publications. Accessed September 26, 2019. https://files.eric.ed.gov/fulltext/ED255267.pdf.

Zook, George F., ed. 1921. National Conference of Junior Colleges, 1920, and First Annual Meeting of American Association of Junior Colleges. Bulletin, 1922. Bureau of Education, Department of the Interior. Accessed September 25, 2019. https://eric.ed.gov/?id=ED540323.

CHAPTER 3

Transfer Students: Challenges and Opportunities for Librarians

Vision without action is a daydream. Action without vision is a nightmare.
—Japanese Proverb

As we have explored, students may transfer college to college, college to university, university to college, or university to university at *any* stage in their academic journey. Taken broadly, however, there are essentially just two ways to look at this: The student who is transferring to our institution is doing so either *with* or *without* an AA degree.

Does the student's transfer status make a difference in library initiatives and librarian-led information literacy instruction? It certainly can and should, particularly if we assume that AA-degreed transfer students have already had multiple exposures to information literacy instruction and have achieved a level of competency comparable to that of native students of similar class rank. The other possible assumption we may make is that non-AA-degreed transfer students will easily transfer their knowledge base on information literacy, whatever it may be, to their new institution's library resources, and build upon that. Research informs us that neither of these assumptions are correct and could actually add to the transfer student's challenges, which, taken on sum, can contribute to the aforementioned "transfer shock," generally defined as a dip in the student's GPA in the semester following transfer.

"Transfer Shock" or "Culture Shock"?

Although "transfer shock" can be attributable to various factors, Lafrance and Kealey (2017) point out that transfer students who arrive as sophomores, juniors, or seniors and have not participated in information literacy instruction at their previous institutions are at risk of falling through the cracks. Although some of these students may encounter a librarian in one of their upper-division courses, many have to fend for themselves when coursework requires research and the use of library services. Because transfer students often have social and academic challenges in adjusting to a new institution, the students' level of competency in information literacy, or complete lack thereof, continues to be an ongoing concern for librarians (Lafrance and Kealey 2017).

In 2015–2016, a group of transfer students at the University of Washington's Seattle Campus shared their experiences through interviews and focus group discussions (Whang et al. 2017). Some of the student concerns included a desire to have their prior academic experience recognized and to be acknowledged as a group of students who are distinct from first-year students. The surveyed students expressed a need to identify resources and sources of support rapidly, concerns about the "culture shock" of transferring from a community college to a large research university, and the importance of forming community on a large campus.

Interestingly, "culture shock" may actually be a more accurate description of what we refer to as "transfer shock." Students in the survey (Whang et al. 2017) expressed feeling "culture shock" when they arrived at the university due to large class sizes, the radical change in scale from community college to the university, uncertainty about academic expectations, and questions about how to form community. One student (Whang et al. 2017) poignantly likened her transfer student experience to an "immigrant experience," where she had left behind her existing community and had to establish a new identity, form relationships, and learn a different culture.

We suggest that the definition of "transfer shock" as a dip in the students' GPA is akin to equating a fever with an illness. In general, a fever by itself is not an illness; an elevated body temperature is instead a symptom, an indication of something else going on. A fever provides an essential measurement to gauge the status of one's health, but a fever alone is typically not the problem. We suggest that like a physical fever, a drop in a student's GPA is not in itself the real issue; however, like a fever, it is measurable and symptomatic of the larger issues our transfer students are dealing with. Just as a medical professional would not think of berating a patient for their illness, but would instead provide sound advice and prescriptions necessary for recovery, let us adopt that mindset for our transfer students, by providing appropriate advice and prescriptive referrals to support students' recovery from "transfer shock."

Vertical Transfer Student Preparedness: A Historical Perspective

Concerns about transfer student preparedness, particularly for vertical transfer students taking the community college to university path, are not new. In 1995 Barbara Townsend (1995) surveyed a small group of community college students who had transferred to a university, in order to learn about their perceptions of the transfer process, as well as their experiences at their new university environment. It is significant that the university used for the study was one Townsend identified as having a commitment to a diverse student body, which would be an indication of support for community college students. Additionally, Townsend acknowledged that many of the faculty at this university prided themselves on a student-centered approach. Thus, she posited that this particular university setting would be compatible with a community college environment and anticipated this would be a "best possible environment for the students" (Townsend 1995).

Survey responses on the transfer process (Townsend 1995) revealed students' perception of having navigated the process either alone or with the help of friends or family members who had transferred, but without assistance from the college. Several respondents acknowledged that university representative visits to the college campus had been helpful but did not appear to comprehend that the college had facilitated that connection for them.

With respect to the academic environment, most survey respondents (Townsend 1995) found the university to be more difficult in content, and several students honed in on the importance of being able to write well in order to succeed at the university. A number of students surveyed noted that university faculty required more writing for assignments as well as for tests than was required at their community college. One surveyed student said, "I have found the key to doing well at the university is being able to write." Students also noted that the colleges gave more multiple-choice tests than the university, and furthermore, at the college, the multiple-choice tests were easier. According to one survey respondent, multiple-choice test questions at the college had "only one right answer and the other ones were off the wall." Additionally, although most of the surveyed students found the university faculty generally helpful, several noted a difference in the faculty between the institutions. This group perceived university faculty as distant and unsympathetic, expecting the student to master the material independently, particularly when the student did not have a strong foundation in subject prerequisites (Townsend 1995).

In 1996, Gail M. Staines, coordinator of library instruction at Niagara County Community College, New York, researched the differences in what we then termed "bibliographic instruction" between community colleges and four-year institutions. Staines's work provided evidence that the colleges focused on teaching *short-term goals,* such as how to locate library materials, while the four-year institutions based instructional programs on *long-term goals,* such as how to create and conduct a search strategy and select suitable search terms. Staines posited that these differences in instructional goals were based on librarian analyses of student needs, which may actually slow the transition for transfer students. Staines (1996) noted, "Community college [survey] respondents indicated they frequently observe transfer students returning to community college libraries to conduct research for undergraduate assignments. Presumably, community college librarians' attention to basic library skills, combined with the assumption among four-year institution librarians that students should already possess such skills, partially explains this tendency among transfer students."

Staines concluded by observing that the findings of this survey illustrated the precarious position transfer students are in, given that college library instruction is remedial and learned outside the framework of the research process, yet upon transfer to a university, these very same students are expected to possess information literacy and critical thinking skills needed for undergraduate research.

Staines outlined four key aspects learned from this study:

1.   A *process* approach is preferable to one that stresses specific resources.
2.   A *progressive model* (or "scaffolding" in current literature), which builds on previous knowledge, is preferred.
3.   *Credit courses* represent the most appropriate means of providing transfer student library instruction.
4.   There may be obstacles to implementation of a credit course. (Staines 1996)

Building on the research of both Townsend and Staines, in 2004 Sylvia Tag, reference and instruction librarian at Western Washington University, Washington, explored the role of librarians in supporting transfer student success. As Western Washington had (and still has) a significant transfer student population, Tag questioned whether the library genuinely understood and addressed the needs of transfer students. Tag observed that transfer students entering at upper-division levels, at least in some departments, would need to "fend for themselves" in order to adjust to a new campus as well as adjust to disparities in academic acculturation between their experience at their previous institution and the experience of native students. Tag also noted that the library had no data on the transfer student population, relying instead on anecdotal information obtained through conversations with transfer students, university staff, and colleagues from area community colleges. Thus, Tag developed a survey in order to gather information on the research experiences of transfer students, with the goal of justifying expanded library services to this population. Survey questions focused on information related to students' previous research experiences and their anticipated use of the library, and an open-ended question allowed for personal expressions of previous and anticipated library use. The survey was distributed at the university transitions fair, held prior to the start of the 2002 fall term.

The completed surveys reflected the experiences of 307 students, or 31 percent of the 981 new incoming transfer students for that semester (Tag 2004). The survey responses described a population of students who were eager to use the library for their continuing education, and the library responded with improved and a wider scope of communication, including designated space for library information in the New Student Programs newsletter and inclusion in the Student Affairs and Academic Support Services brochure. The library newsletter was included in the information packets for transfer students, and the library initiated a web page for transfer students (https://library.wwu.edu/use/toplinks-transfer), which was also linked from the Admissions, Academic Support, and New Student Programs web pages. The library expanded their scope in other ways as well, by keeping current on additional, but not library-centric, literature on transfer students (also used in the preparation of this publication) and participation in university-wide committees.

Student responses to the 2002 library survey (Tag 2004) are just as valid today in informing our work with transfer students and include the following:

Question: What would you like to know about doing research at the college or university level?

Tag's survey responses included the following:

- How to get around the WWU library, because each library is different
- Familiarization with the library setup would be useful
- More about campus library
- Where do you start? The library is huge! (and confusing)
- How to access information in the most efficient way
- The best way to effectively research a topic
- Credible resources—how to find them and determine credibility
- How to use databases
- How to find very specific scholarly resources
- How to make it easier!
- Which databases are used at WWU, best searches to use, etc..
- How do I go about finding people who can help?

- I would like to learn how to be a more effective researcher
- I have been instructed on how to use the library at the community college level which is much smaller. I would like instruction on using a library at the university level
- I would like to know how the books are arranged (such as Dewey Decimal System) to be able to find books easier
- College or Library of Congress call number system (Tag 2004)

This sampling of student responses (Tag 2004) helps us to appreciate that some things have not really changed. Transfer students may have attained some level of competency in information literacy, but the structure, services, and resources of university libraries are significantly richer and more complex than resources at the typical community college library, a reality acknowledged by one of Tag's survey respondents. Navigating these resources successfully will likely prove challenging. It makes sense, both then and now, that transfer students, whether with or without an AA degree, would need library support at their new institution in order to succeed academically.

Concerns Continue

Although some of the aforementioned research is 25 years old, the findings are still valid, and in many cases, the needs of transfer students, particularly in terms of information literacy, are still largely unmet.

For example, building on Staines's work, McBride, Gregor, and McCallister (2017) observed there is still a difference in how information literacy is taught between colleges and universities. They found that community college librarians taught the use of resources outside the framework of the research process, whereas librarians at four-year institutions expected transfer students to possess the information literacy skills necessary to conduct upper-level research. Staines's work had suggested that librarians should design information literacy instruction for transfer students and that this increased communication between two- and four-year institution librarians would only enhance this endeavor. McBride, Gregor, and McCallister (2017) conclude, "It is noteworthy that academic librarians have largely ignored this call."

In a similar vein, and also based in part on the work of Staines, librarians at the University of Colorado Boulder (Roberts, Welsh, and Dudek 2019) designed a survey to determine what supportive measures Colorado college and university libraries offer to transfer students. They learned that although the majority of library professionals at four-year institutions agreed that there is a need for transfer-specific instruction, *only four institutions out of the 20 surveyed indicated they had a designated library orientation specific to transfer students* (italics ours). None of the two-year institutions reported a designated library orientation for transfer students. In addition, over half of the two-year institutions and 80 percent of four-institutions have a presence at their institutions' new student orientation, which includes transfer students. *However, only 12.4 percent of surveyed libraries had a presence at orientations meant specifically for transfer students* (italics ours). Few institutions, either two- or four-year, reported any collaborative endeavors with other campus departments to participate in transfer student activities, and of the 29 libraries surveyed, only one (a four-year institution) reported offering transfer students a welcome event specifically sponsored by the library. Roberts, Welsh, and Dudek (2019) note, "There is strong agreement between two- and four-year library professionals that information literacy is integral to the library mission and is an effective use of budgetary resources and staff time. Yet, according to the survey responses, notable differences exist between general and transfer-specific library instruction statistics and attitudes, which suggests that transfer students may be missing academic library services."

To bring this discussion full circle, we followed up with both Gail Staines (1996) and Sylvia Tag (2004) to see if their perspectives had changed since their original and oft-cited research. Both graciously agreed to contribute an update on the information literacy needs of transfer students for this publication.

Dr. Gail Staines is a university librarian at the James C. Kirkpatrick Library at the University of Central Missouri, Missouri, and strongly supports the need to improve collaboration and communication between college and university librarians to support student information literacy outcomes. She provided the following timely recommendations (email communication, July 19, 2019):

- Make information literacy a general education goal/outcome at the institutional level.

- Create cross-institutional collaborative relationships—for example, one-day summits with faculty and librarians from community colleges and four-year institutions to develop common information literacy objectives and share ideas, conduct effective pilot testing to see what is effective, and redesign course syllabi to emphasize information literacy.

- Identify librarians to work with transfer students.

- Use active learning strategies and pedagogies in instruction.

- Understand that transfer student library experience is very diverse.

- Get the word out that library and information literacy skills are key to academic success.

- Community college librarians: Understand the most frequent transfer paths, (i.e., to pursue a bachelor's degree in nursing or biology), and then work with faculty to develop and teach.

- Use multiple instructional methods, such as tutorials, librarian, and faculty collaboration to target upper-level undergraduate courses that are research based or intensive or discipline specific.
- Work together at a programmatic level.
- Integrate information literacy into online courses (Staines 2019).

Professor Sylvia Tag is an associate professor at Western Washington University. She explained that the purpose of her original (2004) research was not for publication; rather, it was to determine whether the university's library outreach and services for transfer students were meeting student needs. Since that time, Professor Tag shared with us that the student population at Western Washington University has reflected additional changes in higher education, including increasing numbers of students who enter the university as 18-year-old juniors due to dual enrollment programs as well as an increase in nontraditional students. Professor Tag noted that nontraditional students include older students, students returning to the university, and students from underrepresented populations. Professor Tag also observed that transfer students still enroll in large numbers for the fall term, but also enroll throughout the year, which makes providing library outreach services at multiple times during the academic year more challenging; however the Western Washington University library has collaborated with other campus departments to support fairs and other events for new students. Professor Tag also shared that the Western Washington University library has made changes to their physical space by removing the reference desk and replacing it with a studio combining research and writing services (https://library.wwu.edu/rws) (email communication, July 8, 2019).

Given what we know now about the challenges many transfer students face as well as the importance of both academic and social engagement in student persistence, the lack of transfer-specific library outreach or instruction appears to be a woefully missed opportunity at many institutions and one that has now persisted for decades. Therefore, if we want to position our libraries as essential to student success and the true "heart of the campus," there is no better time than the present to support our transfer students.

Self-Referenced versus Norm-Referenced and "Transfer Shock"

While some university faculty may describe vertical transfer students as "underprepared," it helps to take a broader perspective on what may initially seem a dismissive and negative view. As Staines (1996) discovered, there *is* a difference in instructional goals in information literacy instruction between colleges and universities. Later, Tipton and Bender (2006) noted that students making the transition from community colleges to universities would experience a difference in both the *content of what they are learning* as well as the *style*. Tipton and Bender (2006) posit that the community college environment tends more toward one that is supportive and nurturing, leading to a difference in grading philosophies between college and university faculty, with colleges tending to inflate grades. When first semester university grades come in, students are often faced with a harsh reality and period of adjustment, resulting from students' moving from the *self-referenced* (comparing the student to their previous performance) grading systems of the college to the more *norm-referenced* (comparing the students' ability with others) grading systems of universities. Thus, Tipton and Bender (2006) believe that this is at least a partial explanation for "transfer shock."

Based on the years of research referenced in this chapter, we suggest that while it is quite likely that most transfer students are not adequately prepared for upper-division university work, we should approach this as the result of *institutional differences* rather than *student shortcomings*. This change in mindset alone may yield positive results as we seek ways to support the academic success of our transfer student population. The easiest approach with the greatest potential for impact is through collaboration.

Collaborate to Make a Difference

If we are in a state with a statewide articulation agreement, then most likely a good number of our AA-degreed transfers (or vertical transfers) are coming to our institution from an established feeder college, and perhaps some of these colleges are within close geographic proximity. Obviously, proximity does not guarantee that the student has received any librarian-led information literacy instruction prior to transfer or that students can apply what they learned seamlessly at their new institution, but it *does* mean there is a collaborative opportunity we may have missed. Consider the following:

Roberts, Welsh, and Dudek (2019) concluded that both two- and four-year librarians have opportunities to positively influence transfer student experiences. Although librarians at two-year colleges may not always recognize the role they can play in preparing students with transferable skills and resources, the various transfer pathways support that two-year institutions do receive transfer students, though not typically at the rates of four-year institutions. Thus, two-year librarians are also on the receiving end for transfer students in addition to preparing students for matriculation to four-year settings. Roberts, Welsh, and Dudek (2019) noted that at four-year institutions, there is a general assumption that a subject-specialist librarian is meeting the needs of transfer students without specific outreach or instruction, stemming from the belief that most transfer students begin their four-year career by transferring into a specific major and degree program. The authors note that addressing the specific needs of transfer students at four-year institutions, whether within discipline-specific contexts or generally through transfer student activities, is a worthwhile focus for four-year librarians. Both two- and four-year libraries need cross-institutional collaboration and strengthening of local networks to help ease transitions for transfer students (Roberts, Welsh, and Dudek 2019).

To be fair, there are reasons behind the lack of specific library initiatives to support transfer student success, and they are as varied as the experiences of transfer students themselves. Although the term "transfer students" sounds homogenous, it is far from that. The only absolute common denominator for transfer students, with the probable exception of dual-enrolled students, is that they have attended at least one institution of higher learning prior to attending ours. With respect to dual-enrolled students, consider that dual-enrolled students are trending younger, this point underscored by a recent conversation between Peggy Nuhn and a *dual-enrolled 12-year-old*. Therefore, whether students graduated from the local community college and are coming as a vertical transfer or are coming to our two-year college as a reverse transfer student after having attended a four-year institution, and every other path imaginable, their backgrounds, educational experience, both good and bad, differ widely. In this environment, a "one-size fits all" approach for information literacy for transfer students will likely prove less than successful. Additionally, transfer students may be identifiable as "transfer students" for only a very short time during the enrollment process and thereafter are absorbed into their new institution. This can make ongoing focused outreach challenging.

As Anna Sandelli (2017) notes, it has been observed that both a lack of data about the transfer student population at the institutional level and a lack of accountability to track this data represent common challenges in supporting transfer students at most institutions. She adds that institution-specific data collection serves several key purposes, including functioning as a resource for developing strategic plans, dispelling myths, and requesting resources or program support (Sandelli 2017).

Tobolowsky and Cox (2012) suggested examining the transfer experience from the institutional perspective could move us closer to providing appropriate supports. They conducted a study at a university in which 20 percent of the incoming class consisted of transfer students and anonymized the institution at the focus of their research as "Research U." Their findings, obtained through in-depth interviews with 17 faculty and staff members with the potential to affect the transfer student experience, give us much to consider including the following:

- Faculty and staff members mentioned two characteristics of transfer students, which made them a particularly challenging population to serve:

- ○ The students' incredible diversity; including race/ethnicity, age, socio-economic status, educational backgrounds; number of entering credits; and major interests.

- ○ The student's frequent false assumptions about the institution. It was noted that the diversity in the transfer group was far greater than the diversity among the direct-entry cohort, and the false assumptions were based on how processes, such as registration and financial aid disbursement, were handled at their previous institutions. Differences in processes resulted in frustration and confusion for students.

- A belief that the university is more concerned with first-time full-time degree-seeking students "because that's what we're rated on." One survey respondent shared that a successful transfer housing option allowing transfer students to share a residence hall, thereby creating a social connection and sense of community, was curtailed to make way for a new housing facility for honors students. According to the survey respondent, this shift reflected the overall sentiment of the university, indicating that "transfer students . . . are an afterthought."

- The survey also revealed a "myth of transfer student success." For some, the visible success of a few transfer students was taken as anecdotal evidence that on sum, transfer students were doing well at Research U. While the transfer students compared favorably with first-year students, when compared with students with a similar number of credits, they were not as successful. It was noted that this "myth" is hard to dispel because of the inconsistent definitions of who transfer students are and the fact that "transfer student" is a transitional status. (Tobolowsky and Cox 2012)

Despite some genuine challenges, including significant diversity among transfer students, librarians need to seek out opportunities to support the academic success of transfer students at our respective institutions. In some colleges and universities, librarians are beginning to increase outreach and instruction specific to transfer students, as we will explore further in chapter 8.

Let us make it our priority to be among them.

Practical Applications of Chapter 3

- Transfer students need an orientation to their new library and new resources, but it should be different and separate from orientations for First Year Experience students. Transfer students are not new to the college experience, and our library initiatives need to acknowledge that.

- Transfer student populations are among our most diverse student populations. They tend to be older, are often married, possibly with children, and working full or part time. Therefore, a "one size fits all" approach for transfer students will likely not be as successful as a focused approach.

- We need to connect with transfer students early in the term. There is research to support that outreach is most effective during the first or second week of the semester. A welcoming "blast" email (putting student addresses in the BCC line to protect their privacy) is simple and can be effective.

- Most transfer students may not be adequately prepared for upper-division university work, but based on years of research, this is far more likely the result of *institutional differences* rather than *student shortcomings*. Adopting this mindset will help us develop effective initiatives.

- Transfer shock is defined as a drop in the student's GPA in the semester (or two) following transfer, but this drop in grades may be more of a symptom of "culture shock." Just as a fever is a measurable symptom for gauging one's health but in itself a fever is not generally considered a health problem; a drop in GPA is measurable and may be symptomatic of larger issues relating to navigating the new institution.

- Build partnerships between institutional departments with similar objectives, such as the writing center or academic success center, and with librarians at established "sending" institutions (feeder colleges) and "receiving" institutions (universities) to accomplish goals.

- There is strength in collaboration. Think of the oft-used expression "TEAM: Together Everyone Achieves More." Collaboration expands our reach and impact and builds and strengthens relationships.

References

Lafrance, Helene, and Shannon B. Kealey. 2017. "A Boutique Personal Librarian Program for Transfer Students." *Reference Services Review* 45(2): 332–45. doi:10.1108/RSR-10-2016-0066.

McBride, Kelly Rhodes, Margaret N. Gregor, and Kelly C. McCallister. 2017. "Bridging the Gap: Developing Library Services and Instructional Programs for Transfer Students at Appalachian State University." *Reference Services Review* 45(3): 498–510. doi:10.1108/RSR-10-2016-0067. https://search.proquest.com/docview/1938958222.

Roberts, Lindsay M., Megan E. Welsh, and Brittany Dudek. 2019. "Instruction and Outreach for Transfer Students: A Colorado Case Study." *College & Research Libraries* 80(1): 94–122. https://crl.acrl.org/index.php/crl/article/view/16925/18608.

Sandelli, Anna. 2017. "Through Three Lenses: Transfer Students and the Library." *Reference Services Review* 45(3): 400–414. doi:10.1108/RSR-10-2016-0074.

Staines, Gail M. 1996. "Moving Beyond Institutional Boundaries: Perceptions toward BI for Transfer Students." *Research Strategies* 14(2): 93–107.

Tag, Sylvia G. 2004. "A Library Instruction Survey for Transfer Students: Implications for Library Services." *Journal of Academic Librarianship* 30(2): 102–8. doi:10.1016/j.acalib.2004.01.001. https://www.sciencedirect.com/science/article/pii/S0099133304000023.

Tipton, Roberta L., and Patricia Bender. 2006. "From Failure to Success: Working with Under-Prepared Transfer Students." *Reference Services Review* 34(3): 389–404. doi:10.1108/00907320610685337.

Tobolowsky, Barbara F., and Bradley E. Cox. 2012. "Rationalizing Neglect: An Institutional Response to Transfer Students." *Journal of Higher Education* 83(3): 389–410. doi:10.1353/jhe.2012.0021. https://muse.jhu.edu/article/477073.

Townsend, Barbara K. 1995. "Community College Transfer Students: A Case Study of Survival." *Review of Higher Education* 18(2): 175–93. doi:10.1353/rhe.1995.0022.

Whang, Linda, Christine Tawatao, John Danneker, Jackie Belanger, Stephen Edward Weber, Linda Garcia, and Amelia Klaus. 2017. "Understanding the Transfer Student Experience Using Design Thinking." *Reference Services Review* 45(2): 298–313. https://www.emerald.com/insight/content/doi/10.1108/RSR-10-2016-0073/full/html.

CHAPTER 4

Information Literacy Designed to Support Transfer Student Success

The process of leaving one set of roles, relationships, routines, and assumptions and establishing new ones takes time. For some, the process happens easily and quickly; however, there are many people floundering, looking for the right niche, even after years.

—Nancy K. Schlossberg (2011, 160)

The Basics of Transition

Transfer students must navigate from familiar to unfamiliar information landscapes at institutions of higher education as they migrate from one school, college, or university to the next academic environment. Though these transfer experiences and transitions may have differing factors at play, Schlossberg (2011) suggests that there are certain features that are common to most transitions—whether job-related, education-related, or life-related situations. Schlossberg (2011) identifies a transition model encompassing the 4S System for coping with transitions:

- situation
- self
- support
- strategies

These four components of transition are helpful for academic librarians to be attentive to when working with transfer students. The transition model (Schlossberg 2011) is perhaps a well-known theory among higher education student services and academic services departments but not so well known in the academic disciplines and probably not common knowledge among academic librarians. Herein we can find, however, a transdisciplinary theory that can be applied to our work and should be useful to provide context and helpful guidance in serving students in transition.

Information Literacy as Tacit Knowledge for Transition

Possessing information literacy competencies provides a knowledge base that enables students to be confident about asking where to go for *support* and *strategies* for using information in their academic environment, wherever that may be. Information literacy can be a cornerstone of one's tacit knowledge (*self*) that can assist transfer students as they *strategically* navigate their new *situations,* academic expectations, and information spaces. Information literacy preparedness means students migrate from one *situation* to another with a knowledge base of information literacy understanding that keeps them confident and realistically *self*-assured. The transfer student *situation* refers to the students' situation at the time of the transition. For instance, what other factors of life are they dealing with? Family responsibilities, caring for an elderly parent, a new job, illness, financial concerns?

The transfer student as *self* refers to their inner strength to cope with the demands of their academic choices and journey, using their tacit knowledge to assist, and their confidence to continue.

The transfer student *support* refers to the support available at the time of transition. This is where academic libraries can play a vital role in assisting our transfer students as well as in being leaders in collaborative work with other academic departments in higher education.

The transfer student *strategies* refer to coping mechanisms in the transition model—such as brainstorming, reframing a situation, or using stress-reducing techniques. This could include the student initiating an appointment for a librarian consultation to address information literacy and the research process more intentionally or visiting a faculty member during their office hours to better understand their assignment.

Transition theory (Anderson, Goodman, and Schlossberg 2011) provides some context for this exploration of how information literacy can be a pathway for supporting transfer student success. Transfer students experience similar transition factors as do employees in a work transition as identified by Schlossberg (2011). The transition model can equip transfer students with a method to evaluate their individual knowledge base or their knowledge assets—what they already know—for the transfer experience.

As academic librarians learn to acknowledge these features of the transition model (Schlossberg 2011), we can better serve our transfer student populations. Whether the student is dual enrolled, transferring vertically, laterally, in reverse, even swirling, or a transient transfer student, information literacy instruction, situated in the library and information science (LIS) discipline, can be a cornerstone—a foundational, transdisciplinary, and trans-institutional—competency that transfer students acquire for a more seamless transition.

Information Literacy across the Higher Education Landscape

What does information literacy instruction look like across the higher education landscape? Community colleges, technical colleges, public state colleges, public universities, private colleges and universities, and for-profit higher education institutions deliver information literacy to students guided by their institutional priorities. This thread—information literacy—connects transfer students to their academic work throughout their higher education journey. Whether they are in a two-year college, four-year university, small or large, public or private institution of higher learning, information literacy is a common denominator of required competencies for academic success. What role does the academic library have to support transfer students? Recently (May 21, 2019), we sat down with Dr. John Budd, professor emeritus, University of Missouri, and asked this same question. He responded that the role most emphatically is "information literacy."

Information literacy as a common denominator for student success is a concept that supports the notion that "the key for transfer success is academic preparation and transparency, as articulated by the institutions that grant the baccalaureate degree" (Handel 2017). However, transfer students possess varying degrees of information literacy competencies as they progress in their academic journey and navigate new academic institutional cultures and requirements of rigor in their classes. Transfer students often possess the characteristics of being motivated and determined (Pun 2018). These assets are beneficial as they continue to work toward graduation at their new institution of higher learning. If transfer students are prepared for their next step toward reaching their academic goals, they are more confident in addressing academic, social, financial, and administrative challenges that may emerge at their new college or university (Strikwerda 2018). Being information literate can be a fundamental contributor to transfer student preparedness and confidence as they move forward in their academic pursuits—no matter the institution where they are studying.

For example, Joo and Choi (2015) found that undergraduate students studying at different academic ranks possess different levels of information searching competencies, which affect use of information or their "use intention" of online library resources. They found that usefulness and ease-of-use were positive influencers for student use intention of online library resources. There were five resource quality factors identified that influenced the use intention of online library resources. The five factors are accessibility, credibility, coverage, currency, and format.

The level of users' searching competencies ultimately resulted in whether they were able to locate the best content or sources for their academic work. This is important to note, as transfer students migrate along their educational pathway with different levels of information literacy competencies as tacit knowledge and are familiar with different online library resources. Hence, the findings from this study—that familiarity with sources and good searching skills had a significant effect on users' use intention at the individual user level—is something to note as we look at the library as part of the transfer students' academic community (Joo and Choi 2015). Interestingly, this study also identified that accessibility to the online library resource had the strongest influence on use intention and that credibility was the least influential. Therefore, our work to make credible sources easily accessible to students should be a heightened objective and priority in academic libraries across the higher education landscape.

Information Literacy—Scoped and Scaffolded

The *Framework for Information Literacy for Higher Education* (American Library Association 2015) shifts the approach of teaching information literacy from using linear information literacy standards (American Library Association 2000) to a nonlinear way of thinking and teaching information literacy.

> The Framework presents a shift in how academic librarians need to think about instruction, because it moves away from standard, learning outcomes, or any prescriptive enumeration of skill and toward a cluster of interconnected core concepts, with flexible options for implementation. (Hess 2015, 772)

This metacognitive approach has been reported to assist in facilitating productive conversations about teaching with faculty and librarians. Metacognition refers to "thinking about one's own thinking," situated in both the disciplines of psychology and educational psychology for over 35 years, and then adopted by practitioners across many disciplines (Fulkerson, Ariew, and Jacobson 2017). The research process as a problem-solving activity requires the engagement of metacognition. The essentiality of reflection (as noted in the definition of information literacy [ACRL 2015]) situates the requirement of the notion that the education and psychology communities first identified—that students learn when engaged in guided reflection (ACRL 2015). The research process is inherently recursive, in that it is a process that can be repeated inherently and across disciplines. The discursive aspect of threshold concepts further defines how learners migrate from novice to expert—or somewhere in between while in the liminal space—moving from topic to topic without order or evidential arguments. Liminality, or the liminal space that learners experience, is this stage when one may begin with some uncertainty regarding a topic or concept, but when they pass through this liminal portal, moving from uncertainty to new and transformative understanding, this is evidence of acquiring a threshold concept (Meyer and Land 2006, as cited in D'Angelo et al. 2016, chapter 2, provided by Dr. Holly Larson; Tucker et al. 2014). The learner experiences an "aha" moment and due to perhaps a new way of thinking introduced by the professor on a specific topic—or simply the learner connecting concepts in a new way than previously attuned to—there is a transformative, irreversible, integrated, and bounded experience the learner has that more emphatically grounds new understanding and that results in more substantially acquired knowledge on a specific topic in a specific discipline.

Using the *Framework* and the threshold concepts represented by the frames leads to conversations that are focused on teaching and how to teach (Latham, Gross, and Julien 2019) and in turn, to conversations about scaffolding information literacy concepts as a tiered approach—to support student learning as they move along a continuum from novice to more expert researchers—using a cluster type of metacognitive critical thinking. This scaffolding of information literacy concepts by course level or some other pathway, depending on the institution, facilitates student learning to build information literacy competencies throughout their academic careers (Dubicki 2019).

One of the best preparedness tools to deliver to students early in their academic career is to teach information literacy early and often in a variety of discipline-specific courses (Kaufmann 2018). Students who are confident about their ability to find, evaluate, and use information well for their coursework have a great advantage as they transfer from one institution to another. This is because they have acquired certain understandings of information literacy as threshold concepts.

Threshold concepts represent portals through which individuals cross and have a transformed understanding for a fundamental concept in a discipline. Threshold concepts have certain features or attributes. Threshold concepts are:

- **Transformative**—this experience is realized as a shift in understanding, perception, and even identity, such that one's values, attitudes, or even the acquisition of newly found confidence as a result of this transformative experience affects one's identity.

- **Troublesome**—this experience lends to the idea of discomfort or a counter-intuitive type of understanding that is exposed or revealed. It requires a bit of "wrangling" or "wrestling," and this may be due to new understandings challenging previously embraced preconceptions, knowledge, or ontological or epistemological prevailing thoughts.

- **Irreversible**—the experience affecting one's perception and understanding is not likely to be unlearned. The transformation of new understanding is situated and can be considered to be not easily reversed.

- **Integrative**—this experience reflects when one makes a connection to a concept or idea or connects new understanding to an idea or situation previously not understood to be connected, or the connection was somehow hidden or veiled. A more unified grouping of understanding of concepts or ideas is now prevalent and relevant to understanding, with an integrated approach to knowledge that was previously not understood.

- **Bounded**—this experience reflects the notion that there are "terminal frontiers" and particularly with regard to conceptual disciplinary ideas and vocabulary that may border or seem to infringe onto thresholds of new or other thresholds of understanding. More importantly, boundedness may assist in the notion of learners acquiring new understanding specific to disciplinary work and transdisciplinary understandings. (Meyer and Land 2006, as cited in D'Angelo et al. 2016, chapter 2)

When students acquire these fundamental threshold concepts for any discipline, they possess an asset that is foundational to their preparation for new experiences in their academic journey. This asset of tacit knowledge or their "knowledge base" of information literacy travels with the transfer student as they work in different information environments—from novice to expert researcher. The notion of acquiring transdisciplinary understanding relates to a holistic approach to threshold concepts. Transdisciplinary research refers to different disciplines that may typically use a variety of methodological approaches but provides for an integration that moves beyond discipline-specific approach to address a research problem or provide for new conceptual understandings (Harvard Transdisciplinary Research in Energetics and Cancer Center 2019). It is a holistic approach to solving complex research questions and provides for crossing discipline-specific methods and combining thoughtful approaches to solve complex investigations.

A transdisciplinary approach to curriculum suggests that integration may dissolve boundaries between conventional disciplines and organizes teaching and learning around the construction of meaning in the context of real-world problems or themes (UNESCO 2016c).

An interdisciplinary approach to curriculum refers to integration of understanding of themes and ideas. It provides opportunity to process meaning rather than product and content by combining contents, theories, methodologies and perspectives from two or more disciplines (UNESCO 2016a).

A multidisciplinary approach refers to ways to adopt pedagogy to the same topic from the viewpoint of more than one discipline. "Frequently multidisciplinary and cross-disciplinary are used as synonyms describing the aim to cross boundaries between disciplines" (International Bureau of Education [UNESCO] 2016b).

To summarize several types of approaches, a ResearchGate post leads us to the inspiration provided by a researcher at the University of Oslo who provides a nice comparison for consideration:

2nd Feb, 2016

Ljubomir Jacić

Technical College Požarevac

As inspired by @Raoof's contribution, I do continue.

- "Intradisciplinary: working within a single discipline.
- Crossdisciplinary: viewing one discipline from the perspective of another.
- Multidisciplinary: people from different disciplines working together, each drawing on their disciplinary knowledge.
- Interdisciplinary: integrating knowledge and methods from different disciplines, using a real synthesis of approaches.
- Transdisciplinary: creating a unity of intellectual frameworks beyond the disciplinary perspectives."

(Jensenius 2012)

A transdisciplinary approach is a holistic approach that embraces multiple disciplinary methods, theory, and thinking to address complex inquiries. Therefore, transdisciplinary understanding by learners crossing thresholds of understandings relating to information literacy concepts and disciplinary content may provide for a high level of synthesis of new knowledge. This metacognitive learning experience has the potential to encourage transfer students to use critical thinking more intuitively in their new situation and with future learning requirements.

Information literacy threshold concepts within the information science discipline are identified by the Association of College and Research Libraries (ACRL 2015) *Framework for Information Literacy for Higher Education* as:

- Authority is constructed and contextual
- Information creation as a process
- Information has value
- Research as inquiry
- Scholarship as conversation
- Searching as strategic exploration

This *Framework* is useful for instructional pedagogy for academic librarians at colleges and universities. Academic libraries and librarians have a unique platform to engage transfer students early in their journey (Robison 2017) by providing intentionally scheduled classes, outreach, or simply conversations with transfer students. This may require—or perhaps we can be so bold to suggest—does require collaboration across campus departments and across institutions to best serve our growing transfer student populations. The *Framework* provides an excellent metacognitive pathway to engage other-discipline faculty to begin conversations about crossing thresholds of understandings by applying information literacy competencies to specific course assignments—thus, enriching student learning in a transdisciplinary scoped and scaffolded but rigorous environment.

In a recent study of transfer students, which focused on understanding their needs and challenges, a survey was administered by the University of Washington academic library (Whang et al. 2017, 298–313). Survey results showed significantly higher levels of confidence among those transfer students who had participated in formal information literacy instruction. The survey findings also indicated that transfer students do need information about their new library, and survey participants suggested small group settings or private communications for receiving this information was preferred. The study also identified a critical window to deliver information literacy instruction and provide information about the library to transfer students. This small segment of time was found to be the period from when transfer students arrive on campus through the second week of class. Though this is quite specific to the University of Washington population of transfer students, perhaps we can take some important takeaways for the importance of scoping and scaffolding information literacy instruction and general library outreach to transfer students on our campuses.

How academic libraries deliver information literacy may look differently, as influenced by the institutional strategic plan and mission, as well as the library mission. The delivery of information literacy is informed by the institutions' information literacy instruction program, liaison relationships, and structure of communication between academic instruction librarians, other faculty, and the local institution community of practice. In addition, other influences impacting how academic libraries deliver information literacy instruction could include instructional designer interventions, e-learning protocols, specific departmental policies, or other department or stakeholder procedures at the college or university.

Beyond what has traditionally been researched on the transfer student experience, such as student level variables including race, gender, GPA, the transfer student experience is also influenced by a variety of subtle institutional influences (Tobolowsky and Cox 2012). These hidden institutional influences can also shape the transfer student experience.

To address subtle institutional influences, Tobolowsky and Cox (2012) suggest using organization theory as a suitable framework to attend to multiple lenses—rational, natural, and open system perspectives—which may be reflected as less explicit influences. Using organization theory provides a theoretical framework to more accurately identify less obvious institutional influence by using multiple lenses to assist us in knowing how to best serve this growing but often invisible population on our campuses. Using organization theory to incorporate a multidimensional approach to examine official policies and structure of an institution and how this may affect transfer students may lead to needed alterations that can be implemented across the spectrum of departments that are influencing and guiding our transfer students.

Partnerships between College and University Academic Librarians

One key factor toward supporting transfer student preparedness and transparency is for faculty and staff at four-year institutions to get to know faculty, staff, and even students of feeder colleges or other universities where transfer students often come from. This collaboration and communication between institutions can deter transfer student failure or minimize transfer shock impacted by higher education cultural, administrative, or bureaucratic barriers or misunderstandings (Strikwerda 2018) and support the transfer student in practical ways (Taylor and Jain 2017).

One of the key findings from a study investigating ways to support students in transition included that two- and four-year college and university partnerships are instrumental to successful transfer student transitions. The research indicated these partnerships between the two-year degree granting institutions and the baccalaureate degree granting institutions is paramount to strengthening the transfer student pathways to effective degree completion and enhanced learning experiences (Rodriguez-Kiino 2013). "When a 4-year campus does not have a strong transfer receptive culture and does not attempt to partner effectively with community colleges [feeder colleges or others], this can result in ineffective outreach, access, and retention for transfer students"

(Taylor and Jain 2017, 279). As noted in chapter 3, it's important for information literacy instruction design for transfer students to be shaped by increased communication between two- and four-year institution librarians (Staines 1996; McBride, Gregor, and McCallister 2017).

Nuhn and Kaufmann conducted a cross-institutional study between state colleges and a university that enjoy a DirectConnect partnership, which provides students graduating with an AA degree from a DirectConnect college to transfer seamlessly to the university. The study investigated the elements of information literacy instruction delivered by the university librarians to the elements of information literacy instruction delivered by state college academic librarians and was presented at the ALA Annual Conference 2018 in a session titled "Building Inclusion: How Can Information Literary Instruction at Two-Year Colleges Help Students Successfully Transition to the University?" (Nuhn et al. 2018, June 23). (See the LibGuide: https://guides.ucf.edu/building inclusion.in "Practical Application of Chapter 4.")

Findings reflected alignment among many of the information literacy elements taught at both the colleges and the university. However, there were several elements where "gaps" in instruction were identified. These "gaps" include:

- Caution when using database-generated citations
- MLA/APA citation resources
- Identifying parts of a citation
- Recognizing a research study
- Avoiding plagiarism
- Understanding the information cycle
- Literature review

An academic librarian from Pensacola, Florida, who attended the ALA presentation reflected via the LIS College Report Card as a guest blogger, that:

When I really started to think about what my students were having the most problems with, I would have to agree with the findings. The biggest thing my students have problems with is citations, even after instruction and in-class and out-of-class practice. Many of my students don't seem to understand the difference between an article title and a journal title. They don't know what those numbers are (volume and issue numbers). They insist on including helpful abbreviations for the volume and page numbers they do include. They don't want to use a citation generator or get help from the writing lab or from me. I don't have an instant solution to the citations problem. I'm still trying to figure out how to give citations more time and/or a more practical approach. I have started to be more mindful about the other topics on the need-more-work list as well.

Still, I have to think that the students attending basic LIS classes are more prepared to go to a university than those who don't, and perhaps other professors (and high school teachers) requiring excellence with citations will help students master this skill. That students are aware of the power of databases and how to use them and that they can navigate a library somewhat successfully is a win in my book.

An outcome from this information literacy element study presented at the 2018 ALA Conference (Nuhn et al. 2018, June 23) resulted in a day-long "Celebration of Librarian Collaboration for Transfer Student Success" event. This inaugural meeting of academic librarians was well attended by librarians and administrative representatives from each of the six partner colleges and from the university. The day began with opening remarks from dignitaries from the host college and university, followed by a keynote address from a university representative, providing an environmental scan of the transfer students as a unique community at the university. The rest of the day was all about librarians talking with librarians—about what we do, what our challenges are regarding instruction and transfer students, and how we might further collaborate to support transfer students at our respective institutions. To collect participant data, there were paper posters situated in the meeting room with prompts for attendees to respond to by writing their comments and then dot stickers for others to indicate they too agreed or supported the statement recorded on the poster. Some polling was randomly done during the day, and participants were invited to complete an exit survey to provide feedback on the day and give suggestions for planning the "Second Annual Celebration of Librarian Collaboration for Transfer Student Success" event. (See chapter 6 for more on this topic.)

This is an example of the possibility of enhancing communications among our shared partners across institutions and the significant conversations, connections, and ongoing goodwill produced by simply but intentionally building bridges between our academic librarian colleagues across institutions to support information literacy instruction for transfer students.

Transfer Student Information Literacy: User Experience in Academic Libraries

The transfer student may find that their information literacy experience at their previous college or university may differ from their new college or university. The transfer student, depending on the type of transfer experience with which they identify: dual enrollment, vertical transfer, lateral transfer, swirling transfer, double-dipping transfer, or transient transfer (see chapter 1 for a detailed review of these scenarios)—may find gaps in their information literacy competencies and preparedness to succeed academically. Due to these various pathways to continue their higher education, transfer students may find that they come underprepared for the information literacy and research process and competencies needed at their new college or university. When students transfer from a two-year college to a four-year university, they most likely have chosen to take on a transition in both content and style of learning (Tipton and Bender 2006). As Schlossberg (2011) identifies *situation, self, support,* and *strategies* to successfully navigate transitions, librarians should recognize the content and style of learning may potentially touch each of these four Ss in the transfer student experience and may impact the student's system of coping with transition.

Therefore, as librarians, we can play a significant role in being a resourceful and user-friendly ally for transfer students as they begin to learn more about their new institution and the resources available to them to be academically successful.

A few of the key findings from a study of transfer students and the library at DePaul University (Alverson et al. 2017) found that:

- Transfer students knew how to use the library physical space but didn't have opportunities to engage with librarians or enhance their information literacy competencies.

- Transfer students reported experiencing "transfer shock"—felt overwhelmed, intimidated, and underprepared for the academic challenges at DePaul, including faculty expectations and navigating campus life.

- Transfer students may not identify as such beyond their first quarter or semester.

A summary of the key findings from a recent transfer student study specific to the role of academic libraries—perceptions of academic librarians—in Colorado (Roberts, Welsh, and Dudek 2019), contextualized with findings from surveys of academic libraries in New York and Ohio, provides the following for consideration:

- There seems to be a trend across 30 years of librarianship—that transfer students have not been identified as a distinct population by academic libraries.

- Two-year college librarians may not recognize their role in preparing transfer students for their next step with transferrable information literacy competencies, resources, and confidence.

- Two-year college librarians also serve transfer students and have perhaps not recognized an opportunity for engagement and enhancement of information literacy competencies.

- Four-year university or college librarians may not recognize the specific need of transfer students, as subject librarians with assumptions of preparedness, or recognize previous potential gaps in information literacy instruction of transfer students.
- Cross-institutional collaboration and strengthening of local networks of feeder colleges or simply local communities of practice may help ease transition and enhance success for transfer students.

Table 4.1 provides a comparative look at the mapped findings from these studies—one which investigates the student or user view and one which investigates the academic librarian view—alongside transition theory.

This mapping of data using transition theory as a lens provides a comparative look at studies revealing student and academic librarian views. This chart indicates that students are asking for support that academic librarians are quite willing and interested in providing. In fact, for each view identified

Table 4.1 Transfer Student and Librarian Views of Transition

Transition theory	Student view *Schlossberg (2011);* *Alverson et al. (2017)*	Librarian view *Roberts, Welsh, and Dudek (2019)*
Strategy	Need opportunities to engage with librarians or enhance their information literacy competencies	Two-year college librarians also serve transfer students and have perhaps not recognized an opportunity for engagement and enhancement of information literacy competencies
Situation	Experienced "transfer shock"—felt overwhelmed, intimidated, and underprepared for the academic challenges	Four-year university or college librarians may not recognize specific need of transfer students, as subject librarians with assumptions of preparedness, or recognize potential gaps in information literacy instruction of transfer students
Support	Challenged with faculty expectations and navigating campus life	Two-year college librarians may not recognize their role in preparing transfer students for their next step with transferrable information literacy competencies, resources, and confidence

(Continued)

Table 4.1   (Continued)

Self	Transfer students may not identify as such beyond their first quarter or semester	Transfer students have not been identified as a distinct population by academic libraries; however, cross-institutional collaboration and strengthening of local networks of feeder colleges or local communities of practice may help ease the transition and enhance success for transfer students

by transfer students in these studies, the academic librarian perceptions align quite seamlessly. The student views and librarian perceptions all align into the 4S categories of transition: *situation, self, support, and strategies*. There seems to be an understanding of what transfer students articulate they need and what academic librarians articulate to be areas they would like to contribute to. Therefore, we understand the *why*, as guided by the four *Ss* in transition theory: *strategy, situation, support, and self*. We also understand the *what*: answered by students and librarians in the studies reflected in the chart. Now to work on the *how*. *How* can academic libraries fill these gaps in transfer student needs and expectations? There is opportunity and interest (Roberts, Welsh, and Dudek 2019) for academic librarians to be a more intentional partner in contributing to transfer student learning and academic achievement. We can more fully engage with transfer student transition needs regarding *situation, self, support, and strategy*. As this distinct population continues to expand, the academic library can be proactive as a collaborator and innovator in supporting transfer students in connecting to our campus communities holistically, socially, and academically.

As noted earlier, the study conducted at the University of Washington libraries (2017) found similar findings as the DePaul study (Alverson et al. 2017). Since transfer students often immediately enroll in upper-division courses, they may miss out on introductory library sessions offered to first- and second-year students. Both studies also identified the transfer student populations with multiple responsibilities such as outside jobs, families, and social networks outside of the academic institution.

Using "design thinking" the University of Washington study outcome helps answer the *how*. The study findings uncovered raising awareness with the library staff of transfer student needs was a good next step. This simple but impactful step of raising library staff awareness of transfer students shifted the focus of the library staff toward building a "collaborative culture" across departments such as First Year Programs, admissions, and other relevant departments. The "design thinking" approach provided a venue for the library to experience internalized and formalized methods of continuous engagement with all users, including transfer students. This operationalized model proved a way for "design thinking" to allow new ideas that are generated for student support to then be incorporated into ongoing library activities—such as marketing, creating a culture of cross-departmental collaboration, and creating innovative solutions to meet user needs. This idea of how and when to build collaborative partnerships will be addressed more fully in chapter 5.

"Transfer shock" is a reality for our transfer students. Academic librarians can take a lead in mitigating this phenomenon by becoming informed of the elements of transition specific to information literacy competencies—once again, raising awareness of the potential gaps in transfer student information literacy competency preparedness. Nuhn and Kaufmann (Nuhn et al. 2018) identified five keys to mitigate information literacy transfer shock:

1. Identify specific elements of information literacy instruction.
2. Align these elements with the *Framework for Information Literacy for Higher Education.*
3. Identify element gaps between college and university expectations.
4. Engage in authentic collaboration across institutions and departments.
5. Fill the gaps.

These five keys can be adapted to a variety of transfer scenarios and communities of practice. Whether you are a librarian at a college or university, there are ways to incorporate these five keys to get started thinking, conversing with colleagues, and strategizing to address information literacy transfer shock for students. (See chapter 6 for more on this topic.)

Information Literacy Relevant to the Real World and Everyday Information

Making information literacy relevant to transfer students can bridge some of the gaps vital to supporting transfer student academic success. The academic library has a key role and wonderful opportunity to engage transfer students early in their transfer experience. A good beginning for academic libraries and librarians includes an awareness of this significant and growing population of students on our campuses. Having a heightened awareness provides opportunity to have a favorable impact on transfer student retention, completion, and engagement with transfer students as they navigate their new campus community. When there is a raised awareness of transfer students at the institutional level, this results in a subtle encouragement to faculty and staff to increase time, energy, money, and other resources to facilitate transfer student success (Tobolowsky and Cox 2012). This refocus at the institutional level provides a platform to take a fresh look at policy and practices that may need to be revised to improve meeting the needs of this sizable and growing student population.

Since information literacy is a common denominator of required competencies for academic success, using information to learn across disciplines bridges thresholds of understanding for transfer students in their new academic setting. Transfer students can possess substantive information literacy competencies, as reflected in their knowledge base and acquisition of certain thresholds of understanding regarding their research process as they arrive on a new campus. More fully prepared and therefore confident, these students can apply information literacy competencies quite readily, mitigating transfer shock and information literacy gaps as they continue to use information literacy as a crosswalk to new understandings in discipline-specific content and their new academic community.

Academic librarians can use the 4S transition model (Schlossberg 2011) to assist in framing a strategic way of thinking to assist transfer students in coping with their transition to attain their academic goals. The transfer student *situation* refers to the students' situation at the time of the transition. The transfer student as *self* refers to their inner strength to cope with the demands of their academic choices. The transfer student *support* refers to the support available at the time of transition. The transfer student's *strategies* refer to coping mechanisms they find useful (Schlossberg 2011).

Academic librarians can and should address each of these areas of transition that our transfer students may find to be part of their journey. Developing intentional options means we identify ways in which we can strategize across institutions, departments, and at the immediate local level to find out how to enhance our transfer student's acclimation to our library resources—including human resources.

The 4S transition model provides structure for analyzing transition (Schlossberg 2011). The academic library can use this model to consider how to optimize support for transfer students as they transition from one institution of higher learning to the next and how to strengthen our resources to support this growing student population on our college and university campuses.

Chapter 5 will explore more specifically some options for academic libraries and librarians to connect the academic library more successfully and intentionally to meet the needs of our transfer student populations.

Practical Applications of Chapter 4

- Recognize information literacy as tacit knowledge: the transfer student's knowledge base—what they know.
- Acknowledge that good searching skills and accessibility to the library sources impact how students use the library.
- Acknowledge threshold concepts—portals through which individuals cross and have a transformed understanding for a fundamental concept in a discipline—to talk about transdisciplinary work.
- Identify ways to integrate and educate faculty about threshold concepts, the specific features or attributes that can be integrated into collaborative teaching and learning pedagogies across a variety of disciplines.

  Transformative—this experience is realized as a shift in understanding, perception, and even identity such that one's values, attitudes, or even the acquisition of newly found confidence as a result of this transformative experience affects one's identity.

  Troublesome—this experience lends to the idea of discomfort or a counter-intuitive type of understanding that is exposed or revealed. It requires a bit of "wrangling" or "wrestling," and this may be due to new understandings challenging previously embraced preconceptions, knowledge, or ontological or epistemological prevailing thoughts.

  Irreversible—the experience affecting one's perception and understanding is not likely to be unlearned. The transformation of new understanding is situated and can be considered to be not easily reversed.

  Integrative—this experience reflects when one makes a connection to a concept or idea or connects new understanding to an idea or situation previously not understood to be connected, or the connection was somehow hidden or veiled. A more unified grouping of understanding of concepts or ideas is now prevalent and relevant to understanding, with an integrated approach to knowledge that was previously not understood.

  Bounded—this experience reflects the notion that there are "terminal frontiers" and particularly with regard to conceptual disciplinary ideas and vocabulary that may border or seem to infringe onto thresholds of new or other thresholds of understanding. More importantly, boundedness may assist in the notion of learners acquiring new understanding specific to disciplinary work and transdisciplinary understandings. Use collaborative relationships with discipline faculty to scaffold and engage transfer students early in their journey (Robison 2017) by providing intentionally scheduled classes, outreach events, or creating partnerships with on-campus or cross-campus transfer institutions.

- Talk about ways to build collaborative work to assist transfer students among colleagues at your institution and with local transfer institutions:

  > Here's an example: LibGuide: https://guides.ucf.edu/buildinginclusion. ALA Annual Conference 2018 in a session titled: "Building Inclusion: How Can Information Literary Instruction at Two-Year Colleges Help Students Successfully Transition to the University?"

- Build collaborative relationships between two- and four-year college and university partnerships. These relationships are instrumental to support successful transfer student transitions.

- Be an advocate to communicate awareness of transfer shock with library colleagues.

- Acknowledge elements of the Schlossberg transition theory for coping with transitions that transfer students face: *situation*, *self*, *support*, and *strategies*.

- Raise awareness of the potential gaps in transfer student information literacy competency preparedness in formal and informal settings.

- Pay attention to hidden institutional influences that could be barriers to supporting transfer student success at your institution.

- Use marketing content to raise awareness of information literacy transfer shock. Infographic: Five Keys to Mitigate Information Literacy Transfer Shock.

References

Alverson, Jessica, Susan Shultz, Jill King, and Morgen MacIntosh-Hodgetts. 2017. *DePaul University Transfer Students and the Library*. DePaul University.

American Library Association. 2000. "Information Literacy Competency Standards for Higher Education." http://www.ala.org/acrl/standards/informationliteracy competency.

American Library Association. 2015. "*Framework for Information Literacy for Higher Education*." http://www.ala.org/acrl/standards/ilframework.

Anderson, Mary, Jane Goodman, and Nancy K. Schlossberg. 2011. *Counseling Adults in Transition: Linking Schlossberg's Theory with Practice in a Diverse World*. Springer Publishing Company.

D'Angelo, Barbara J., Sandra Jamieson, Barry M. Maid, and Janice R. Walker, eds. 2016. *Information Literacy: Research and Collaboration across Disciplines*. Perspectives on Writing. Fort Collins, CO: WAC Clearinghouse.

Dubicki, Eleonora. 2019. "Mapping Curriculum Learning Outcomes to ACRL's Framework Threshold Concepts: A Syllabus Study." *The Journal of Academic Librarianship* 45(3): 288–98. doi:10.1016/j.acalib.2019.04.003. https://www.sciencedirect.com/science/article/pii/S0099133319300825.

Fulkerson, Diane, Susan Ariew, and Trudi Jacobson. 2017. "Revisiting Metacognition and Metaliteracy in the ACRL Framework." *Comminfolit* 11(1): 21–41. doi:10.15760/comminfolit.2017.11.1.45. https://search.proquest.com/docview/1927088053.

Handel, Stephen. 2017. "Transfer Students Deserve Better Road Maps." *Chronicle of Higher Education*. Accessed September 11, 2019. https://www.chronicle.com/article/Transfer-Students-Deserve/238772.

Harvard Transdisciplinary Research in Energetics and Cancer Center. 2019. Accessed September 11, 2019. https://www.hsph.harvard.edu/trec/about-us/definitions/.

Hess, Amanda Nichols. 2015. "Equipping Academic Librarians to Integrate the Framework into Instructional Practices: A Theoretical Application." *Journal of Academic Librarianship* 41(6): 771–76. doi:10.1016/j.acalib.2015.08.017. https://www.sciencedirect.com/science/article/pii/S0099133315001755.

International Bureau of Education [UNESCO]. 2016a. "General Education System Quality Analysis/Diagnosis Framework, Interdisciplinary Approach." Accessed September 11, 2019. http://www.ibe.unesco.org/fr/node/12230.

International Bureau of Education [UNESCO]. 2016b. "General Education System Quality Analysis/Diagnosis Framework, Multidisciplinary Approach." Accessed September 11, 2019. http://www.ibe.unesco.org/en/glossary-curriculum-terminology/m/multidisciplinary-approach.

International Bureau of Education [UNESCO]. 2016c. "General Education System Quality Analysis/Diagnosis Framework, Transdisciplinary Approach." Accessed September 11, 2019. http://www.ibe.unesco.org/en/glossary-curriculum-terminology/t/transdisciplinary-approach.

Jensenius, Alexander Refsum. 2012. *Disciplinarities: Intra, Cross, Multi, Inter, Trans—Alexander Refsum Jensenius*. http://www.arj.no/2012/03/12/disciplinarities-2/.

Joo, Soohyung, and Namjoo Choi. 2015. "Factors Affecting Undergraduates' Selection of Online Library Resources in Academic Tasks." *Library Hi Tech* 33(2): 272–91. doi:10.1108/LHT-01-2015-0008. https://search.proquest.com/docview/1684436490.

Kaufmann, Karen F. 2018. "Sociocognitive Relevance of Information Literacy: The Impact on Student Academic Work." PhD thesis. Queensland University of Technology. https://eprints.qut.edu.au/123999/

Latham, Don, Melissa Gross, and Heidi Julien. 2019. "Implementing the ACRL Framework: Reflections from the Field." *College & Research Libraries* 80(3): 386.

Meyer, Jan, and Ray Land. 2006. "Threshold Concepts and Troublesome Knowledge: Issues of Liminality." In *Overcoming Barriers to Student Understanding*, 43–56. Routledge.

McBride, Kelly Rhodes, Margaret N. Gregor, and Kelly C. McCallister. 2017. "Bridging the Gap." *Reference Services Review* 45 (3): 498–510. doi: 10.1108/RSR-10-2016-0067. https://search.proquest.com/docview /1938958222.

Nuhn, P., K. Kaufmann, R. Mulvihill, and M. Tracy. 2018, June 23. "Building Inclusion: How Can Research Instruction at Two-Year Colleges Help Students Successfully Transition to the University?" [Conference Presentation]. June 21–26, 2018.

Pun, Raymond. 2018. "Helping Transfer Students Succeed: General Tips & Strategies for Academic Librarians." *Credo* (blog). Accessed September 11, 2019.

Roberts, Lindsay, Megan E. Welsh, and Brittany Dudek. 2019. "Instruction and Outreach for Transfer Students: A Colorado Case Study." *College & Research Libraries* 80(1): 94. https://crl.acrl.org/index.php/crl/article/viewFile/169 25/18608.

Robison, Mark. 2017. "Connecting Information Literacy Instruction with Transfer Student Success." *Reference Services Review* 45(3): 511–26. doi:10.1108/ RSR-10-2016-0065.

Rodriguez-Kiino, Diane. 2013. "Supporting Students in Transition: Perspectives and Experiences of Community College Transfer Students." *Journal of Applied Research in the Community College* 20(2): 5. https://search.proquest .com/docview/1640488156.

Schlossberg, Nancy K. 2011. "The Challenge of Change: The Transition Model and Its Applications." *Journal of Employment Counseling* 48(4): 159–62. doi:10.1002/j.2161-1920.2011.tb01102.x. https://search.proquest.com /docview/912809137.

Staines, Gail M. 1996. "Moving Beyond Institutional Boundaries: Perceptions toward BI for Transfer Students." *Research Strategies* 2(14): 93–107.

Strikwerda, Carl. 2018. "Why Community Colleges Are Good for You." *Chronicle of Higher Education*. Accessed September 11, 2019. https://www.chronicle .com/article/Why-Community-Colleges-Are/242359.

Taylor, Jason L., and Dimpal Jain. 2017. "The Multiple Dimensions of Transfer: Examining the Transfer Function in American Higher Education." *Community College Review* 45(4): 273–93. doi:10.1177/0091552117725177.

Tipton, Roberta L., and Patricia Bender. 2006. "From Failure to Success: Working with Under-Prepared Transfer Students." *Reference Services Review* 34(3): 389–404. doi:10.1108/00907320610685337.

Tobolowsky, Barbara F., and Bradley E. Cox. 2012. "Rationalizing Neglect: An Institutional Response to Transfer Students." *Journal of Higher Education* 83(3): 389–410.

Tucker, Virginia M., Judith Weedman, Christine S. Bruce, and Sylvia L. Edwards. 2014. "Learning Portals: Analyzing Threshold Concept Theory for LIS

Education." *Journal of Education for Library and Information Science* 55(2): 150–65. https://www.jstor.org/stable/43686977.

Whang, Linda, Christine Tawatao, John Danneker, Jackie Belanger, Stephen Edward Weber, Linda Garcia, and Amelia Klaus. 2017. "Understanding the Transfer Student Experience Using Design Thinking." *Reference Services Review* 45(2): 298–313. doi:10.1108/RSR-10-2016-0073.

Connecting the Library to Transfer Students

On Collaboration: "Incremental adjustment at the margins will not suffice, alteration in fundamental practice will be needed."
—David Lewis, dean of the Indiana University–Purdue University, Indianapolis, 2007

Using Schlossberg's transition theory to guide our work, let's explore ways to connect transfer students to our academic libraries. Let's not tinker around the edges (Tinto 2008)—as mentioned in chapter 2 but look at ways to use transition theory to address "transfer shock" and be intentional in uncovering our role in supporting transfer students.

How or what role do academic libraries play to *support* transfer student success as they reach to their own inner strengths or *self*? How do academic libraries more effectively and *strategically* collaborate and build partnerships with academic librarian colleagues and other-discipline faculty to address information literacy competencies? How can we more effectively address barriers to teaching and conversing about information literacy and using information to learn?

There is a potential opportunity for the library to connect the student's inner strength or *self* to cope with their new institutional and local community of practice regarding their academic work and research. Providing additional or value-added *support* such as guidance or referral to other departments, administration, colleagues in the library, faculty liaisons, or even contacting colleagues at other colleges or universities may be opportunities for the library. Identifying *strategies* for transfer students to use for engaging their information literacy competencies across disciplines can be a significant connecting point for academic librarians to support transfer students in their journey to graduation. There may be barriers that are part of the transfer student's *situation* relating to the library or information literacy competencies and research skills. Recent evidence-based research reveals that the library can be a key player as a provider of local campus knowledge and be a "library as place" for transfer students looking for a community to connect to (Harrick and Fullington 2019).

Transfer Student Situation

The transfer student's *situation* may reveal some barriers to their successful transition to a new academic environment, including the new library at their college or university (Taylor and Jain 2017).

Figure 5.1 is Twitter post that succinctly illustrates and exposes some of this dilemma.

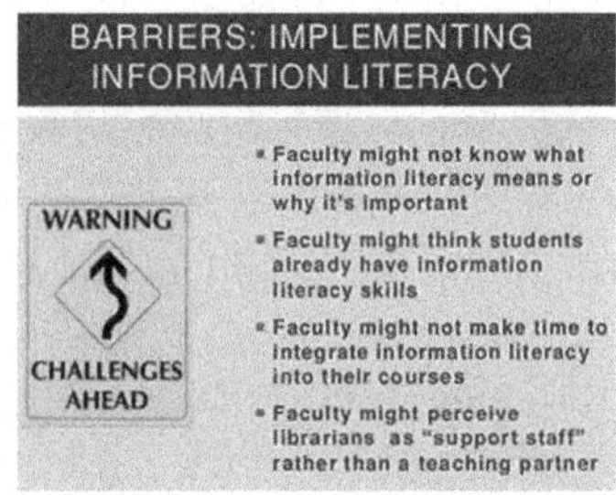

B for BARRIERS: One thing we have come up against in our project is the misunderstandings around information literacy, what it means and how it can be incorporated, not to mention how the librarian is perceived . . . please help us to overcome these barriers!

Twitter Post 2/13/2019 @ILSpaces **#AtoZInfoLit #infolit**

Figure 5.1   Information Literacy Barriers.

How can we build bridges and engage in scholarly conversations across and between institutions of higher learning where transfer students engage in the academic research process and need support for their research and information literacy competency enrichment to support their new *situation*?

Barrier Breaker 1: How to Talk about Information Literacy with Faculty

One potential barrier identified is how faculty librarians or teaching librarians can effectively communicate with other faculty to bridge understandings of the value of integrating information literacy into the course curriculum, assignments, and assessments and work more seamlessly as collaborators. When this is addressed effectively, transfer students—perhaps all students—are positively impacted by our effective communications. When we professionally acknowledge the strengths of the discipline faculty who is the content expert, and the library faculty who is the information literacy expert, a new and refreshing dynamic occurs. Students are presented with a model of higher education collaboration and pedagogically sound transdisciplinary teaching that enables and empowers a new way of critically thinking about their assignment. They now have permission—if you will—to explore, ask questions, be willing to fail a bit to find new and perhaps unexpected ways to apply sources they find to answer their thesis or research question for an assignment. There is not a tug of war between professors as discipline experts and professors of library science or information literacy experts as professors, but rather, an organic and supportive environment for students and faculty to engage and expand knowledge and the scholarly conversation in an interactive and scholarly manner.

To address this barrier, librarians at UNC Wilmington (UNCW) inaugurated an Information Literacy Faculty Fellows (ILFF) program in spring 2018 (Crowe, Pemberton, and Yeager 2019).

This program trains faculty and instructors from across the university in the knowledge practices, dispositions, and threshold concepts embedded in the *Framework*. Faculty develop concrete plans for integrating one or more of these concepts into their courses by working with liaison librarians and each other. Their hope was to develop a community of practice at UNCW surrounding information literacy and to embed the *Framework* throughout the curriculum. The program encourages librarians and teaching faculty to view information literacy as a shared responsibility, one that doesn't end at the library door but is integrated throughout the academic experience.

The first cohort of 10 faculty met weekly for six workshops, each focusing on one frame of the ACRL's *Framework for Information Literacy for Higher Education* (ACRL 2015). Stipends were provided to faculty who completed all the workshops and submitted a concrete assignment, lesson plan, or syllabus that reflected integrating one or more of the IL *Framework* concepts. This first faculty cohort had a 100 percent participation rate of both workshop and final project submission completions.

Assessing perceptions of the Faculty Fellow program was a key component to learn what to do differently to improve the program. Faculty participated in a first assessment per their application to the program. Faculty selected from the application pool provided a preprogram reflection assessment of their familiarity and understanding of information literacy concepts as well as their student's familiarity. Perceptions of the program were gathered from the ILFF faculty and librarians participating in the program. The faculty final project was evaluated by the participating librarians. Finally, a post one-year assessment of the impact of the program for fellows, their department, and students is planned.

The ILFF was found to provide some significant discoveries in terms of ways to work with and collaborate with discipline faculty across disciplines. For example librarians learned that the knowledge practices and dispositions of the *Framework* were found to be useful to faculty, but expanded definitions and concrete examples of way the *Framework* could be applied were needed. Also needed was more time for collaboration on assignment creation, information literacy session development, and one-on-one discussions to brainstorm on creative but effective ways to integrate information literacy and students into the conversations. One outcome showed that perhaps combining some of the *frames* in a discussion could be a useful tool to consider active learning ideas and other pedagogical approaches to teaching discipline content while also teaching information literacy competencies.

This was a barrier-breaking/bridge-building opportunity to update the teaching faculty's understanding of information literacy concepts and to reestablish teaching information literacy as a collaborative partnership between teaching faculty and librarians. This also was an attempt to move beyond what academic librarians often refer to as "one-shot instruction" to a more integrated, systematic, and program-conscious intention of including information literacy into disciplinary work.

Using a variety of pedagogical approaches, the *Framework* encourages these kinds of conversations across disciplines and among faculty. For example, active learning, problem-based learning, inquiry-based learning and self-directed learning, evidence-based practices, and independent research allow student learning to draw on their previous experiences, can be fostered, and provide pathways to more effective and transformative learning for students. This points to a type of curriculum design called informed learning (Bruce 2008; Bruce and Hughes 2010; Maybee et al. 2013; Maybee 2015, 2018), where there is a focus on information literacy and content learning at the same time. This metacognitive information experience provides students with an intentional and explicit focus on using information within a context (Maybee 2018; Bruce and Hughes 2010). This could be especially impactful for transfer students who arrive with different understandings and perspectives of how to use information to learn, based on their current knowledge base and previous experiences.

As academic librarians, we can assist transfer students in overcoming barriers based on their *situation* by providing this diverse population on our campuses a pathway to transformative learning. This can be accomplished using a pedagogically sound approach to teaching—information to learn within a context. This begins by building teaching collaborations with discipline faculty.

Barrier Breaker 2: Teaching Collaborations

There are many ways for discipline faculty and library faculty to collaborate to both scope and scaffold information literacy instruction (Dubicki 2019) for transfer students. This intentional work can be effective as a tiered approach to move transfer students along the learning continuum as information literacy competencies are learned and applied to research and other academic assignments. Dubicki (2019) used a syllabus study to learn that faculty-defined student learning outcomes, when mapped to the ACRL *Framework* threshold concepts, was an effective approach to build collaborative work with faculty and effectively scope and scaffold information literacy competencies into the curriculum. Scaffolding information literacy concepts by course level keeps students moving forward and toward crossing new thresholds of understanding throughout their academic journey. For transfer students, this is especially poignant for their learning and continued progress as critical thinkers and 21st-century lifelong learners.

Latham, Gross, and Julien (2019) did an exploratory study with librarians to learn their perceptions of and experience with the *Framework*. The study revealed that perhaps a barrier to building effective teaching partnerships lies within our own discipline. Academic librarian perception challenges toward the *Framework* and teaching partnerships—once identified—may assist in moving toward embracing some of the successful strategies identified in this recent study. *Framework* perception challenges by the librarians in this study reveal the following:

- Teaching time and discipline-faculty allowance for information literacy instruction.
- One-shot instruction limits opportunities for scaffolding information literacy instruction.
- *Framework* concepts (nebulous, nonlinear) versus standards skills (concrete, linear)—a difficult migration.
- Assessment of student learning using the framework.
- Perception of the framework as elitist.

Successful strategies were also identified in this study in terms of academic librarian perceptions and include:

- Training to work with other librarians using the framework.
- Having conversations with other librarians about teaching.
- The conceptual nature of the framework has more value in conversations with discipline faculty—it's "meatier" and results in more effective conversations about teaching.
- Focus on the frames most relevant to a session or course assignment.

Assessment of student learning was an area that was perceived as challenging by librarians. There perhaps is a need to shift from standards type of thinking for assessment to a bigger picture of assessment—looking at student progress in a longitudinal approach rather than in a one-shot/one-session assessment model. This supports the threshold concept model and that these frames can be scoped and scaffolded to course-specific student learning outcomes (Dubicki 2019). To assess student learning of the *Framework* concepts, it could require a pivot—and that we look at assessment over the course of their education. To do this, one suggestion is to require an entry-level library and information science (LIS) course and then use a student capstone course to assess information literacy competencies reflected in their final coursework or thesis.

Barrier Breaker 3: Assessment: A Friend to Building Partnerships

Using assessment tools as a "barrier breaker" may be a consideration for colleges and universities' academic librarians to consider. If colleges are working toward assessing student learning outcomes based on the American Library Association Framework (2015), then those results may be useful for universities and other colleges to also take note of as they formulate information literacy instruction for transfer students. However, using the *Framework* requires understanding and shifting from an outcome "counting" type of assessment to using threshold concepts as the cornerstone to create assessments that reflect student learning. "Threshold concepts help us teach what cannot be counted" (Hofer, Hanick, and Townsend 2018, 179). This shift from assessing what can be counted to big ideas requires some reconceptualizing of information literacy to an understanding and application of context and integrated use of information to learn and make assessments realistic and integral to student learning and the mission of the institutions of higher learning (Rockman 2002; Hofer, Hanick, and Townsend 2018). Moving from a one-shot instruction skills–based type of thinking for assessing learning of information literacy skills, our profession is tasked with envisioning an approach that is unfamiliar and perhaps a bit daunting. However, as a profession, we can migrate to this "concept" way of thinking and learn together ways to assess learning of information literacy, wrapped in the application of threshold concepts. There is still the need, however, for some of the skill-based "bibliographic instruction" (Hofer, Hanick, and Townsend 2018, 184). Interestingly, perhaps, what we find is that the *Information Literacy Standards* (2000) are perhaps resident in the ACRL *Framework* (2015). In fact, this is what Nuhn and Kaufmann (Nuhn et al. 2018) found when they mapped instruction elements used in pre- and post-framework teaching modules of information literacy used at the University of Central Florida. This empirical data may inform gaps that are evidenced in information literacy instruction for transfer students. The data from this study will be useful to explore further how to prepare universities and two-year college institutions on ways to coordinate and facilitate transfer student information literacy preparedness (Oakleaf 2018).

For librarians to assess learners crossing threshold concepts of understanding and becoming well acquainted with the notion of liminality and the iterative type of learning experiences that happen, we can be more effective in building assessment type of approaches that are relatable to our institutional cultures of teaching and learning. We can also partner with discipline faculty and converse about threshold concepts in various disciplines and how to perhaps build concept assessments of learning more holistically.

This approach to assessment of information literacy bodes well for supporting transfer students, as they will be able to apply their "crossing of thresholds of understanding" in information literacy and discipline content to other institutions—whatever that may look like.

Perhaps using the *Framework* brings new hope for more authentic or "real world" assessment options, since information literacy is now situated and acknowledged as an integrated threshold concept type of metacognitive learning and understanding environment. This environment includes recognizing the metacognitive way that students cross thresholds of understanding across disciplines as an integrated and reflective experience. Kaufmann (2018) describes this experience as analogous to a kaleidoscope—reflective and intertwined. Kaufmann's (2018) research investigated student perceptions of the relevance of information literacy, as they experience using information literacy to complete assignments. In this metacognitive environment, students are using information to learn, also identified as informed learning (Bruce 2008; Hughes and Bruce 2010; Maybee 2015).

There are three key principles of informed learning that can inform curriculum design and are used to build student awareness of information literacy competencies (using information) and discipline content.

- Building on learners' prior experiences.
- Concentrating on both learning to use information and subject content.
- Simultaneously focusing on subject content and using information. (Bruce et al. 2017)

Informed learning design (Maybee 2015) borrows from backward design (Wiggins and McTigue 2005) and may guide our collaborative work with discipline faculty to build courses, assignments, and assessments that more effectively address student learning as a metacognitive experience. This could look like a holistic approach to building collaborations for transfer student success.

The informed learning design process consists of three stages:

1. Identifying critical aspects of intended learning, which include both using information and subject content. For example, explicitly state that students will be using the frames to engage in the research process to complete their assignment. Ask students to consider what frames (concepts) they are applying as sources to support their research assignment.

2. Defining assessment methods for gauging students' increased awareness of critical aspects associated with using information and subject content. For example, ask students using a postlecture online survey to rate their perceived increase in confidence or competence in applying information literacy to complete their academic work. An example of these types of questions is provided here. This is an online survey created by Kaufmann and used at the end of every face-to-face lecture.

Online Survey: Your thoughts . . . Research and Information Literacy

1. Please indicate your level of confidence using library resources at the beginning of this session.

   Very confident
   Somewhat confident
   Confident
   A little confident
   Not at all confident
   Other:

2. Please indicate your confidence level to use library resources at the end of this session.

   Very confident
   Somewhat confident
   Confident
   A little confident
   Not at all confident
   Other:

3. Please share one (or more!) new things you learned during this session.

4. How will you use or apply what you learned today to your academic work?

5. Please rate the relevance of using information literacy competencies for your assignments.

   Highly relevant (1)—Not at all relevant (5)

6. Please rate the impact to your research process of defining information literacy and introducing the six information literacy frames?

Highly impactful (1)—Not at all impactful (5)

7. What question, if any, do you have that wasn't answered during this session?

8. What was your favorite part of this session?

3. Here are some examples of immediate post-instruction survey questions found in the newly launched ACRL Project Outcome Survey tool (https://acrl.projectoutcome.org/) that is freely available to academic libraries. These surveys can be customized for your institutional needs. There are four quantitative questions ranked on a Likert-type scale from strongly disagree (1) to strongly agree (5). There are two qualitative questions as well.

1. I learned something new that will help me succeed in my classes.

2. I feel more confident about completing my assignments.

3. I intend to apply what I just learned.

4. I am more aware of the library's resources and services.

5. What did you like most about this session?

6. What else could the library do to help you success in your classes?

4. Determining activities that enable students to learn about critical aspects associated with subject content by intentionally using information. For example, collaborate with faculty to integrate shared vocabulary during research lectures (library instruction/information literacy instruction) as they work on finding an article on their research topic (discipline/assignment specific), which requires metacognitively connecting their information experience to their assignment requirements.

These three stages are summarized below:

During stage one, the designer of an informed learning environment examines past teaching interactions or initial evaluations to identify students' current experiences and uses the conclusions to determine intended changes in students' awareness of using information and subject content to be focused on in the course. In stage two, methods for assessing the changes in students' awareness throughout the course are selected. The learning activities determined in stage three help students to foster new awareness and the ability to use information to learn as defined in stage one. (Bruce et al. 2017, 13)

A less holistic but perhaps excellent step in using assessment in a more traditional pathway includes options like what the librarians at UNC Wilmington have initiated—a program called "Bridges to Information Literacy at UNC Wilmington." They have created an Information Literacy Exam for Transfer Students (University of North Carolina Wilmington 2019).

Librarians at the University of Maryland developed an "aha moment" assessment (Gammons and Inge 2017) an active learning–based lesson plan grounded in the ACRL's *Framework for Information Literacy for Higher Education*. The lesson plan revisions that began in spring 2015, were informed by the ACRL's *Framework for Information Literacy for Higher Education*. The revised teaching outline included an introduction to threshold concepts via a student-centered lesson plan. To apply the *Framework*, the lesson plans shifted form a lecture-based search strategy focus to active learning that supported and introduced higher-level critical thinking skills. The new lesson plan addresses each frame and includes activities such as:

- *Research as inquiry/searching as strategic exploration:* brainstorming for students to craft a research question and identify relevant keywords for database searching.

- *Authority is constructed and contextual/information creation as a process:* an evaluating activity where students examine sources for credibility and suitability for class assignments.

- *Scholarship as conversation:* was explored via librarian-led small group discussions with students on ways to identify topics and analyze multiple perspectives on a topic to strengthen understanding.

The pilot lesson plan resulted in a transition away from purely quantitative skills–based assessment plan to a revised analysis process. The process included the creation of an "aha moment" rubric and the creation of a coding system to appropriately code responses based on the seven framework dispositions identified in the lessons.

The pilot resulted in the following revisions for collecting student responses and assessing the instruction and learning:

1. Revised rubric to include six framework dispositions and one knowledge practice.

2. Developed a more robust coding process to analyze student responses, "developing," "proficient," and "advanced" levels of competency.

3. Added two categories to the rubric: "other" to account for responses that didn't fit one of the seven categories and "comfort level with the library website, physical spaces, or library instructor."

Traditional assessment methods were found to be inadequate, and the librarian practitioner-researchers created an assessment strategy that combined "the scalability of a survey with the intentionality of qualitative research" (Gammons and Inge 2017, 170). The *Framework* instigated this significant revision and revival for teaching information literacy in a holistic manner with a new approach to teaching, grounded in threshold concept theory, recognizing the metacognitive learner needs and providing a more iterative, student-centered teaching environment with a critically grounded assessment model mapped to the ACRL *Framework for Information Literacy for Higher Education*. Gammons and Inge's (2017) study provides an example of how we can reimagine how to teach and assess information literacy teaching and pedagogy for program-level approaches and assessment while integrating the *Framework* into our teaching environments and communities of practice. This revised active-learning approach was a shift from skills-based lectures. The new four-question survey was developed to measure skills to an information literacy curriculum that focuses on active learning and supports and teaches higher-level critical thinking approaches and competencies. This is grounded in threshold concepts, a theory that informed the development of the ACRL *Framework for Information Literacy for Higher Education* (2015).

This reimagining and building on assessment options may be a pathway to build bridges for cross-departmental and institutional conversations on ways that make sense to assure transfer students are equipped with information literacy competencies for real-world applications and success.

Using whatever means of assessment that seems to work for your community of practice is key. Almost 20 years ago Rockman (2002) suggested that assessment of a common baseline of information literacy experiences for all students, including transfer students, and integrated across central courses is a valuable contribution the library can make to student learning. This sage advice, though now using ACRL *Information Literacy Framework for Higher Education* (2015) rather than the *Information Literacy Standards* (2000), is still a pertinent and relevant bridge to building partnerships with faculty and establishing information literacy as an integrated part of the curriculum with higher education decision-makers and stakeholders. Determining how best to use assessment in a way that supports transfer student initiatives at your institution of higher learning is what should be explored and implemented. For example, providing a post-instruction survey such as the newly developed ACRL Project Outcome Survey could be advantageous for consistent data collection and benchmarking of student learning outcomes of information literacy concepts. Using assessment strategies can guide the work of information literacy assessment that connects the crossing of threshold concepts of understanding contextually across disciplines, thereby providing a metacognitive lift in student learning. The lift in learning can then be built upon in the next information experience by students in a more advanced class in the same discipline or applied to an information experience in a different discipline. This learning that builds upon already acquired knowledge—transformed into tacit knowledge—equips students to be critical thinkers and prepares them for real-world application of information literacy.

Transfer Student Support

Barrier Breaker 4: Building Collaborative Partnerships

The importance of building collaboration cannot be understated. However not every collaboration is good collaboration, and there is some helpful guidance we can glean from our friends in business. There are common elements of good collaborations that can span the fields of education, business, or libraries. First, the collaborative project should be approached strategically with an end goal identified. Second, the organization should already foster a culture of collaboration—to readily overcome a variety of differences between organizations or departments. Finally, recognize that collaboration that fosters deep commitment achieves the greatest impact (Gashurov and Kendrick 2013). This idea of deep commitment to achieve the greatest impact leads us back to Tinto (2008) and determining not to tinker around the edges. When the elements of good collaboration are evident, we should be intentional in pursuing those collaborative partnerships to reach the identified goal or goals of the project.

Once again, we librarians can benefit from the work of colleagues in other disciplines to apply theory that is relevant to our work. Just as Schlossberg's transition theory has value for our work with transfer students in academic libraries, we can also learn from the leaders in business ways to build collaboration into our work. Brad Maihack, retired executive with 40 years' experience directing business operations and leading global teams at Hewlett-Packard and engaged with high-tech and innovation-centered Silicon Valley companies, says that collaboration is the key to "building a better human existence" (2019).

In the *San José State University Washington Square Magazine* blog post titled "Job Maestro: How to Promote Purposeful Collaboration," Maihack (2019) suggests this "social innovation happens at the intersection of art, design, tech, engineering, business, social sciences—and our individual human experiences." Perhaps looking at social innovation and the innovations needed for moving the academic library forward with more collaborative work could benefit from knowledge in social innovation. The following tips are suggested to promote purposeful collaboration and "unleash collaborative innovation" (Maihack 2019). Here are Maihack's tips to consider:

Be clear about what you personally want to accomplish.

Make sure your goals are clear to your audience. People need to understand what you're talking about to really collaborate with you.

Attract the right people who share your passion and specific focus. You need an interdisciplinary team that can see the world through different lenses and therefore understand solutions from different points of view, whether that's finance, technology, human services, sales, or distribution.

Understand the ecosystem for which you're innovating. It's amazing how many people attempt to solve social problems, and they don't even know what the current social services or community infrastructure is, who the stakeholders and clients are, or the people who are currently providing support and funding. Invite the community in, and be proactive in engaging the right partners to find a place in the ecosystem where you can be successful.

Experience the problem. Everybody on your team has to understand the problem of the community, rather than just trying to drive a solution. Have your team go out and experience a day in the life of the community or the client. Live it, watch the person go through their day, read about it. Understand why they're doing what they're doing. Understand what the challenges are. When you come back together, you will be talking about a very clear problem as seen from your own points of view. Then you can start to brainstorm possible solutions or elements of solutions, create a small set of innovative ideas to evaluate and prototype, and then go back to your clients to test those ideas.

Listen and be patient. Social innovation can be slow. You have to bring people along. Seek to really understand and appreciate very diverse points of view, and be confident that you're not giving up your point of view because you're listening. The first meeting you go to is not a debate. You will hear opportunities present themselves that you may never have thought about.

Unfortunately, many collaborations by the academic library have not prospered due to poor communication or lack of communication, lack of focus (i.e., goals not identified), or a lack of leadership (Gashurov and Kendrick 2013). Leadership and management have distinct qualities, and to have successful collaborations, leaders are needed. Gashurov and Kendrick (2013) identify several elements that make academic library collaborative partnerships succeed:

- The importance of common culture.
- Find partners that are open to innovation.
- Leaders are needed for transformation.
- Commitment to change.
- Recognize that successful collaborations add value. (Gashurov and Kendrick 2013)

What are some keys to successful collaborations, specifically pertinent to academic libraries in the context of supporting transfer students? Reflecting on Maihack's (2019) social innovation elements and elements identified in the library literature (Gashurov and Kendrick 2013), we find table 5.1 provides a look at common elements to successful collaborations that academic librarians may be keen to attend to.

What Lewis (2007) identifies to be required for successful academic library collaborations as real change echoes Tinto's (2016) concern regarding student persistence. The need for collaborative work that moves beyond incremental changes at the margins at institutional levels can result in

Table 5.1   Elements of Successful Collaborations

Library Literature	Business Literature
The importance of common culture	Experience the problem
Find partners who are open to innovation	Attract the right people
Leaders are needed for transformation	Understand the ecosystem
Commitment to change	Listen and be patient
Recognize that successful collaborations add value	Be clear about what you personally want to accomplish
	Make sure your goals are clear to your audience
Gashurov and Kendrick (2013)	Maihack (2019)

successful collaborations that support student persistence. Real changes and alterations in fundamental practice are needed (Lewis 2007), leading us to refrain from simply making small changes on the edges or margins.

This collaborative higher educational environment requires institutional levels of support for academic library policies and structures. Administrative stakeholders are most likely looking for data that they can point to in order to support resources and funding that will provide the needed staffing and expertise in the academic library to more fully support the transfer student population at your college or university.

This institutional support is essential; otherwise the transfer student support that the library is seeking to disseminate may be impeded by institutional policy or culture. This may be exhibited by subtle and often hidden institutional influences or attitudes and by the institution's cultural ethos.

These academic library collaborations include stakeholders across the institutional higher education landscape such as:

- administrators: academic affairs, deans, department chairs,
- discipline faculty and program managers,
- library directors,
- faculty librarians,
- technical services librarians,
- e-learning,
- disability support services,
- student services (financial aid, advising), and
- transfer students as collaborators.

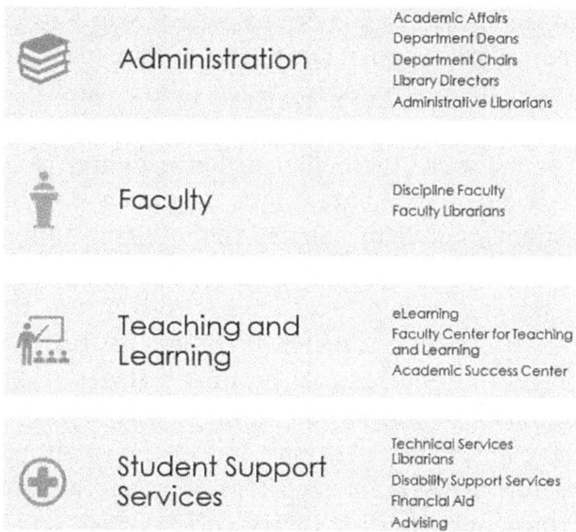

Figure 5.2   Institutional Collaboration Landscape.

This landscape of collaborators (see Figure 5.2) may seem to be a hierarchical tree, but rather, we suggest it is a relationship tree where communication, shared goals, and leadership roles are clearly defined.

Collaboration within and across institutions of higher learning is vital for transfer student support. A 2019 case study in Colorado investigating transfer student needs as a distinct population in two- and four-year institutions found that collaboration is the key to effective interventions for transfer students including: building partnerships, improving communication and increasing the knowledge of resources—physical and human—at different institutions (Roberts, Welsh, and Dudek 2019). Moving away from institutional silos provides academic librarians a wonderful platform to help transfer students recognize the transferable skills they've acquired at one institution and confidently build on those skills at their next institution of higher learning.

Barrier Breaker 5: iSchool Curriculum—Transfer Students as Distinct Populations Training for Diversity Equity and Inclusion

One way to ensure academic librarians are prepared for and aware of the transfer student populations they serve is to look at academic librarian training. The iSchool curricula is a good place to start in terms of evaluating an awareness of this student population who will be served in academic libraries. Dr. Sandra Hirsh, Associate Dean for Academics, College of Professional and Global Education at San José State University, and president-elect for the Association for Library and Information Science Education (ALISE) notes, "Transfer students are a critical user population that is sometimes overlooked in libraries and in LIS education. As iSchools prepare the next generation of academic librarians, it is critical that the content offered in courses like academic librarianship and information literacy be updated and expanded to embrace new user populations and user engagement techniques and ensure the needs of a broader range of users, like transfer students, are being met." iSchool courses or segments of courses that address transfer students and how the academic library can support them may be an option to better prepare 21st-century library professionals graduating with master's degrees in library and information science. This is a pathway toward raising awareness for those entering the library and information science profession as educators who are prepared to be inclusive in working with transfer students. Specifically, academic librarians can then be attentive to potential opportunities to serve transfer students in their communities of practice in a way that is effective and productive. This proactive approach can be a praxis toward equity and inclusion for our growing population of transfer students in colleges and universities. iSchools can take the lead in preparing the next generation of information professionals—LIS graduates—to teach information literacy to diverse populations, including transfer students.

In a recent survey of information literacy practices in academic libraries across the United States (Julien, Gross, and Latham 2019), findings provide data to inform how to prepare librarians for instructional work using the ACRL *Framework for Information Literacy for Higher Education*. The data can inform course content and curriculum guidance for iSchool and master's degree programs that prepare librarians to deliver instruction. The findings from the survey suggest certain areas to pay attention to including:

- formalizing assessment of student learning and formalizing evaluations of information literacy instruction programs,
- developing marketing expertise, and
- emphasizing pedagogical innovation and practices that are fitting to the community of practice where academic librarians are providing instruction.

Interestingly, these same areas of concern are echoed by Canadian information literacy instruction survey data where the importance of student, faculty, and administration support are needed for information literacy integration and pedagogical infusion into curriculum is needed (Julien, Gross, and Latham 2018).

The opportunity for students in iSchools who are preparing for the challenges identified in this survey, which instruction librarians face in academic libraries, may be the catalyst to open up discussion and strategic thinking about how to address barriers that seem to be enduring in our academic librarian communities as we teach information literacy. The impact has the potential to be quite phenomenal, if iSchool curricula incorporates ways for preparing MLIS students to be innovative and collaborators in the classroom and then in their professional roles that unfold. Perhaps the idea of not just being ready for transfer students but recognizing their place as significantly impacting presence in information literacy instruction delivery modalities—in classrooms, on campus, and online—and therefore raising the notion that we have a variety of levels of novice to expert information-literate students in a variety of disciplinary contexts that we teach.

This global list of iSchools is a nonprofit organization that focuses on information science, technology, library science, and information. Each member school or program has certain strengths and specialties. They share and support the foundational interests of the organization: the relationships between information, people, and technology.

An advanced degree in library and information studies is vital for future librarians who wish to work in schools, government agencies, hospitals, and more. *U.S. News* has a list of the best library and information studies programs—as ranked in 2017. These are the top schools for a master's degree in library and information studies. Each school's score reflects its average rating on a scale from 1 (marginal) to 5 (outstanding), based on a survey of academics at peer institutions. The methodology used by *U.S. News* for iSchool rankings is provided online.

U.S. News typically provides a list of schools in the United States with the most transfer students. The list is primarily universities, but we can see that approximately 1,500–10,000 transfer students could be part of a distinct group of students entering our campus communities each year. This is important, as these students consider themselves to be a unique and distinct group of students from other undergraduates due to:

- prior experiences,
- shortened timeline at the university, and
- need to balance academic work and family commitments. (Whang et al. 2017)

This notion that transfer students see themselves as a distinct group of students is an important consideration for academic libraries to more effectively work to mitigate information literacy transfer shock (see chapters 3 and 6). This notion can be more fully integrated into iSchool curricula to raise awareness for new information professionals as they enter the profession of academic librarianship. Being intentional with curriculum design at the iSchool level ensures a balanced approach to equity, diversity, and inclusion training for emerging academic librarians.

The next few sections of this chapter will move from talking about barriers and address how academic libraries can more intentionally connect directly to our transfer student populations.

Transfer Student Strategies

Information Literacy Teaching Methods That Work and Marketing That Matters

Methods That Work

How do students learn, and what can instructors do to make that happen? Results from a grassroots assessment project of 25,000 students at 27 institutions reveal that a simple approach can produce big results. Faculty who make the process of teaching and learning explicit to students—particularly for those who don't know what to expect in college—help students succeed. This approach—"transparent teaching"—suggests that if the tacit curriculum is made very plain and explicit, even students who aren't engaged in discussion or miss the point of an assignment or are overwhelmed can recover and learn if there is explicit instruction.

While teaching at Harvard, Mary-Ann Winkelmes first became curious about what students learned, and what learning they would take with them after completing their course with her. As the associate director of Harvard's Derek Bok Center for Teaching and Learning, Professor Winkelmes wondered if her students knew how to learn, beyond learning about Renaissance frescoes.

Transparent teaching protocol can be distilled into three questions when faculty are creating assignments and is designed to be an effective technique for faculty to improve learning.

Task—what exactly they are asking students to do

Purpose—why students must do it

Criteria—how the work will be evaluated (Berrett 2015)

Connecting the Dots

This idea of "transparent teaching" has taken some ground in higher education as an effective tool for assignment creation and for building recognition of transferrable skills and learning for students. Recognizing that students often did not see the relevance of assignments in her psychology course, Professor Tanya Martini ran an experiment to investigate this dilemma. She learned that students typically don't connect how the skills they learn in one context transfer to a different one—even if the skills an assignment was addressing are explicitly communicated. Martini learned that students often see these skills in a narrowly focused context or situation-specific way. Bridging the idea that these are meta-skills that could be transferred to other disciplines, learning environments, the workplace, and our everyday situations was not a natural or even invited consideration for students. Therefore, the explicit and transparent articulation of connecting certain competencies to other contexts with concrete examples encourages critical thinking and learning (Supiano 2019).

Scaffolding and Threshold Concepts

In addition to being explicit and transparent in teaching information literacy, learning theory reminds us that reinforcement and scaffolding are important for students to develop understanding and learn information literacy competencies. This is especially effective when integrated into discipline coursework and scaffolded across the learning journey for students in higher education. The notion of scaffolding information literacy instruction is also supported by the idea of learners moving along the scale of acquired threshold concepts from novice to expert researchers (see chapter 4). Novice learners need explicit instruction when new information is being presented to them, as they are engaging their "working memory"; whereas minimal or guided instruction tends to be effective with more expert researchers who possess a knowledge base that supports more independent inquiry for learning (Kessinger 2013). The importance of scaffolding information literacy instruction is situated as foundational, as related to the notion of threshold concepts, as the learner acquires more than a new core concept—but a new understanding, way of thinking, interpretation or way of viewing something—whereby they cross through a liminal space, so they can continue to progress in their learning (Kessinger 2013).

Scaffolding is not a new concept for teaching pedagogy but perhaps hasn't been addressed specifically for information literacy instruction. A mixed method instruction program assessment at the University of Wyoming (Bowles-Terry 2012) found some direct correlations to the value of scaffolding information literacy learning outcomes to both the freshman-level and upper-division classes in every major. There are different learning outcomes that are appropriate for students who are at different stages along their academic pathway to graduation. The path and student experience may look differently for each student; however, designing information literacy instruction programs with a cohesive and nonrepetitive scaffolded approach is valuable, from the student perspective. Findings from this mixed methods study tell us that academic librarians should have different learning objectives for lower-division (freshman) and upper-division classes. This is important to recognize for transfer students, as information literacy instruction for classes are appropriately scaffolded for the class level and discipline. Transfer students may, however, need a short tutorial or video to provide a baseline of library orientation as they begin their academic work at their new college or university. These online tutorials or videos, as a refresher library orientation, can seamlessly be offered during the instruction session with the librarian, assuming transfer students engage with a librarian for instruction.

This tiered approach to information literacy instruction was suggested by students in the focus groups of the study and cited that a visit to the library for orientation as freshmen to get a basic introduction to the library resources and services followed by a subject-specific session would be the most valuable approach to benefit students. To further support this approach to information literacy instruction, the quantitative academic transcript analysis in Terry-Bowles' (2012) study "shows a significant relationship between upper division information literacy instruction and GPA at graduation" (p. 89). The scaffolding of freshman library instruction with additional subject-specific upper-level course information literacy instruction is an approach that students suggest is valuable to them, and the GPA data reflects a positive impact on student learning and academic success. For transfer students, this scaffolded approach is to be noted so that academic librarians are attentive to this distinct and growing population on our campuses and we have instruction practices that address their needs for information literacy preparedness. Having clearly defined information literacy goals for students at each level of their academic journey and providing a scaffolded approach to teaching information literacy competencies can be impactful for student learning and their successful completion of academic studies.

Perhaps one approach to scaffolding information literacy for transfer students is to offer an information literacy research class for all incoming transfer students. This opportunity allows for not only ensuring there is a baseline of information literacy competency knowledge for these incoming students but also serving to build community among these new students on our campuses. Whether this is offered as an online or on-campus course, transfer students will meet other transfer students, and the opportunity to connect with this distinct community early in their experience at the college or university is a comfortable and low-risk assist with making new connections in the academic environment. This transfer student research class offered in the first term of their entry at a new campus gives them solid footing for learning research skills, information literacy competencies, and learning how to apply these in subsequent classes and offers the opportunity to build relationships with peers and the librarians. This class when taken early in their program sequence provides students with the opportunity to enhance their academic experience by building confidence and competencies for using information well in their academic work.

Ideally a holistic approach to teaching information literacy based on learning theory with the emphasis on teaching pedagogies and building learning outcomes in partnership with faculty is a pathway to build learning success. Building information literacy instruction outcomes across the curriculum that recognizes possible stopping and starting points of students at the college or university enables scaffolding to fill gaps and teach learners—at whatever stage they may be in crossing thresholds of understanding—to progress in their learning journey (Kessinger 2013). Informed learning (see chapter 4) as a pedagogical approach to information literacy is a way to provide our transfer students the platform to practice using information in their general education context and prepare them to apply those concepts in their majors and be better prepared for the higher-level disciplinary contexts they will eventually engage with as they work toward completing their degrees.

Library Marketing That Matters to Transfer Students

Marketing that matters means academic libraries articulate clearly how information literacy competencies are essential for students to succeed academically—as critical thinkers—and prepare students to be successful life-long learners. Transfer students, as a distinct population, may especially benefit from marketing that is explicit in terms of identifying services, hours, and resources, as their previous academic library may have had vastly different offerings.

The basic premise of good communication and marketing is to know our audience and target marketing to transfer students may be an effective strategy to employ in order to enhance the transfer student's *strategy* for capitalizing on library resources and services at their current college or university.

Academic libraries can market specifically to transfer students as a target market. Here are some ideas curated from a few successful forays by academic libraries:

- Transfer student kick-off events marketed cross-divisionally during "Welcome Back Week" including:
    - library tours led by returning transfer students and
    - library transfer student social—an informal event hosted in the library with librarians and advisors (Pun 2018).

- Raise awareness of transfer students with full library staff as part of staff development by hosting a panel of transfer students that share their challenges and how the library might make the transition easier (Whang et al. 2017).

- Library orientation for transfer students—a specific session for this this distinct population (Boone 2017).

- Library initiative to establish a transfer student success group—a network of campus partners to collectively reach out to transfer students as a distinct population. Partners might include student life, advising, financial aid, feeder institutions (sending and receiving), writing center, academic success center, honors program, research opportunities, and study abroad (Alverson et al. 2017).

- Implement a required research/information literacy course (one credit/online or on campus) for all incoming transfer students in their first semester. Use a programmatic approach to address gaps in information literacy competencies and prepare these new students for resources needed for academic work (Alverson et al. 2017).

- Cross-institutional library marketing for transfer students—building on teaching and library initiatives for sending and receiving librarians—innovate for target marketing to transfer students.

Transfer Student Self and Inner Strength

Transfer student self-efficacy and confidence can be a building block for their academic success. The academic library can be a leader to assist with building information literacy competencies for transfer students by intentionally finding ways for these students to have library instruction early in their transfer experience at their new institution. Grigg and Dale (2017) found a relationship between transfer students having library instruction in their classes and transfer students subsequently seeking and receiving additional assistance from a subject librarian. Whang et al. (2017) found similar findings in his survey of incoming transfer students at the University of Washington. There were higher levels of confidence among those transfer students who had participated in formal information literacy instruction. As we more fully embrace the knowledge and theory that students use information to learn, which has been identified as informed learning, we may take a more systematic and theoretical approach to integrating information literacy into curriculum and classes, which in turn has the potential to build student confidence and self-efficacy—both in using information competencies and content knowledge. The *Framework* gives us threshold concepts as guideposts for assessment and flexible conversations with faculty across disciplines. These tools can guide us as information professionals and library faculty to more effectively enhance and influence learning and academic achievement for transfer students who are transitioning.

The notion that transfer students arrive with information literacy competencies as needed to be successful academically is perhaps where we should start to converse in the context of teaching and learning. Let's consider that students are familiar with a variety of educational course designs and philosophies. For instance, the mission of two-year colleges is often quite different than a four-year university; therefore, when they make this transfer, they experience a transition in content, with new or different expectations by faculty and different approaches and orientations in grading. For example, community college students have often experienced a nurturing environment where they are accustomed to a more self-referenced norms grading climate versus the university grading, which typically uses a norm-referenced grading system (Tipton and Bender 2006). This shift can be a bit alarming, and transfer students' self-confidence may be challenged. As Stephen Handel, associate vice president for undergraduate admissions in the University of California system, suggests "The key for transfer success is academic preparation and transparency" (Handel 2017, 13). Using these *strategies*, the academic library can play an integral role in preparing transfer students with information literacy competencies and being transparent about the scaffolding of using their current knowledge base to build on as they engage with more challenging research assignments and content.

Whether we are academic librarians receiving transfer students or academic librarians sending transfer students, we can be a contributor to building well-prepared transfer students for academic success as they journey toward degree completion.

Identifying potential barriers to transfer student support in the academic library is the first step toward addressing how we can more effectively engage and support our transfer student community on campus. Coupling the barrier awareness with elements of transition can further empower our position as academic libraries to be proactive in working alongside our students and other departments on our campuses to be effective collaborative "change agents" in our everyday work in the library.

The transfer student *situation* in transition can be proactively addressed as we consider ways to talk with other faculty about information literacy, build teaching collaborations with the transfer student in the sphere of awareness, and remember that assessment can bridge our way to building effective pedagogical conversations to serve stransfer students as we teach.

The transfer student *support* needs include being mindful of way to build collaborative partnerships across disciplines and even looking at ways to more intentionally train future library and information science professionals in our iSchools to raise awareness of the expanding transfer student populations on our campuses.

Engaging transfer student transition *strategies* to address potential barriers could include examining our teaching methods—like explicit instruction—and using strategies such as being sure to connect the dots and scaffold information literacy instruction across lower- and upper-level classes. Reflecting on our marketing efforts may also reveal new approaches to reaching our transfer students effectively.

Finally, addressing barriers that may be situated in the transfer student experience of their *self* and *inner strength* can be addressed as we build confidence and guide them to realize their own experiences are assets to build on as they continue toward achieving their academic goals, and be a voice of professional "cheerleader" and academic support.

Practical Applications of Chapter 5

- Create a Faculty Fellows Program to instruct and engage faculty as collaborators on your campus and to integrate information literacy as the norm into assignments, syllabi, and programs at your institution.

- Invigorate, and reform the information literacy instruction program at your institution using the *Framework for Information Literacy for Higher Education* (ACRL 2015) and threshold concepts as the foundation for new student-centered, concept-based lessons and assessments.

- Reconceptualize information literacy assessment from "what can be counted" to "threshold concepts," "big ideas," and "metacognitive pathways" that make assessments realistic, real-world focused, and integral to student learning and the mission of the institutions of higher learning.

- Build collaborations with discipline faculty to build the framework concepts into assignments and long-term assessments of crossing thresholds of understandings in the discipline and in the application of the *Framework for Information Literacy for Higher Education* (ACRL 2015).

- Seeking collaboration within and across institutions of higher learning is vital for transfer student support—be intentional. Find, and build collaborative partnerships.

- Think about social innovations to build innovative collaboration—how to connect art, design, tech, engineering, business, social sciences—and our individual human experiences.

- Offer an information literacy research class for all incoming transfer students.

- Provide online tutorials or videos as a refresher library orientation specifically for transfer students as a seamlessly tiered approach to information literacy instruction.

- Provide an invitation to transfer students for a follow-up meeting with the librarian—perhaps even a subject-specific session—to benefit them.

- Raise awareness in your academic library of the transfer student transition elements and potential barriers to academic success that are at play including: *situation, support, strategies, self,* and *inner-strength.*

- Use the transfer student *situation* to proactively talk with other faculty about information literacy to build teaching collaborations with the transfer student situation in mind; use assessment as a topic to engage in effective pedagogical conversations to serve transfer students as we teach.

- Use the transfer student need for *support* as an opportunity to be mindful of ways to build collaborative partnerships across disciplines and institutions, leading to more intentionally train future library and information science professionals in our iSchools to raise awareness of the expanding transfer student populations on our campuses.

- Use specific *strategies* that address the transfer student transition experiences to examining our teaching methods—like explicit instruction; connect the dots and scaffold information literacy instruction across lower- and upper-level classes. Reflect on new approaches of marketing library information to reach transfer students more effectively.

- Recognize the unique transfer student experiences of *self* and *inner strength*, which can be leveraged to build their confidence and guide them to realize their own experiences are assets to use as they continue on their journey toward achieving their academic goals; be a voice of the professional "cheerleader" and information expert that provides needed academic and research support.

References

Alverson, Jessica, Susan Shultz, Jill King, and Morgen MacIntosh-Hodgetts. 2017. *DePaul University Transfer Students and the Library.* DePaul University.

American Library Association. 2000. *Information Literacy Competency Standards for Higher Education.* http://www.ala.org/acrl/standards/informationliteracy competency.

American Library Association. 2015. *Framework for Information Literacy for Higher Education.* http://www.ala.org/acrl/standards/ilframework.

Berrett, Dan. 2015. "The Day the Purpose of College Changed; After February 28, 1967, the Main Reason to Go Was to Get a Job." *Chronicle of Higher Education* 61(20). https://search.proquest.com/docview/1651188862.

Boone, Rick H. 2017. "Community College Student Perceptions of University Transfer Barriers." ProQuest Dissertations Publishing. https://search.pro quest.com/docview/1896981231.

Bowles-Terry, Melissa. 2012. "Library Instruction and Academic Success: A Mixed-Methods Assessment of a Library Instruction Program." *Evidence Based Library and Information Practice* 7(1): 82–95. doi:10.18438/B8PS4D.

Bruce, Christine Susan. 2008. *Informed Learning*. Chicago: Association of College and Research Libraries. http://bvbr.bib-bvb.de:8991/F?func=service& doc_library=BVB01&local_base=BVB01&doc_number=017109104&seq uence=000001&line_number=0001&func_code=DB_RECORDS&se rvice_type=MEDIA.

Bruce, Christine Susan, Andrew Demasson, Hilary Hughes, Mandy Lupton, Elham Sayyad Abdi, Clarence Maybee, Mary M. Somerville, and Anita Mirijamdotter. 2017. "Information Literacy and Informed Learning: Conceptual Innovations for IL Research and Practice Futures." *Journal of Information Literacy* 11(1): 4. doi:10.11645/11.1.2184. http://urn.kb.se/res olve?urn=urn:nbn:se:lnu:diva-63778.

Bruce, Christine, and Hilary Hughes. 2010. "Informed Learning: A Pedagogical Construct Attending Simultaneously to Information Use and Learning." *Library and Information Science Research* 32(4): A2–A8. doi:10.1016/j. lisr.2010.07.013. https://www.sciencedirect.com/science/article/pii/S074 0818810000733.

Crowe, Stephanie, Anne Pemberton, and Vonzell Yeager. 2019. "Information Literacy Faculty Fellows Program: Building a Faculty-Librarian Framework Community of Practice." *College & Research Libraries News* 80(5). doi: 10.5860/crln.80.5.285. https://crln.acrl.org/index.php/crlnews/article/view /17752.

Dubicki, Eleonora. 2019. "Mapping Curriculum Learning Outcomes to ACRL's Framework Threshold Concepts: A Syllabus Study." *Journal of Academic Librarianship* 45(3): 288–98. doi:10.1016/j.acalib.2019.04.003. https:// www.sciencedirect.com/science/article/pii/S0099133319300825.

Gammons, Rachel, and Lindsay Inge. 2017. "Using the ACRL Framework to Develop a Student-Centered Model for Program-Level Assessment." *Comminfolit* 11(1): 168–84. doi:10.15760/comminfolit.2017.11.1.40. https:// search.proquest.com/docview/1927093489.

Gashurov, Irene, and Curtis L. Kendrick. 2013. "Collaboration for Hard Times: Insights into What Makes Academic Library Partnerships Succeed." *Library Journal* 138(16): 26.

Grigg, Karen Stanley and Jenny Dale. 2017. "Assessing and Meeting the Information Literacy Needs of Incoming Transfer Students." *Reference Services Review* 45 (3): 527–539. doi:10.1108/RSR-10-2016-0076.

Handel, Stephen. 2017. "Transfer Students Deserve Better Road Maps." *Chronicle of Higher Education*. Accessed September 11, 2019. https://www.chroni cle.com/article/Transfer-Students-Deserve/238772.

Harrick, Matthew, and Lee Ann Fullington. 2019. "'Don't Make Me Feel Dumb': Transfer Students, the Library, and Acclimated to a New Campus." *Evidence Based Library and Information Practice* 14 (English Language): 77–91. doi:10.18438/eblip29512.

Hofer, Amy R., Silvia Lin Hanick, and Lori Townsend. 2018. *Transforming Information Literacy Instruction: Threshold Concepts in Theory and Practice*. Santa Barbara, CA: Libraries Unlimited.

Kessinger, Pamela. 2013. "Integrated Instruction Framework for Information Literacy." *Journal of Information Literacy* 7(2). doi:10.11645/7.2.1807.

Latham, Don, Melissa Gross, and Heidi Julien. 2019. "Implementing the ACRL Framework: Reflections from the Field." *College & Research Libraries* 80(3): 386. https://crl.acrl.org/index.php/crl/article/viewFile/17397/19219.

Lewis, David W. 2007. "A Strategy for Academic Libraries in the First Quarter of the 21st Century." *College & Research Libraries* 68(5): 418–34. doi:10.5860/crl.68.5.418. https://search.proquest.com/docview/199377182.

Maihack, B. 2019. *Job Maestro: How to Promote Purposeful Collaboration.* SJSU Washington Square Magazine. http://Blogs.Sjsu.Edu/Wsq/2019/12/05/Job-Maestro-how-to-Promote-Purposeful-Collaboration/.

Maybee, Clarence. 2018. *IMPACT Learning.* Cambridge, MA; Kidlington, UK: Chandos Publishing.

Maybee, Clarence Dale. 2015. "Informed Learning in the Undergraduate Classroom: The Role of Information Experiences in Shaping Outcomes." http://trove.nla.gov.au/work/201620103.

Maybee, Clarence, Christine S. Bruce, Mandy Lupton, and Kristen Rebmann. 2013. "Learning to Use Information: Informed Learning in the Undergraduate Classroom." *Library and Information Science Research* 35(3): 200–206. doi:10.1016/j.lisr.2013.04.002. https://www.sciencedirect.com/science/article/pii/S0740818813000352.

Nuhn, P., K. Kaufmann, R. Mulvihill, and M. Tracy. 2018, June 23. "Building Inclusion: How Can Research Instruction at Two-Year Colleges Help Students Successfully Transition to the University?" [Conference Presentation]. June 21–26, 2018.

Oakleaf, Megan. 2018. "Northeast Florida Library and Information Network (NEFLIN) Assessment Program 2017–2018 Final Report." https://neflin.org/wp-content/uploads/2018/10/Assessment-Project-Final-Report.pdf.

Pun, Raymond. 2018. "Helping Transfer Students Succeed: General Tips & Strategies for Academic Librarians." *Credo* (blog). Accessed September 11, 2019. http://blog.credoreference.com/helping-transfer-students-succeed-general-tips-strategies-for-academic-librarians.

Roberts, Lindsay, Megan E. Welsh, and Brittany Dudek. 2019. "Instruction and Outreach for Transfer Students: A Colorado Case Study." *College & Research Libraries* 80(1): 94. https://crl.acrl.org/index.php/crl/article/viewFile/16925/18608.

Rockman, Ilene F. 2002. "Strengthening Connections between Information Literacy, General Education, and Assessment Efforts." *Library Trends* 51(2): 185. https://search.proquest.com/docview/220462753.

Supiano, Beckie. 2019. "How One Professor made Her Assignments More Relevant." *The Chronicle of Higher Education* 65 (25): A32. https://search.proquest.com/docview/2199253589.

Taylor, Jason L., and Dimpal Jain. 2017. "The Multiple Dimensions of Transfer: Examining the Transfer Function in American Higher Education." *Community College Review* 45(4): 273–93. doi:10.1177/0091552117725177.

Tinto, Vincent, 2008. "Access Without Support is Not Opportunity." *Inside Higher Ed*. Accessed September 17, 2019. https://www.insidehighered.com/views/2008/06/09/access-without-support-not-opportunity.

Tinto, Vincent. 2016. "From Retention to Persistence." *Inside Higher Ed*. Accessed September 17, 2019. https://www.insidehighered.com/views/2016/09/26/how-improve-student-persistence-and-completion-essay.

Tipton, Roberta L., and Patricia Bender. 2006. "From Failure to Success: Working with Under-Prepared Transfer Students." *Reference Services Review* 34(3): 389–404. doi:10.1108/00907320610685337.

University of North Carolina at Wilmington. "UNCW Information Literacy Exam." Accessed September 18, 2019. https://library.uncw.edu/info_lit/information-literacy-exam-transfer-students.

Whang, Linda, Christine Tawatao, John Danneker, Jackie Belanger, Stephen Edward Weber, Linda Garcia, and Amelia Klaus. 2017. "Understanding the Transfer Student Experience Using Design Thinking." *Reference Services Review* 45(2): 298–313. doi:10.1108/RSR-10-2016-0073.

Wiggins, Grant, and Jay McTighe. 2005. *Understanding by Design*. 2nd ed. Alexandria, VA: Association for Supervision and Curriculum Development.

CHAPTER 6

Communication and Collaboration between College and University Librarians

Collaboration that fosters deep commitment achieves the greatest impact.
—Gashurov and Kendrick (2013)

Building collaborative work opportunities between librarians at different campuses and institutions is best situated by our communication and institutional structures. Cross-institutional collaborations among academic librarians may also hinge on common knowledge about transfer student information literacy competencies.

As mentioned in the introduction, the authors of this book are faculty librarians who enjoy a collegial relationship at separate institutions—Seminole State College of Florida and the University of Central Florida. A unique and vibrant partnership exists between these institutions, and an enhanced articulation agreement, marketed as DirectConnect to the University of Central Florida (UCF) guarantees acceptance to AA-degreed students within the DirectConnect partnership area. Six area colleges are part of the DirectConnect partnership, with Seminole State being the second-largest partner in terms of the numbers of DirectConnect matriculating students. DirectConnect has given UCF a large transfer student population—in the 2017–2018 academic year, 51 percent of UCF's transfer student population came from DirectConnect colleges—and fueled UCF's growth to one of the largest universities in the United States.

Perhaps this experience could be beneficial to other college and university librarians beyond Florida's borders, not only because of the growing numbers of transfer students nationwide, and the number of statewide articulation agreements within the United States but also because of the many established institutional transfer pathways throughout the United States. Although a number of states are presently without a "statewide guaranteed transfer of an associate degree" articulation agreement, a number of specific institutional agreements have been crafted with the intent of creating a clear pathway for students to obtain a baccalaureate degree.

Assessment Research Project

An assessment project guided by a research question prompted an inquiry into the role of academic libraries and how they support transfer students. It was initiated and supported by the Northeast Florida Library Network (NEF-LIN Assessment Project: 2017–2018), which provided a faculty team of renowned experts to guide our assessment project work. Our research question asked: How can library instruction at two-year colleges help students successfully transfer to the university? We and others who participated in this project were the recipients of an exceptional team of well-respected experts: Megan Oakleaf, Martha Kyrilidou, Kristine R. Brancolini, and Amanda Albert (Oakleaf 2018).

Furthering this research agenda, the relationship between our institutions has served to foster our communication and collaboration. In the partner-college relationship, we serve many of the same students, interact with many of the same discipline faculty, cover the same research desk, and eat lunch in the same break room. This is as an advantage in our work that few other librarians would have, and we believe that this institutional and collegial relationship provided the perfect platform for us to research the ways in which information literacy instruction is taught to native UCF students and compare that to how information literacy instruction is handled for UCF's partner college students (Lorenz speech). Further, because Florida is a leader in the statewide articulation agreement movement, we are geographically positioned to be aware not just of this partnership but of various designated transfer pathways within the Florida University System and Florida's 28 colleges.

The original research question "How can library instruction at two-year colleges help students successfully transfer to the university?" was investigated, and the methodology and findings are shared in the following sections of this chapter. This case study is provided for readers to learn how a simple research question can blossom into subsequent collaborative work and presentation opportunities and guide future research on similar or related topics to further the scholarship and dissemination of research in our discipline of library and information science. We can embrace the identity of practitioner-researcher to enhance our understandings and therefore improve our teaching and pedagogy in our respective academic library communities of practice. This identity of practitioner-researcher bridges our discipline as transdisciplinary and situates our research and findings to inform not just our work but, as is the case in the example of our findings, to learn about ways to more effectively collaborate across departments and institutions of higher learning to support transfer students and mitigate transfer shock.

This research is evidence of ways in which the Scholarship of Teaching and Learning (SoTL) can further the discovery of effective pedagogy, theory, and application for effective work in transdisciplinary work in higher education (Chick 2019).

Research Design and Methodology

The two-stage sequential study embarked upon to investigate the previously stated research question included a stage-one content analysis, and then an online survey was developed and administered for stage two.

The content analysis began by reviewing what primary elements of information literacy were included in two distinct sets of UCF online instruction modules. The first set of modules is delivered in a Canvas web course titled "Introduction to Library Research Strategies." The second set of modules, titled InfoLit, is a UCF proprietary program with 12 separate modules. The online InfoLit modules, created in a proprietary platform, are available only to the university faculty and students and are not open access or shareable with anyone outside the institution. UCF faculty may integrate these InfoLit modules into their courses and have the flexibility to integrate selected modules or the full InfoLit module content into their courses. This provides faculty options for delivery of specific content at specific times in the course, thereby having the option to scaffold the modules as needed in their courses.

The content analysis, which led to the identification of the major elements of information literacy delivered in the university online modules, were categorized as a list of information literacy elements into "basic" and "advanced" topics. After this determination, the elements were aligned or "mapped" to the ACRL *Framework*. With the content analysis completed, the key elements of information literacy instruction were identified as what was typically offered by the University of Central Florida subject librarians. To further validate the content analysis, triangulation was used by piloting the survey with two UCF librarians and one UCF library administrator. Triangulation is used in research to support validation of data by using more than one method to collect data for the research topic. In this case, the elements of information literacy as basic and advanced topics were further examined by mapping the elements to the ACRL *Framework for Information Literacy for Higher Education* and then also piloted with UCF librarians and an administrator.

This was intended to learn if the elements identified in the content analysis were valid and that the sequence and presentation of the elements in the survey were accurate. This categorization was useful to inform the survey design. After the successful pilot and editing the survey based on the pilot results, the survey was sent via email to one partner college instruction librarians (fall 2017). The survey included first asking the partner college instruction librarians to identify the information literacy elements they typically include in information literacy instruction sessions—online and on campus. We provided lists of information literacy elements and asked which elements of information literacy they routinely covered in "one shot" classes, in face-to-face interactions at the desk, through chat, and any other modality. We learned from these results to modify the survey and provide a space in the survey for respondents to list any other elements they included, which were not listed on the survey.

Finally, the revised survey was sent to the six other UCF DirectConnect partner college instructional librarians (spring 2018). Twenty-three responses were received. Due to the relatively small survey population, librarians were not asked to identify their institution to preserve anonymity.

Using Google Forms, a simple survey was designed informed by the results from stage-one content analysis. There are many options for survey platforms, and often there are specific options available specific to institution licenses and preferences. Survey Monkey, Qualtrics, Microsoft Forms, Google Forms, and LibWizard are platforms that are typically available for easy access, intuitive survey design, and development and, very importantly, provide user-friendly data management of survey results. A great resource to consider is Miller and Hinnant's (2018) book titled *Making Surveys Work for Your Library: Guidance, Instruction and Examples.*

Be sure to take the time to communicate with your institution's research department—such as institutional research or center for distributed learning or other such area—to learn not only of options concerning survey platforms and administration but also any institutional review board (IRB) requirements that should be addressed.

The 2018 ALA presentation titled "Building Inclusion: How Can Research Instruction at Two-Year Colleges Help Students Successfully Transition to the University?" was selected as one of the ACRL transforming teaching and learning topics at the conference. A brief summary was published in the **CRL News Reporter September 2018** (College & Research Libraries 2018):

A full room of visitors came for the ACRL sponsored panel presentation titled: *Building Inclusion: How Can Research Instruction at Two-Year Colleges Help Students Successfully Transition to the University?*

This session shared preliminary findings from a study which looked at whether library instruction at the college level adequately prepares students for transition to university-level research assignments; and which elements needed at the university level could be incorporated into information literacy instruction for transfer students. The mixed methods research design included qualitative content analysis followed by a quantitative online survey. The content analysis identified elements of information literacy instruction at the university and was aligned and mapped to the ACRL *Framework* (2016). An online survey was developed, based on the content analysis, to inquire what content was included in information literacy instruction for college students. Preliminary findings identify potential gaps in information literacy instruction between the university and colleges. The practical implications and value of the study provide empirical data to inform the gaps that are evidenced in information literacy instruction for transfer students. This study provides data for universities and two-year college institutions to better prepare for coordination and facilitation of transfer student information literacy preparedness.

As noted in chapter 4, we found five keys to mitigate "transfer shock":

- Identify elements of information literacy instruction.
- Align elements with the ACRL *Framework*.
- Identify information literacy element gaps between colleges and universities.
- Engage authentic collaboration.
- Fill the gaps.

An infographic was created and distributed to the audience at the conference presentation, and a LibGuide, including the presentation slides, was created for future reference.

The research from this project has been disseminated in print or presentation as follows:

- ALA EBSS—2018
- NEFLIN Annual Presentation—2018
- Florida Summit on Transfer Student Success—Poster—2018

- Celebration of Collaboration—2019
- SSC Faculty Welcome Back—2019—Scaffolding to Support Transfer Student Success: SSC & UCF DirectConnect
- Book—*Supporting Transfer Student Success: The Essential Role of College and University Libraries*, 2020

The findings from this research confirm findings from Kaufmann's recent doctoral study investigating the relevance of information literacy to college students (Kaufmann 2018). This study identifies what makes information literacy relevant to college students when students use information literacy competencies (ILC) to complete an assignment.

The doctoral mixed methods study identifies student perceptions of the relevance of information literacy to complete assignments (quantitative) and identifies the factors that make information literacy relevant to them (qualitative) (Kaufmann 2018). The quantitative findings reveal that students find information literacy to be relevant or highly relevant to the successful completion of academic work. The qualitative findings identify that there is a metacognitive way in which multiple factors are in play that contribute to college student successful application of information literacy to complete academic assignments. This may be more useful using an analogy to a kaleidoscope. Certain factors of relevance are both reflective and refractive, thereby creating variations of understandings of both disciplinary content and information literacy competencies, all at once. This metacognitive user experience with information is predicated by the students' knowledge base and the pathway or crosswalk the student is using to cross new thresholds of understanding.

The factors of relevance that make information literacy relevant to students are pathways to thresholds of understandings across disciplines for students to successfully learn disciplinary content (Meyer and Land 2003; Wiggins and McTighe 2005; Tucker et al. 2014). Using information to learn (Maybee 2015; Bruce 2008) about additional disciplinary content—such as economics or psychology— is the kaleidoscope experience (Kaufmann 2018) that is transformational for student learning. These factors of information literacy relevance, identified by users, are pathways to crossing liminal spaces to new understandings related to information literacy competencies and the disciplinary content required to be attained for successful completion of knowledge attainment and course completion. The kaleidoscope of reflective and refractive information experiences enhances critical thinking and learning.

What are the factors that make information literacy relevant to college students? Three types of factors were identified: an uber factor, nine key factors, and 11 dimensional factors. The factors that make information literacy competencies useful and meaningful (sociocognitively relevant) to students are dimensional, dynamic, variegated, and diverse while at the same time are intertwined and influence the impact, usefulness, and meaningfulness of information literacy when applied to student academic work.

The uber factor identified as knowledge base is the factor of origin, foundational to what matters when students applied ILCs to their academic task. The nine key factors of information literacy relevance are:

1. digital literacy
2. academic discipline
3. ILC awareness
4. acquiring new knowledge
5. real-world application
6. research process
7. critical thinking
8. scholarly conversation
9. curiosity/passion/motivation

The 11 dimensional factors of information literacy relevance are:

1. user-friendliness in digital environments
2. user experience in digital environments
3. current information
4. authoritative sources
5. ILC articulated
6. ILC integration
7. ILC instruction
8. personal relevance
9. professional relevance
10. organizing information
11. comprehension

The factor relationships are related and reflective in a somewhat diffused hierarchy. Hierarchy lends to the meaning of a higher to lower order or rank of factors, whereas diffusion lends to the meaning of spontaneous movement of any kind or type of factor but stems from a shared origin. The origin of relationship in this diffused hierarchy of factors is the uber factor knowledge base. The key and dimensional factors then spontaneously are present in the student experience or perception of the sociocognitive relevance of information literacy. The spontaneous presence of factors that make information literacy relevant reflects the metacognitive way students experience and perceive information literacy competencies to be useful and meaningful for their academic work (Kaufmann 2018, 194).

These findings show an intertwined and diffused hierarchical relationship among all the factors: uber, key, and dimensional—analogous to a kaleidoscope—both reflective and intertwined. The factors or *things* that impact user-relevance perceptions of information literacy help us understand the way students may find metacognitive pathways toward crossing information literacy and disciplinary liminal spaces to new understandings. These findings can be used for improving pedagogical work to impact student success, supporting academia goals such as retention and completion, and improving how to communicate the value of information literacy competencies as transferable competencies from academia to the real world (Kaufmann 2018, 2–3).

Taking this current user-relevance research into consideration, how can academic libraries more successfully be partners to ensure transfer students are well prepared for their research assignments? Let's be diligent to incorporate the factors that make information literacy relevant into coursework and assignments by sharing research-based data and guiding our work more intentionally as faculty partners across disciplines and institutions. (See chapter 5—Faculty Fellows.)

"Celebration of Librarian Collaboration for Transfer Student Success"

Early in the transfer student information literacy research, we realized that there had never been an opportunity for the university and DirectConnect partner college librarians to even meet as a cohort, much less to collaborate, learn from each other, and to network—despite our geographic proximity. There had never been a formal recognition of the fact that we all—eventually, at least—teach many of the same students. Appreciating that communication and collaboration is essential to the success of any large endeavor, and with the research survey findings in hand, we set about remedying this lack of an avenue for communication and collaboration with respect to information literacy instruction between the university and college librarians with the goal of a daylong workshop.

This endeavor began by assembling a planning committee, including librarians from the University of Central Florida, as well librarians as from several of the partner colleges, all working together to design a day that was informative, which fostered collaboration and was also fun. Having the colleges represented on the planning committee also helped create an early "buzz" about our event at the various college campuses. To emphasize the goal of building collaborative partnerships, the event was named a "Celebration of Librarian Collaboration for Transfer Student Success." The planning committee worked together and identified a date at the end of the final exam week that would support librarian attendance from all institutions.

The importance of building a strong planning committee is quite important—a committee of individuals who are invested in the outcome and will follow up with various assignments and, perhaps more importantly, who also will raise questions or concerns along the way so that those can be addressed at the outset—cannot be underestimated. A good committee is invaluable, and we had a wonderful group of colleagues with which to design this event.

The college planning committee members obtained email addresses for all instructional librarians and library administrators at their respective institutions. Several emails were sent to anticipated attendees prior to the event. A LibGuide was created featuring the event logo (see Figure 6.1), designed by Cynthia Dancel, Senior Art Specialist, UCF Libraries, incorporating iconic structures from UCF and each of UCF's partner colleges.

The LibGuide also included the tentative program, an RSVP function to facilitate planning as well as a campus map.

The "celebration" was planned to take place toward the end of the fiscal year, when obtaining approval for travel requests may have been challenging. It was therefore a priority by the planning committee with the support of the hosting institutions to provide the event without a registration fee and for lunch to be provided. The university library and the host partner college shared expenses to host the lunch and other conference refreshments. A notebook featuring the event logo was provided to everyone attending and some prizes for drawings during the event were additional "perks" for attendees. To keep the lunch budget in tow, we relied upon a grocery store deli for sandwich and salad platters (less expensive than individual boxed lunches) and included selections for vegan and vegetarian attendees. The

Figure 6.1 "Celebration" Event Logo.

event was held at a centrally located partner college campus, where parking was plentiful and free.

To encourage mixing and mingling among attendees, tables were designated with signs in specific colors, and colored dot stickers corresponding to the signage were randomly placed on programs, which were slipped inside the notebooks. Attendees were encouraged to sit at the table with a dot color that matched the dot on their program. Evaluation forms were included in the notebook so that attendees could jot their ideas throughout the day. We also had large easels set up with oversized notepads and markers so that attendees could share their thoughts on common concerns such as the limitations of a "one shot" instruction session.

The college president, Dr. Georgia Lorenz, and the university associate vice president, Dr. David Mealor, provided welcome remarks, which served to underscore the symbiotic relationship between our institutions, with the college president eloquently emphasizing the role of information literacy and librarians in preparing students for academic success and for success as future employees. Dr. Jennifer Sumner, executive director, UCF Online Connect Center and Strategic Initiatives for UCF Connect, who has worked closely with transfer student issues and barriers, gave our keynote address. The balance of our program consisted of sharing the results of our survey, a presentation from a librarian from teaching and engagement with updates on the progress of new information literacy modules, which will be informed by the survey results, a panel of university subject librarians sharing insights, and a "round table" period in which all could mingle to learn of new initiatives from the various colleges, which were requested in advance. The college news office was also at hand to take pictures for a follow-up college newsroom article. At the conclusion of the event, some final remarks were given, a door prize was awarded, and attendees were given a certificate of attendance for professional development documentation.

The excellent feedback received from the event, and the subsequent review of the feedback at the postevent planning committee meeting, guided the planning committee to next steps that would include a webinar and a planned "Second Annual Celebration of Librarian Collaboration for Transfer Student Success."

The concept of the "Celebration of Collaboration for Transfer Student Success" is easy to replicate in a manner that suits your individual needs. Here are the major takeaways:

- Begin your event proposal process with library administration.
- If approved, begin communication on your event with the librarians at your partner or feeder institutions—beginning communication via email on shared concerns is an easy starting point.

- Librarians at feeder institutions are also involved in your state library association; can you leverage that relationship to build stronger connections between the two library systems?

- Learn more about information literacy instruction at your partner institution(s). This is a two-way street to simply be better informed. Are there areas that should or could be aligned between the feeder college and university in order to support transfer student acclimation and success?

- Would it be beneficial for you to design a simple survey?

- One basic approach to support your shared student population is to determine which databases the college has in common with the university and acknowledge that in information literacy instruction. Begin to prepare students for the transition to a university library in this way.

- A huge budget is not essential for a successful collaborative event. You can start by a hosting half-day sessions with coffee, pastries, and complimentary on-campus parking.

- Librarian responses to the large notepad question, "What instruction activity or practice do you think has the biggest impact on transfer student success?" received the following responses:

  ○ Supporting career research and transfer institution assignments.

  ○ Listening to students at point of need and letting them know they are supported by library staff and librarians throughout their course of study.

  ○ Teaching them how to navigate a new system to find the answers they need.

  ○ Letting students know the university will be a bit different and that coaches exist there specifically to help with transfer.

Table 6.1 outlines the stakeholders, the level of involvement, and some notes that may be helpful for planning a similar event.

Chapter 7 will address how academic librarians can support virtual transfer students.

Practical Applications of Chapter 6

- Be intentional—build collaborations across institutions for transfer student information literacy success with colleagues at neighboring colleges and universities, and particularly those with articulation agreements already in place.

Table 6.1   Stakeholder Support for Planning a Multi-Institutional Event

Person or Group and Order of Contact	Level of Involvement	Notes
Administration	Low to medium commitment of their time. Obtain administrative support of event first and learn the degree of financial support that will be available for refreshments and so on	Start early if you'd like administrators to attend or give a "Welcome" address, as their calendars are often booked far in advance
Library department heads	Low to medium time commitment. Department head buy-in is essential to create an in-house "buzz" about your event, so they can plan for as many to attend as staffing allows	Department heads can have helpful suggestions for individuals to serve on the planning committee as well as other helpful suggestions
Event planning committee	Significant time commitment. Highly involved	Committee should be representative of all stakeholders; a good committee is essential to a successful event. Be respectful of their time; send agendas in advance of meetings
Graphic artist	Time commitment varies	Work with your graphics department early so that you can "brand" your event with a logo
Attendees	Low time commitment	Send "Save the Date" emails with a tentative agenda early on and ongoing updates. Creating an event LibGuide is useful for obtaining RSVP responses. Provide a certificate or similar "artifact," which could be useful in a tenure or promotion portfolio. Provide a survey form at the outset so that they can note thoughts throughout the event

- Use research methods to document collaborative work of transfer student information literacy initiatives and successful collaborative work both within and across institutions.

- Be a partner collaborator, and seek to present and publish your work to disseminate new knowledge in this area of transfer student success and the role of academic libraries.

- Use innovative strategies to build collaborations (see chapters 4 and 5, Practical Applications).

- Plan and host an event that includes local colleges and universities where transfer students are typically migrating. See this example illustrated with tips in the LibGuide: https://guides.ucf.edu/buildinginclusion.

- Use regional and statewide resources—professional organizations and consortia—to build innovations and strategies to serve transfer students holistically, such as the NEFLIN example illustrated in this chapter.

- Be creative and leverage resources—both human resources and financial resources—to build partnerships that benefit students and the invested colleges and universities working with transfer students.

References

Bruce, Christine Susan. 2008. *Informed Learning*. Chicago, IL: Association of College and Research Libraries. http://bvbr.bib-bvb.de:8991/F?func=service& doc_library=BVB01&local_base=BVB01&doc_number=017109104& sequence=000001&line_number=0001&func_code=DB_RE CORDS&service_type=MEDIA.

Chick, Nancy L. 2019. "Theory and the Scholarship of Teaching and Learning: Inquiry and Practice with Intention." In Melissa Mallon, Lauren Hays, Cara Bradley, Rhonda Huisman, and Jackie Belanger, eds. *The Grounded Instruction Librarian: Participating in the Scholarship of Teaching and Learning*. Chicago, IL: Association of College & Research Libraries.

College & Research Libraries. 2018. "ACRL in New Orleans: ACRL Programs at the ALA Annual Conference." *College & Research Libraries News* 79(8). doi:10.5860/crln.79.8.438. https://crln.acrl.org/index.php/crlnews/article /view/17249/18975.

Gashurov, Irene, and Curtis L. Kendrick. 2013. "Collaboration for Hard Times: Insights into What Makes Academic Library Partnerships Succeed." *Library Journal* 138(16): 26. https://link.gale.com/apps/doc/A343753744 /GRNR?u=lincclin_scc&sid=GRNR&xid=e3d10556.

Kaufmann, Karen F. 2018. "Sociocognitive Relevance of Information Literacy: The Impact on Student Academic Work." Queensland University of Technology. https://eprints.qut.edu.au/123999/.

Maybee, Clarence Dale. 2015. "Informed Learning in the Undergraduate Classroom: The Role of Information Experiences in Shaping Outcomes." http://trove.nla.gov.au/work/201620103.

Meyer, J., and R. Land. 2003. *Threshold Concepts and Troublesome Knowledge: Linkages to Ways of Thinking and Practising Within the Disciplines* (pp. 412–424). Edinburgh: University of Edinburgh.

Miller, Robin, and Kate Hinnant. 2018. *Making Surveys Work for Your Library: Guidance, Instructions, and Examples.* Santa Barbara, CA: Libraries Unlimited.

Oakleaf, Megan. 2018. "Northeast Florida Library and Information Network (NEFLIN) Assessment Program 2017–2018 Final Report." https://neflin.org/wp-content/uploads/2018/10/Assessment-Project-Final-Report.pdf.

Tucker, Virginia M., Judith Weedman, Christine S. Bruce, and Sylvia L. Edwards. 2014. "Learning Portals: Analyzing Threshold Concept Theory for LIS Education." *Journal of Education for Library and Information Science* (2): 150. http://db26.linccweb.org/login?url=http://search.ebscohost.com/login.aspx?direct=true&db=edsgao&AN=edsgcl.369065399&site=eds-live.

Wiggins, Grant, and Jay McTighe. 2005. *Understanding by Design.* 2nd ed. Alexandria, VA: Association for Supervision and Curriculum Development.

Connecting the Library to Support Virtual Transfer Students

Technology and philosophy are both tools for living, and the best tools remain useful over long periods of time. Though we barely realize it, every day we use connective tools that were invented thousands of years ago. Similarly, great ideas have no expiration date.

Hamlet's Blackberry: Building a Good Life in the Digital Age,
by William Powers (2010, 79)

Virtual library services and resources are ubiquitous for both local and online students, creating access as a great equalizer that supports student research, reading, and curriculum. The virtual platform provides academic libraries a ready but perhaps untapped or unrecognized resource to more fully enhance and market our services and resources to virtual transfer students. Online students are as much a part of the campus community as on-campus students, and they seek to connect to the academic community. Making explicit how the library provides access to information, instruction, and guidance for students—specifically transfer students—can improve our work in equity, diversity, and inclusion by more creatively and intentionally creating venues that speak directly to transfer students. As a distinct, unique, and growing population on our campuses, college and university libraries may find an untapped audience to more directly engage with as we work toward assisting virtual transfer students in their coursework.

There are innovative ways for colleges and universities to provide community connections for online learners. For example, online student governments can provide representation for the unique interests, needs, and welfare of the online learning community (LaPadula 2003), as both Washington State University and the British Open University have explored. Excelsior College in New York created a website called the Electronic Peer Network—an online space for students to find study partners, join online study groups, chat with other students and staff, and find additional resources to support their academic work and engage socially with other online students (LaPadula 2003). Pun (2018) suggests some simple and seamless ways to connect with our online transfer students or any who engage virtually more readily:

Personalized emails—send to new transfer students from subject librarians targeted to majors or send a personalized email to the incoming transfer students from the online librarian or liaison librarians, whatever seems to be a good fit for your community of practice. Find a way to reach out early via email with the incoming transfer students at your institution. Be sure to include international students as well—because they are transfer students too! Check with the registrar or transfer office to obtain this information.

Student-focused newsletters—get the library included with campus or department newsletters or other communications to students; ask for a space to specifically communicate with transfer students. If you have a transfer student office, student services/affairs or student life office, find out how the library might partner and reach out to transfer students in these systematic communications that are reaching the students on your campus.

Integrate into courses that transfer students typically enroll in—find ways to connect and communicate in a meaningful way via a personal librarian program, as embedded librarians, getting some space in the course syllabus with contact information; open some research workshops in the online course space; talk with faculty to find ways to more prominently and explicitly reach out to transfer students.

Create a LibGuide for transfer students—a guide that contains general library information but can also link to other course guides or general campus information. The guide could include the areas of transition they may be working through to assist them with the explicit connection to potential barriers or challenges they are facing—the four *Ss* of transition (Schlossberg 2011; Anderson, Goodman, and Schlossberg 2011): *situation, self, support, and strategies.*

Online Transfer Students as a Community on Campus

The literature seems to be replete with emphasis that distance learners and transfer students seek a sense of belonging to their academic institutions (LaPadula 2003; Ziegenfuss, Dwyer, and Larsen 2019). The student-centered approach to learning—perhaps what is missing from online services—proves to be valuable for us to consider to more effectively meet the needs of online students and more particularly online transfer students. Perhaps this combination of distance learner and transfer student can better define this unique and distinct student population in our quest to address diversity, equity, and inclusion more emphatically as academic librarians. The use of the library and how it has changed over time regarding access to computing and technology was acknowledged in 2003 by Kuh and Gonyea. However, as technology continues to infiltrate our everyday information lives, our students become more adept and confident with a variety of information platforms where they are both consumers and content creators. Transfer students—part of a diverse community, which includes international students—can be both proficient and familiar with digital technologies (Jackson 2005).

Switzer (2008) acknowledges these distinct characteristics of transfer students and distance learners. The *situation* of transfer students, as online learners, can be more accurately viewed through the lens of Schlossberg's (2011) transition theory to more directly guide the academic librarian in effectively working with this distinct student group. For instance, Switzer (2008) found that research consultations or appointments with librarians were found to be particularly useful for online transfer students—guiding them in one-on-one sessions to overcome barriers to research or technology. Inviting our online transfer students to meet with a librarian by appointment either on campus, on the phone, or online using a meeting room platform with screen-sharing, such as Zoom, can address this *situation* for virtual transfer students. The screen-sharing allows both the student and librarian to share their screens and show examples of problem areas and solutions in real time. Providing these appointment options in terms of different ways to meet are important for students to realize that the librarian is interested and available to provide *support* in a variety of appointment options. During the research consultation, the transfer students can ask questions and provide examples of where they may be "stuck," and the librarian can assess the best way to assist and provide resource suggestions and introduce resources that the institution has that the virtual learner may not be aware of. These research appointments as options for online transfer students may be communicated via the course learning management system, where either the professor or the embedded librarian communicates these options and reaches out to students in courses. These appointments may also be listed in the course or discipline LibGuide that students access online.

Online tutorials for were found to be very effective, as verified by pre- and posttutorial tests. This was significant since students fall into both the category of distance student as well as transfer students (Switzer 2008). Online tutorials can be created on generic topics as well as specific topics related to course assignments. These handy and 24-7 accessible instructional tutorials can be a seamless and friendly way to engage online transfer students. Online tutorials can be included as an effective *strategy* to enhance student engagement and ease anxiety regarding online learning resources by providing a visual and auditory learning environment that mimics some of the features on an on-campus lecture. The online tutorials, therefore, reinforce the online transfer students' *self*, by enhancing confidence, by providing visual and audio components in the digital environment at their transfer institution.

Using instant messaging (IM) or chat for online learners also has proved to be useful and effective (Switzer 2008). These online communication platforms emerging for chat reference with enhanced capabilities may be an effective option for academic libraries to consider. This option can be used as a more prominent reach to impact online transfer students to enhance research and information literacy competency applications to their academic coursework. For example, some chat reference platforms offer screen-sharing capabilities with the integration of systems like Zoom. Chat reference is a great "in the moment" and immediate engagement with a library staff person or librarian to provide information or research assistance that the online learner needs. Chat reference delivery options can be tailored to the institution and could be a consortia–type delivery or individual library managed platform. The academic library can use chat reference to connect readily and in a user-centered and user-friendly modality to support online transfer students as they navigate new library resources and perhaps even new ways to communicate with a librarian. The chat window can be placed strategically in online LibGuides, online courses via the course management system, on the library homepage, and on librarian websites or course guides, making the chat easy to find, access, and use. This can provide a way to more fully engage students in research consultations and provide more effective visual and auditory sensory touchpoints for students.

In LaPadula' s (2003) study of online students, 92–97 percent of those surveyed rated their experience with the library as being satisfied. They also indicated interest in having additional student services available online such as a book club, chat rooms, and additional technical assistance on how to do research online. It is important to recognize that distance learners need to access support services in the same way they access instruction. This includes easy access from a distance and at times that fit their schedules, which may include different time zones. These virtual realities for online students and particularly online transfer students can guide our work as academic librarians to meet them where they are—in their time zone, with their research needs, and with their information literacy knowledge base. This aims to more effectively connect them to their community and more specifically to their academic library and the librarians who can assist them to be successful in their new academic environment.

The Library Online

Websites

The library website is a first go-to online resource for students. We can present a user-friendly and inviting space for students to enter for academic and research support and human engagement. When our library websites are well designed, current, and created with the student researcher in mind, the opportunity to enhance student engagement and reduce library anxiety is the information experience we want to provide for our online user communities. Each institution is self-directed by institutional priorities and strategic plans. However, we can look at how these may align or have similarities where we can work together to build on shared priorities in the academic library communities in which we work.

Usability studies can be an effective tool in enhancing our library websites. When we enlist assistance from our users and learn what makes sense to them, the impact can be substantial. This process can be a bit tedious, but it may result in more effective student engagement and learning using library resources for their academic work. This includes the decisions related to our library discovery platforms, catalog protocols, and other technical services and cataloging functions and services such as an interlibrary loan.

The academic library competes with commercial enterprises—such as Google and Bing—for student ease of use for searching, finding, and locating relevant sources for assignments. Twenty-first-century users are accustomed to seamless online experiences for online shopping and other search functions. When they meet with slow and less-than-seamless results while searching in our library catalog or databases, they often are perplexed, frustrated, and are apt to return to the less cumbersome experience of using a web-based search engine to try to find credible and authoritative sources using the internet. This can lead to yet another set of perplexities and frustrations for our students if they are not well versed in evaluating websites and internet sources for authority, credibility, and scholarly quality. As academic librarians, being good listeners to our users—and attentive to our transfer students—can result in making needed and informed changes to our online searching environments. This may require collaborations with our information technology departments in order to ensure seamless or at least shared understandings of user needs in order to serve our transfer students as well as the general student population at large in effective ways. In turn, our users may experience an enhanced searching experience and find relevant sources more readily with the assistance of barrier-free access to library resources.

This might include, for instance, a single sign-on for users. This simple but significant institutional technology decision can make a huge difference for transfer students. More broadly, this type of decision can positively impact the institution and its users across the technology landscape, which is integrated and necessary for the daily work of students, faculty, and staff.

This may be an institutional challenge for many of us. However, recognizing the significance, could be quite beneficial to our transfer student population. How can we more effectively communicate this to our institutional partners and administrative thinkers? Perhaps there are innovators in our faculty librarian communities who can formulate best practices of communications to assist with this challenge.

To this end, combating "fake news" and the insistent challenges to our 21st-century information ecology is a constant struggle for all learners in higher education. The opportunity for academic librarians and our partner discipline faculty to instruct and inform our students of the value of acquiring real-world information literacy competencies for their academic success and the application and relevance of these competencies to their lifelong learning cannot be understated.

Specifically for transfer students, highlighting the "fake news" or misinformation concepts could be included as an informational tab on the library website or in a LibGuide created for transfer students at both sending and receiving institutions or by having the library web team be explicit in including this critical thinking challenge of "What is fake news?" in the information literacy online content for both students and faculty. There is an abundance of literature and resources on the subject of "fake news" that could easily be adapted or adopted for colleges and universities and delivered online for virtual transfer students to easily access as integrated into the library website and other library instructional materials provided in courses. Not only does explicitly recognizing the concept of "fake news" raise awareness of this phenomenon but also provides for inviting critical thinking as a bridge for transfer students across the curriculum and across institutions as they use information to complete their assignments The International Federation of Information Association (IFIA) has produced a key document to assist us and all learners across the world with a valuable and relevant document to guide us in evaluating and assessing information as critical thinkers in a democratic way. Figure 7.1 is the infographic, titled, "How to Spot Fake News," and has been translated into over 40 languages.

Access to Sources and Content for Learning and Academic Work

One of the key components of the online academic library includes access to databases and e-books. These gateways are invaluable for students working to complete assignments that require credible sources, often with specific parameters as required by their professor. Though perhaps these incredible online credible sources are at our students' fingertips 24-7 with their login

Figure 7.1 How to Spot Fake News.

Source: https://www.ifla.org/publications/node/11174 9. IFLA [CC BY 4.0 (https://creativecommons.org/licenses/by/4.0)]

credentials, the usability and familiarity of navigating these sources may not be resident for transfer students. For students who are new to the institution, accessing and navigating these required resources may not lead to a successful and enjoyable information experience. The importance of providing online library tools, tips, tutorials, and guides for the online learning community can make this library experience more profitable and enhance learning.

Directing students to links to the ACRL website that addresses the *Framework* and provides an easily accessible and findable tool for students to use when working remotely will keep them connected to the library as a distinct community. This online ACRL guide could be an effective resource for our online transfer students to use for their *self*-directed efficacy (Schlossberg 2011). Herein, the academic library can be a conduit to support online transfer students and create the sense of community. Why re-create content that has already been identified to be helpful and vetted as reliable? Using the ACRL *Framework* online resources is a great starting point for directing students and faculty to reliable information that will be useful for research and writing.

If more institutional-specific information is needed, video content, RSS feeds for researching specific types of content, and even information directing them to other departments on campus could be included in a LibGuide that would be beneficial at an institutional level. This guide could include links to campus departments to assist students, if they find a gap in their financial aid package, need some advising assistance, or need some counseling or mental health guidance or support while continuing with their studies. Librarians tasked with LibGuide creation using an institutional format is a good start. Transfer students may find themselves in a new and unanticipated *situation* (Schlossberg 2011), which impacts a new transition that they have encountered. Knowing they can go to an online source easily found on the library website, to provide needed and "just in time" information can be a *support* and *strategy* (Schlossberg 2011) for these online transfer students to use during a transition that occurs while studying at their new college or university.

In addition, faculty librarians collaborating with discipline faculty to create assignments and provide the needed step-by-step instructions for using certain library resources is a solid step that can be taken to enhance effective online learning. As Shank and Dewald (2003) explained, when we link library resources to course assignment requirements, connecting the dots for students as to relevance, it is more likely that students will access and use library resources to complete their academic work. This leads us back to the topic of academic librarians working in partnership with instructional designers and discipline faculty to intentionally build a collaborative posture to engage cross-departmental work (see chapters 4 and 5). One area to fully investigate is the use of no-cost textbooks and course materials to students. This can include library e-books, library e-textbooks, and finding OER course materials that may be available and easily adapted to current course curricula with faculty collaboration (chapter 9).

Academic librarians can take the lead in engaging faculty and deans in conversations surrounding the options and opportunities to more fully consider ways to bridge scholarly content with course design and syllabus integration. The conversations could—in fact result in more innovative ideas and movement toward integrating information literacy, current literature (using RSS feeds and journal alerts) into learning management systems (LMS) and assignment design that engages students with real world applications of their research and readings to the disciplines or areas of interest they are pursuing.

Using course syllabi has been found to be an effective way for librarians to partner with discipline faculty and access services, the bookstore, and learning management folks in the e-learning and instructional design areas, to effectively assess pathways for learners to engage with and find effective instructional spaces and tools (Parrot and Daniel Lindsay 2017; Maybee et al. 2015; McGowan, Gonzalez, and Stanny 2016). This could perhaps be replicated by the work of University of Maryland librarians as cited in chapter 5. This is not a "one way is the only way" scenario, but rather an approach to bridge instructional design, using applied theory across disciplines, to engage students using meta-literacies, which lead to the student experience of meta-cognitive learning. This includes using information to learn (informed learning) and other proven pedagogies for online learners to find success as they navigate sources, resources, technology, information, and faculty expectations. Virtual learners are guided to be critical thinkers and find avenues to apply their own learning to the scholarly conversation they have engaged in with the scholarly sources they have located using various modalities in their online learning experiences.

The academic library as a teaching resource can be further expressed as relevant to our online transfer students when we integrate our resources in the learning management systems (LMS) at our colleges and universities. This can assist our online transfer students as they learn to navigate not just a potentially new LMS but also a new library website and new library online resources. When we intentionally recognize the value of making a seamless, user-friendly, single-sign on experience for our online learners a priority, we are saying—essentially—that they matter, are important, and that we are here to support their academic success. When online learners find continual barriers to ease of access to sources and delivery systems for learning—it interrupts their learning. However and whenever we can facilitate more seamless information experiences, the academic library can work to engage our learners and guide them toward transformative learning experiences.

The Library Transfer Student Community Online

"Embedded librarianship" has been a noteworthy but perhaps ambiguous term that seemed to emerge in the literature. What is an embedded librarian, and how do we serve online transfer students? Dewey (2004) seems to be the inaugural entry in terms of the literature, and defining this role at least in the timeline of our work is influential in teaching and learning. However, we see more defining roles, definitions, and scoping of embedded librarianship presented by Matthew and Schroeder (2006). They suggest there is a missing human element. Herein lies wonderful advantages and challenges—namely, librarian availability and the scoping and feasibility of this endeavor.

The largest challenge is scalability and support for the academic librarians who are committed to the teaching and learning of students but are not fully supported in terms of resources and funding by the institution. This is clearly stated in the literature:

Some faculty members have come to rely on the program after two years and expect library assistance automatically each semester. While a testament to the program's success, this expectation can prove problematic because CCV does not have enough librarians to provide the service in every online class. Consequently, some faculty have been turned away after a predetermined number of courses has been reached. This points to a larger concern, which is the inability—given a finite number of librarians—to continue to grow the program in its current form. (Matthew and Schroeder 2006, 64)

This results in the challenge of sustainability of the embedded librarian program. Alternative approaches that may support the sustainability of an embedded librarian include looking at additional types of modalities to deliver instruction to students. One approach involves creating library courses for specific curricular areas, which may also include a scaffolded approach that could prove to be beneficial to online transfer student learners, even perhaps be more impactful to learning and applying information literacy competencies specific to the discipline. Another consideration is using videoconferencing—offering scheduled online conferencing availability by librarians, like office hours, where online transfer students could engage with librarians in a research or reference consultation by sharing screens and dialoguing in a pseudo face-to-face environment (Matthew and Schroeder 2006).

This type of human resource deficit could perhaps be also reckoned by institutions creating new types of librarian positions that can serve not just the online transfer student but focus on the online services, teaching and learning materials, and delivery modalities in a more holistic way. This could include positions such as a diversity, equity, and inclusion librarian. The position vacancy announcement for the diversity, equity, and inclusion librarian at the University of Florida reads as follows:

The George A. Smathers Libraries at the University of Florida seek an innovative, engaged individual to serve in the newly created Diversity Equity and Inclusion (DEI) Librarian position, focused on the development of a comprehensive and strategic DEI program. The Libraries are critical contributors to the University's ambitions regarding diversity, equity, inclusion and awareness. We recognize DEI as guiding principles and understand differences between people from the full spectrum of human and social identities as assets. These values help sustain excellence and fairness within our workplace, and enhance the relevance and accessibility of our facilities, services and collections, for communities we serve.

Through a participatory Strategic Directions development process in 2018, the Libraries committed to better understanding and fostering a more inclusive workplace. As one element in our efforts, the DEI Librarian position will help the Libraries' team members recognize, understand, value and embrace our differences as crucial to our communal work. As part of the development and implementation of a DEI program for the Libraries, the DEI Librarian will serve as the Libraries' Campus Diversity Liaison (CDL), working within a network of peer positions from across the University as well as serving as a liaison within the Libraries. We seek a capacity builder who will create, in collaboration with people of diverse cultural backgrounds and origins, races, ethnicities, genders, sexual orientations, and perspectives, meaningful dialogue and change.

The DEI Librarian will participate in national dialogues within the United States and globally that promote the establishment of professional practices in libraries and programs to enhance the opportunities of minority and underrepresented groups in the library profession. The DEI Librarian will pursue professional development opportunities, including research, publication and professional service activities in order to advance their field and meet library-wide criteria for tenure and promotion. (posted June 20, 2019, on the fla-facrl@lists.fsu.edu listerv)

This is a new position that has been created to serve the students and facilitate library team members' awareness of the diverse student populations that faculty librarians and library staff serve as well as to collaborate across the university to enhance the work and relevance of the library to students, staff, faculty, and the administration.

The Human Element and Online Learners

Beyond embedded librarians and positions for academic librarians that are more directly focused on serving our online learners—including transfer students—our library desk staff, student workers, and technical services staff should be noted as collaborators within the library who are key to making our online transfer students feel connected to library content, resources, and services. Often users engage with staff by calling on the phone. This technology is as relevant today as when it first emerged as a transformative communication tool in 1876, when Alexander Graham Bell was awarded the U.S. patent for the invention of the telephone ("Telephone | History, Definition, & Uses" 2019). The telephone is as relevant today—or perhaps more relevant—as it was when first introduced and continues to be a tool and modality that is impactful for our work in the library.

Though students and faculty may access the library using the library website, accessing LibGuides or online tutorials, or even using chat, often the timeless and handy phone conversation seems to fill the need and make a research or reference inquiry turn into a wonderful human–to–human interaction that adds depth, breadth, empathy, and nuanced understandings because of the tone of the conversation or the assurances provided to the inquirer that information as needed can be acquired or located and/or that a referral to a source that can assist is easily made. For instance, perhaps the transfer student really needs to request an interlibrary loan (ILL) or speak directly to a subject librarian or librarian who is the liaison to a department that is best suited to their inquiry. All of this "in the moment" service with the human element in play can connect our online transfer students to the library community in a way that other modalities perhaps are not well suited to delivering. The phone can bridge a gap for our online transfer student to connect to our wonderful human resources who provide exceptional communications and service. Marketing the library phone service intentionally can perhaps make the transfer student potential interactions on the phone a more effective and enjoyable touchpoint for enhancing community at the academic library.

In summary, there are varied ways for the academic library to support our virtual transfer students. As a distinct community we can see how these specific areas as touchpoints and communication points can provide more relevant interactions that support academic success. Table 7.1 illustrates some collaboration and communication items for consideration that may be relevant to your specific community of practice.

Online transfer students are in transition and are looking for ways to connect to the academic community where they are working toward a degree or certificate completion. This journey will inevitably impact their professional trajectory toward achieving goals that are meaningful to them. The academic library can play an essential role in supporting their academic success.

Table 7.1   Online Library Communication Touchpoints

Communication Touchpoints	Communication Delivery Modalities
Library faculty teaching online learners	LibGuide for transfers students
	E-books licensed by the library
	E-textbooks licensed by the library
	OER (open educational resources)
The human element	Online video chat reference
	Transfer student librarian/Outreach librarian
	Diversity, equity, and inclusion librarian
	Marketing the phone

Communication Touchpoints	Communication Delivery Modalities
Teaching resources	LibGuide integration with LMS (learning management system)
	Embedded librarian
	Online services librarian
	Scholarly communications librarian
	Emerging technologies librarian
	Research librarians
User-friendly access	Single sign-on
	User-friendly access to content
	Short "how to" videos with accompanying PDF instructions on "how to" access to library resources
	Using consistent language for easy recognition and understanding of terminology showing up in online library spaces

Practical Applications of Chapter 7

- Create library-related information pathways for transfer students such as personalized emails, transfer student newsletters; integrate librarians into courses that transfer students typically enroll in.

- Create a LibGuide for transfer students.

- Create online appointments for transfer students using Zoom or other web-based synchronous meeting venues, which provide more effective visual and auditory sensory touchpoints for students.

- Invite transfer students to personalized appointments with research librarians on the phone, in person, or online.

- Be online in chat references to accommodate transfer students.

- Market the phone as a user-friendly and effective option for transfer students to get in the moment and efficient guidance for research and other institutional referrals.

- Train library staff to be attentive to transfer students' unique questions and needs.

- Introduce the concept of "fake news" in online spaces, including the library website and courses, to promote awareness, and invite critical thinking across the curriculum: See this IFLA source to use for discussions with students and faculty: **How to Spot Fake News, https://www.ifla.org/publi cations/node/11174**

References

Anderson, Mary, Jane Goodman, and Nancy K. Schlossberg. 2011. *Counseling Adults in Transition: Linking Schlossberg's Theory with Practice in a Diverse World.* Springer Publishing Company.

Dewey, Barbara I. 2004. "The Embedded Librarian." *Resource Sharing & Information Networks* 17(1–2): 5–17. doi:10.1300/J121v17n01_02.

Jackson, Pamela A. 2005. "Incoming International Students and the Library: A Survey." *Reference Services Review* 33(2): 197–209. doi:10.1108 /00907320510597408.

Kuh, George D., and Robert M. Gonyea. 2003. "The Role of the Academic Library in Promoting Student Engagement in Learning." *College & Research Libraries* 64(4): 256–82. doi:10.5860/crl.64.4.256.

LaPadula, Maria. 2003. "A Comprehensive Look at Online Student Support Services for Distance Learners." *American Journal of Distance Education* 17(2): 119–28. doi:10.1207/S15389286AJDE1702_4.

Matthew, V. and Schroeder, A. 2006. "The Embedded Librarian Program." *Educause Quarterly.* https://er.educause.edu/-/media/files/article-downloads /eqm06410.pdf.

Maybee, Clarence, Jake Carlson, Maribeth Slebodnik, and Bert Chapman. 2015. "'It's in the Syllabus': Identifying Information Literacy and Data Information Literacy Opportunities Using a Grounded Theory Approach." *Journal of Academic Librarianship* 41(4): 369–76. doi:10.1016/j.acalib.2015.05.009. http://www.sciencedirect.com/science/article/pii/S0099133315000993.

McGowan, Britt, Melissa Gonzalez, and Claudia J. Stanny. 2016. "What Do Undergraduate Course Syllabi Say about Information Literacy?" *Portal: Libraries and the Academy* 16(3): 599–617.

Parrott, Justin, and Beth Daniel Lindsay. 2017. "Utilizing Syllabi to Support Access Services and Beyond: A Case Study." *Journal of Access Services* 14(1): 29–38. doi:10.1080/15367967.2017.1281138.

Pun, Raymond. 2018. "Helping Transfer Students Succeed: General Tips & Strategies for Academic Librarians." *Credo* (blog). Accessed September 11, 2019. http://blog.credoreference.com/helping-transfer-students-succeed -general-tips-strategies-for-academic-librarians.

Schlossberg, Nancy K. 2011. "The Challenge of Change: The Transition Model and Its Applications." *Journal of Employment Counseling* 48(4): 159–62. doi:10.1002/j.2161–1920.2011.tb01102.x. https://search.proquest.com/doc view/912809137.

Shank, John D. and Nancy H. Dewald. 2003. "Establishing Our Presence in Courseware: Adding Library Services to the Virtual Classroom. (Communications)." *Information Technology and Libraries* 22(1): 38. https://search. proquest.com/docview/215830692.

Switzer, Anne T. 2008. "Redefining Diversity: Creating an Inclusive Academic Library through Diversity Initiatives." *College & Undergraduate Libraries* 15(3): 280–300. doi:10.1080/10691310802258182.

"Telephone | History, Definition, & Uses." 2019. *Encyclopedia Britannica.* Accessed September 30, 2019. https://www.britannica.com/technology/telephone.

Ziegenfuss, Donna, Jamie Dwyer, and Dale Larsen. 2019. "Exploring the Challenges and Opportunities of Library Outreach for Transfer Students: A Cross-Institutional Collaboration." (Conference Proceedings.) ACRL, 2019. http://www.ala.org/acrl/sites/ala.org.acrl/files/content/conferences/confsandpreconfs/2019/ExploringChallengesandOpportunitiesofLibraryOutreach.pdf.

CHAPTER 8

Niche Academic Library Initiatives That Support Transfer Student Success

A common thread running through research regarding transfer students is that academic libraries recognize their position on campus as possibly strategic to easing or eliminating some of the barriers and challenges transfer students encounter.

—Harrick and Fullington (2019, 78)

This chapter explores some of the niche initiatives that academic libraries may consider extending in support of transfer students on our campuses. There are various successful strategies that academic libraries can use and adapt for the local campus communities and to build collaborative partnerships across departmental and program–delineated organizational structures at the college or university.

Here are some suggestions identified in the literature that address millennials and certain subpopulations at the University of Cincinnati, including transfer students (Tenofsky 2005). Included is the way the library can position itself as collaborators with student services to impact millennial transfer populations. Here are some highlights for consideration as your library team begins to build a strategic plan to maximize potential opportunities to support the transfer students at your campus.

On Collaborations

1. Create a unified library message: Collaborate with librarians at your institution and with transfer partner institutions to create messages using the same vocabulary and invite transfer students to engage.
2. Be proactive, and use all staff resources: Be attentive to staff, librarian, and faculty needs as collaborative work ensues, for seamless inter- and intra-institutional effective collaborations.
3. Position librarians in key places: Being aware of on-site, online, embedded, and liaison-ready librarian work in various modalities could be beneficial.
4. Work with existing collaborations, and start small: Be cognizant of small but impactful progress.
5. Be student centered: Recognize all the work is to benefit students—the ultimate goal in teaching and learning.

On Assessment

1. Use existing resources.
2. Use existing groups.
3. Debrief with staff.
4. Use course-integrated instruction.

Though libraries do not always have a seat at the table when discussions on supporting transfer students is on the agenda in higher education circles, the recognition of our place at the table in the library and information science community may be indicated by the two special issues on "Transfer Students and Students in Transition" Volume 45, Issues 2 and 3, published by *Reference Services Review* in 2017. In these two issues 25 articles were published on the topic of transfer students, and the role of academic libraries in supporting their success was published. Topics included literature reviews; information literacy; boutique personal librarian programs for transfer students; information literacy instruction; and how to include games, design thinking, fake news, and supporting teaching practicum while also addressing transition theory and transfer shock and higher education (Ivins, Copenhaver, and Koclanes 2017). Assessment, a common reader program connecting information literacy with transfer student success, and other relevant topics were published in these two volumes dedicated to addressing transfer students and the academic library as a key player to provide both informal and formal support in the transition and transfer student information experience. The following are some recent transfer initiatives to consider as relevant for adapting to your library.

Transfer Student Librarians and Library Initiatives

Creation of a Boutique Personal Librarian Program

Librarians at Santa Clara University, California, a four-year private institution with an undergraduate enrollment of approximately 5,500 students, initiated a "boutique personal librarian" program for transfer students in 2015 (Sandelli 2017). They described this as a user-centric model focusing on personalized, tailored information delivery, which involved learning as much about their users as possible at the outset. The librarians initiated contact with the assistant dean of the campus academic advising center to discuss the concept and obtain demographic information on the newest group of transfer students as well as to learn what institutional supports were already in place. The initial group of transfer students was relatively small, which was ideal for piloting this new initiative. Two designated personal librarians contacted the students by email, using the students' names in their messages, congratulating them on their acceptance to the university and inviting the student to meet with their personal librarian one on one. The personal librarian also included some information about themselves in their initial contact email, including a photo, to make a connection and facilitate the introductory meeting. In addition, the librarians developed templates for contacting the students three times during the term on the following schedule:

- Week 1 or 2 was the introductory message;
- Week 5 (the midpoint of the term) was a follow-up during a peak time for students to be working on assignments; and
- Week 8 was a friendly reminder of their availability to provide research assistance as the term ended as well as notification of extended library hours during the final exam period. (LaFrance and Kealey 2015)

Nearly three-quarters of the students contacted by email in the pilot responded to at least one email, and over 60 percent took advantage of the introductory meeting opportunity. For the full launch, 136 transfer student names were distributed among 11 librarians. They found that while not all students took advantage of the opportunity, those that did found it very helpful; in fact, one student responded, via survey, as follows:

> I really like the Personal Librarian program. I am a transfer student and when I was Assigned my first research paper at Santa Clara I really liked the fact I had a specific Person to contact. Not only that but she showed me all the databases that [the University] has to offer and how to use them. (LaFrance and Kealey 2015, 340)

Based on the number of interactions between librarians and transfer students, the program has been a success. To keep it sustainable, and to keep participating librarians engaged, they began to assign each designated personal librarian a minimum of 20 transfer students to ensure there would be some degree of student follow-up. They noted that close collaboration with other campus units involved with transfer students was key to a successful program.

Creation of a Transfer Services Librarian

The University of North Carolina Wilmington (UNCW 2019) is one of 17 campuses within the University of North Carolina system and has an undergraduate enrollment of approximately 14,000; the campus library has a staff of 51 with 25 serving as librarians.

In reviewing available information on the transfer student population, it became clear that there were significant demographic differences between the makeup of the overall student body and the transfer student population. During the fall 2016 semester, most transfer students were men (47%, compared to 38% of incoming first-year students). In addition, the transfer student group reflected more ethnic diversity than the incoming first-year class.

As noted in chapter 6, in 2018, the authors initiated a survey of college instructional librarians at the six institutions within the DirectConnect partnership with the University of Central Florida (UCF). The purpose of the survey was to determine which elements of information literacy the college librarians typically covered in information literacy instruction and to compare that with the elements of information literacy covered in online modules at the university. (See chapter 6.) Since DirectConnect is an enhanced articulation agreement, guaranteeing admission to UCF upon attainment of an AA degree, our concern was that misalignment in information literacy instruction could disadvantage the DirectConnect AA-degreed transfer student population and would also have implications for students transferring from an area college prior to earning their AA While the survey revealed areas of alignment between the university and partner colleges, it also revealed areas with gaps. This information, as well as an opportunity for learning more about transfer students and networking, was shared at a daylong professional development event—the first ever between our institutions—for librarians and library administrators from the university and the partner colleges. This "Celebration of Librarian Collaboration for Transfer Student Success" was enthusiastically supported and attended. Next steps include a webinar as well as a second annual celebration event.

Creation of Niche Library Marketing for Transfer Students

As noted in chapter 4, marketing explicitly to transfer students can raise awareness of specific resources and services needed for this group of new arrivals on our campuses. They may come with ready knowledge of the kinds of academic sources that might be in the academic library, but may not be sure how to ask about what their new library has to offer. Though confident about some kinds of research, perhaps their new college or university seems much larger or smaller than what they are accustomed to. Therefore, having marketing slogans, taglines, easy-to-follow directions for access, and ways to say to transfer students "Hey, we're glad you're here" can be effective for creating community connections easily, even subtly, but with effecting engagement and setting at ease newcomers on our campuses.

When there is cross-institutional marketing that specifically speaks to the transfer student audience, this enhances the opportunity for the library to be in lockstep to more effectively chime in to conversations with dual-enrolled students, vertical transfer students, lateral, swirling, or other types of students (see chapter 1) who are somehow fit as a transfer student. The library can then be prepared to talk about scenarios that are specific to the transfer experience and create dialogue that supports the student engagement not only on campus but more specifically with the library. The library can talk about the kinds of collections available, technologies and how to access various learning platforms, how to request an interlibrary loan, or get to certain types of content that is of interest to the student. These casual but informative conversations with transfer students about the library can support the transfer student quite effectively while subtly engaging Schlossberg's transition model (2011) for coping with transitions. The four tenets of the model address *situation*, *self*, *support*, and *strategies* (see chapter 4). When the academic library is prepared to market explicitly and intentionally to transfer students, opportunities for building community and engaging our students both academically and socially can be impactful interactions that bring support for our new students.

Creation of Transfer Student Identity in the Library

The intentional "niche" marketing plan for transfer students has perhaps an unintentional but important potential result—which is building transfer student identity in the library. When the library creates messages that are intentionally directed at the transfer student population—as well as other niche segments in our campus communities—this can bring a new way for students to identify with our library spaces. This can be both online and on campus. These new identities are quite important for transfer students to acquire. Much the same as using an athletic logo, slogan, or mascot that represents the team or institution to connect fans to the college or university, the academic library has an opportunity to market in the same way—perhaps even capitalizing on the institutional team representation. It matters how we market the library—what we call ourselves—for students, including transfer students, to be able to quickly and easily identify with who we are and what we do. For example, if the institutional athletic logo is "Titans" perhaps the transfer student logo could be "Transfer Student Titans." Connecting transfer students to identify with or be associated to their new institutional identity or logo may enhance their connection to the academic community.

The term "library" can have many different meanings for different people and continues to emerge in meaning in the 21st century. Being diligent to self-identify who we are and what the library does on our campuses is really a very basic but important and powerful tool to create identity for students. This can also build community around our work and the student academic and community experience as they visit the library on campus or online.

Creation of Pathways to Workplace for Transfer Students

While the academic library typically seems to be a place for academic support, we can also partner with our higher education colleagues to build transferrable skills for the workplace. In fact, the more we can connect real-world applications of the academic work students are doing—specifically relating to information literacy—the more relevant information literacy is to students (Kaufmann 2018). This idea of real-world application, not just of information literacy for lifelong learning but across disciplinary content, can be a factor that provides students, and especially transfer students—as they progress toward completing their academic goals—motivation and persistence (Tinto 2016) to finish and complete their degrees. This also supports the transition model areas of *self* and *strategies*, which Schlossberg (2011) suggests assist with a successful transition experience. This "niche" application of building and identifying transferrable skills for transfer students may be a turnkey area for the library to self-identify and be effective contributors to transfer student success in the areas of *self* and *strategies* relating to information literacy and transdisciplinary engagement of academics and real-world applications for transfer students.

Creation of Pathways to Degrees for Transfer Students

Librarians have a key role for transfer student success in completing and receiving the degree that they have as their goal. As we teach information literacy to students, it is imperative to recognize our role as faculty partners in the discipline of library and information science (LIS) alongside our colleagues in other disciplines to make real-world application of concepts and theory for our students to their professional aspirations.

As we teach information literacy (IL) integrated into course curriculum and to support assignment completion success, recognizing this important role will enhance our work with other faculty and enhance student successes as they work toward degree completion.

Specifically, for transfer students, key findings from a recent study indicate that excellence in IL teaching of college transfer students is associated with the frequency of four IL teaching activities, including:

- providing library orientations and instruction,
- teaching about databases and other electronic resources,
- teaching research skills, and
- teaching students in one-on-one interactions. (Lance, Rodney, and Schwarz 2010)

Perhaps the most poignant finding in this list is the idea of the effectiveness of teaching students in one-on-one interactions. This idea of personal appointments or consultations could be a very inspirational and transformative notion for academic librarians. The notion of waiting for students to come to a reference desk for assistance perhaps has evolved to a different type of interaction with academic librarians, due to the changes in access to information. Rather than having to come to the physical library for research work where students would be in physical proximity to stop in to the research desk with questions, now they access research sources differently—from a variety of access points. Therefore, being intentional in our approach to invite, promote, and elicit one-on-one interactions via research appointments on the phone, online, in video chat, or using IM chat service is needed to more successfully work with and communicate with both students and faculty to enrich and assist learning.

Creation of New Institutional Partner Relationships for Transfer Students

How is higher education addressing the needs of transfer students? Developing additional institutional partnerships with interested higher education partners to make transfer student options more evident and student centered is one approach. One recent example is the creation of new partner relationships for seamless transfer student transition to a fully online university. Seminole State College of Florida recently announced a new partnership with the University of Florida's "UF Online" program. This program provides seamless transfer for students with an AA degree to continue their studies in an online program to acquire their bachelor's degree. This partnership complements the current partnership in place with UCF and with the current bachelor's degrees offered at Seminole State.

An additional partnership between Seminole State College and Complete Florida provides new opportunities for transfer students to complete certifications or degrees, for which they have credentials already accumulated, to work toward crossing the finish line! Transfer students can capitalize on their current bank of academic credentials and move forward to complete additional credentials to enhance their workplace, profession, and life choices.

These types of programs make our work more effective when we know we can partner—even across state boarders sometimes—to assist students as they work to acquire the credentials needed in their professions.

Exploring how niche academic librarian roles can support transfer student success is reviewed and challenged in this chapter. The hope is that what may be a good fit for your community of practice is prompted for thoughtful discussion and contemplation by instruction librarians, administrators, and other stakeholders who are decision-makers in higher education.

As we work toward more collaborative, inclusive, and equitable discussions to empower our work and guide our students, let's consider how the academic library has a significant role in supporting our transfer student populations.

To that end, chapter 9 will explore the open access, more specifically, the open educational resource topic, and how we might consider our role in this segment of academic librarianship and the 21st-century learning information ecology.

Practical Applications of Chapter 8

- Create niche marketing to transfer students as is applicable to your institution.

- Be proactive to identify the best ways to connect and communicate to transfer students in the academic library.

- Be intentional to collaborate to promote transfer student initiatives with partner universities and high schools.

- Create opportunities for transfer student identity in the library.

- Adopt a library-centered transfer student logo like an athletic logo by adopting the school logo and adding "Transfer Student" to the brand.

- Create buttons for academic library staff to wear during the first few weeks of each term that says "We love transfer students."

- Create a transfer student boutique personal librarian if funding is provided.

- Host a transfer student seminar in the library as our colleagues at UNC Wilmington.

References

Harrick, Matthew, and Lee Ann Fullington. 2019. "'Don't make Me Feel Dumb': Transfer Students, the Library, and Acclimated to a New Campus." *Evidence Based Library and Information Practice* 14 (English Language): 77–91. doi:10.18438/eblip29512.

Ivins, Tammy, Kimberly Copenhaver, and Alyssa Koclanes. 2017. "Adult Transitional Theory and Transfer Shock in Higher Education: Practices from the Literature." *Reference Services Review* 45(2): 244–57.

Kaufmann, Karen F. 2018. "Sociocognitive Relevance of Information Literacy: The Impact on Student Academic Work." Queensland University of Technology. https://eprints.qut.edu.au/123999/.

Lafrance, Helene, and Shannon B. Kealey. 2017. "A Boutique Personal Librarian Program for Transfer Students." *Reference Services Review* 45(2): 332–45. doi:10.1108/RSR-10-2016-0066.

Lance, Keith Curry, Marcia J. Rodney, and Bill Schwarz. 2010. "Collaboration Works—When It Happens! the Idaho School Library Impact Study." *Teacher Librarian* 37(5): 30. https://search.proquest.com/docview/609464978.

Sandelli, Anna. 2017. "Through Three Lenses: Transfer Students and the Library." *Reference Services Review* 45(3): 400–414. doi:10.1108/RSR-10-2016-0074.

Schlossberg, Nancy K. 2011. "The Challenge of Change: The Transition Model and Its Applications." *Journal of Employment Counseling* 48(4): 159–62. doi:10.1002/j.2161-1920.2011.tb01102.x. https://search.proquest.com/docview/912809137.

Tenofsky, Deborah. 2005. "Teaching to the Whole Student: Building Best Practices for Collaboration between Libraries and Student Services." *Research Strategies* 20(4):284–99. doi:10.1016/j.resstr.2006.12.023.

Tinto, Vincent. 2016. "From Retention to Persistence." *Inside Higher Ed*. Accessed September 17, 2019. https://www.insidehighered.com/views/2016/09/26/how-improve-student-persistence-and-completion-essay.

University of North Carolina Wilmington. 2019. "Library Resources for Transfer Students." Accessed September 30, 2019. https://library.uncw.edu/transfer_students.

CHAPTER 9

Textbook Affordability Initiatives That Support Transfer Student Success

"Nothing says 'Welcome to College' like exorbitant textbook prices."
—Andre Perry, columnist and David M. Rubenstein
Fellow at the Brookings Institution

A Growing Problem

The high cost of textbooks has become increasingly troubling in recent years. In fact, in 2016 the U.S. Bureau of Labor Statistics released data indicating that for a 10-year period, from January 2006 to July 2016, the Consumer Price Index for college tuition and fees had increased 63 percent, while over that same period, consumer prices for college textbooks increased 88 percent (Bureau of Labor Statistics 2016).

In 2013, the Student Public Interest Research Groups (https://studentpirgs.org/) conducted a survey of 2,039 students from more than 150 different university campuses. That survey revealed that 65 percent of student respondents had decided against buying a textbook because it was too expensive. Additionally, the survey found that 94 percent of the students who had foregone purchasing a textbook were concerned that doing so would hurt their grade in a course, and nearly half of all students surveyed said that the cost of textbooks impacted how many and which classes they took each semester (Senack 2014). Based on this information, it is not difficult to make a correlation between textbook affordability, students' grades and graduation timeline, and the potential impact on performance-based funding metrics.

Granted, the high costs of textbooks affect **all** students, not just transfer students. However, given what we have learned about the financial challenges of many transfer students, the potential for them to be particularly vulnerable to the effect of spiraling textbook costs is especially concerning. As librarians we may recognize, but not have an opportunity to ameliorate, many of the cost increases affecting our students, such as increases in tuition or campus housing costs; however, textbook affordability is being increasingly linked to library services, and as this is the lane we drive in, this is where we have the potential to effect meaningful change. If you have believed until now that purchasing textbooks was not part of your library's mission, please consider the following:

According to the report "Open 101: An Action Plan for Affordable Textbooks" (Vitez 2018) released in January 2018 by the Student Public Interest Research Group (PIRG), several factors influence the cost of textbooks. The report noted that the textbook market does not function like a normal marketplace, where companies compete for their share of the market and the laws of supply and demand affect the price of the product. Instead, students must purchase the materials assigned by a professor, who may or may not be considering price among other factors when assigning materials. Although students may be able to save money with some types of digital materials and through the used books market, publishers have found ways to keep prices high and diminish the cost-saving impact of these alternatives. Many professors who adopt publisher materials for their courses now require students to purchase costly products such as access codes, which hide homework and quizzes behind an online paywall. These products are typically bundled with print or digital textbooks, which make them more expensive, and students usually cannot find the bundle for sale anywhere but at the campus bookstore, which locks them into paying the full price. Then, at the end of the term, the student's access to the online material expires, which renders the other material in the bundle valueless in the market for used materials, meaning the student cannot recoup a portion of their initial cost. Although existing federal statue regulates the practice of bundling, it includes sizeable loopholes, which allow the practice to continue (Vitez 2018).

Some institutions are beginning to address the textbook issue, one recent example being Brown University. According to a *Chronicle of Higher Education* article by Beckie Supiano (2019), Brown has a relatively modest population of low-income students, given that just 14 percent of Brown students receive Pell Grant funds, a widely used marker of low-income status. Nevertheless, Supiano noted the issue of a growing gap between the cost of attending a college or university and what portion of that cost of attendance is covered by financial aid has been true at Brown as well. Brown's open curriculum provides students with great latitude in selecting courses; however, low-income students avoided those courses with more expensive books and materials, and according to Richard M. Locke, Brown's provost, "Some students felt they were trading off books for food" (Supiano 2019). As a result, Brown University started a pilot program to buy required textbooks for some low-income students, and according to the university website, beginning with the 2019–2020 academic year; Brown planned to expand the pilot program from 85 students to approximately 1,100 first-year students who receive university scholarship funds as part of their financial aid packages, including enrolled undergraduates from all class years who have a $0 parent contribution, as determined by the financial aid office (Brown University 2019).

While this is certainly excellent progress at one institution, it is noteworthy that Brown University's Investment Office website states the university has an endowment of $3.8 billion and according to a January 2019 article in the *Chronicle of Higher Education*, Brown ranks among the top 30 highest endowments of national institutions ("Which Colleges have the Largest Endowments?" 2019). Therefore, the financial feasibility of a significant number of other colleges and universities following suit by providing textbooks is highly unlikely.

"Nothing Says 'Welcome to College' Like Exorbitant Textbook Prices"

An opinion column by Andre Perry (2018) titled "Nothing Says 'Welcome to College' Like Exorbitant Textbook Prices" recently put the textbook scenario into perspective. After a self-described "stunned" father reported that he had paid $700 for his freshman daughter's textbooks at Louisiana State University, the columnist noted that $700 per semester for textbooks, or $1,400 per year, represented nearly 7 percent of the 2018 poverty line income of $20,780 for a family of three. Additionally, the column (Perry 2018) reported that the current pricing structure has caused students to become creative in accessing textbooks, including initiating a "book share" arrangement, whereby students get together with friends to purchase a single set of texts and use them collectively. Middle- and low-income students are hardest hit by these prices, particularly when the cost of a single textbook could feed a family of four for a week. "Families can't eat textbooks," he concluded. "And they can't afford them either."

Dr. Penny Beile, associate director of libraries at the University of Central Florida, Orlando, Florida, gave us a lot of great foundational information for this book. An active proponent of textbook affordability initiatives, she described the necessity of a student's prioritization of limited funds as akin to Maslow's "Hierarchy of Needs." Just as "self-actualization," the top of Maslow's pinnacle of needs depends upon an individual's ability to meet basic essentials such as food and shelter before achieving self-actualization, similarly students must first meet their basic essentials: tuition and fees, housing and food, before they can buy textbooks (Figure 9.1). If, after

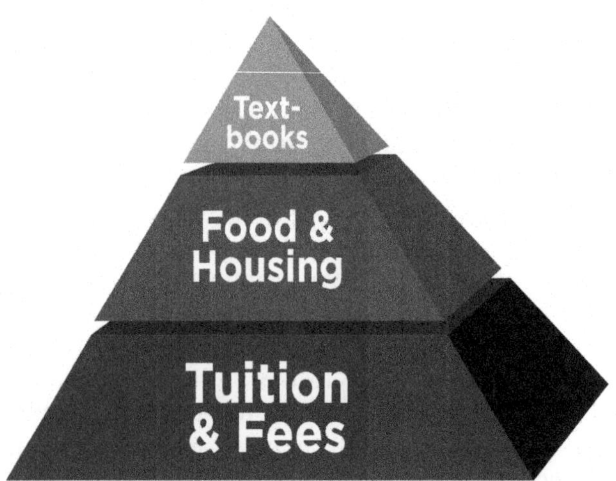

Figure 9.1 Student Hierarchy of Educational Expenses.

essentials are paid, no funds remain, then students cannot purchase their textbooks (Interview with Dr. Penny Beile, University of Central Florida, May 23, 2019).

In this environment, and when textbook purchases may negatively affect student enrollment, thereby affecting students' progression toward a degree, it has become increasingly clear that librarians need to be proactive in supporting students' need for access to affordable textbooks. This may necessitate a change in our thinking, since not long ago our collection development policies may have specifically stated that our library does not purchase textbooks, and in the interest of full disclosure, the authors have defended that policy to students many times over the years. However, due to the increasingly harsh financial realities of purchasing textbooks, many libraries have implemented or are working through the implementation of textbook affordability initiatives to support their students and institutional missions and provide a solid way to assess the library's positive impact on that mission. Supporting access to information is a core value of libraries; supporting our students is essential, and supporting student success supports institutional priorities.

Textbook Affordability Initiative Options: An Overview

Several options exist with respect to textbook affordability initiatives, which range from relatively clear cut to highly involved and labor intensive, with many variations and combinations in between. We will begin by exploring available options, which generally fall into three broad categories:

- Building a print reserve and/or e-textbook collection.

- Increasing OER (open educational resources) awareness in faculty and encouraging them to consider adopting open-access fully formatted e-textbooks through OER resources such as OpenStax. We are referring to this as **OER Level 1**.

- Working with interested faculty, particularly for classes in which an OER textbook is not available or suitable, to create course resources using a variety of OER educational materials. We are referring to this as **OER Level 2**.

Advantages and considerations of these three options are as follows.

Print Reserves/e-Textbooks

This option provides students access to textbooks by purchasing print textbooks for reserve-status library use and/or purchasing e-textbooks generally, allowing for multiple concurrent users (depending upon the class, it may not always be essential to purchase concurrent user access, allowing for a potential cost savings).

Advantages

Students often like having a print book, and depending on scale, generally this initiative can be in place relatively quickly and with modest additional demands on staff time. Community college students (vertical transfer students, see chapter 1) will likely be accustomed to the library having textbooks on reserve, so they may arrive on campus with this expectation, and if it is not available, potentially perceive this as decreased support, which could contribute to transfer shock. Additionally, you may discover that your library collection already contains some titles identified as course-adopted texts. When a textbook is already available in the collection, particularly as an e-book, you can notify the faculty member so that their bookstore record (such as Barnes & Noble's "Faculty Enlight") has a note informing students who are shopping for textbooks to "Go to Class First." Students will learn of their free online option in class and before they purchase a nonreturnable textbook.

Considerations

Certainly, initial funding will be a primary consideration, and updating the textbook collection will be an ongoing expense, as new editions will regularly be needed to replace older editions. The library will need to consider how to prioritize spending. Possible options include purchasing textbooks for classes with historically large enrollments, purchasing textbooks for classes with the most expensive textbooks, or purchasing for classes with high "DFW" rates (classes with high numbers of final grades of D or F, or high numbers of withdrawals) (Beile 2019).

Obviously, reserve print titles do not support online students, and if reserve status is restricted to library use only, then books are available to local students only during times the library is open.

Open Educational Resources

Open educational resources are broadly defined as "the open provision of educational resources, enabled by information and communication technologies, for consultation, use, and adaptation by a community of users for non-commercial purposes" (UNESCO 2002). Within the context of higher education, OER is understood to include free online learning content, software tools, and accumulated digital curricula that are not restricted by copyright license and thus are available to retain, reuse, revise, remix, and redistribute. OER also refers to free open textbooks that can replace traditional, commercially produced, and expensive textbooks (Colvard, Watson, and Park 2018).

As an aid to understanding, for this publication we have broken our OER discussion into two levels with **OER Level 1** referring to adoption of an open source textbook and **OER Level 2** referring to creation of course content from individual open access sources.

The term "OER Level 1" does not imply in any way that there is not a good measure of work involved for a faculty member who is adopting an open source textbook; clearly there is, which is why financial incentives for faculty to do this are so important. Adopting an open source textbook means the faculty member will need to revise lesson plans, assignments, assessments, and everything else they would need to do relative to changing to a new text, but without the advantage of having prepackaged materials available from a traditional bundled textbook with access codes. However, from the librarian's perspective, *at least conceptually*, OER Level 1 adoption is a relatively straightforward process; although it is likely librarians will be called upon to troubleshoot, for both faculty and students, a myriad of issues that can occur in the adoption of an OER textbook. These issues can range from difficulties in downloading materials or printing portions of the text, something students often prefer to do, as well as the compatibility of the OER source with your institution's choice of learning management system (LMS).

Although OER Level 1 can provide an excellent option in many cases, it is not a panacea. It is not realistic to think that every traditional textbook should be replaced with an OER textbook; simply put, not every textbook has an OER equivalent. There has been good success resulting in significant savings for students in using OER textbooks in general education or core courses, however (Beile 2019).

Similarly, with respect to OER Level 2, it is not realistic to expect that librarian liaisons and e-learning departments will be able to collaborate with faculty to revise, reuse, and remix materials from a variety of sources to create a semester's worth of course resources for every class and every major. That is neither desirable nor sustainable. However, when there is interest, a need, and sufficient time, OER Level 2 can provide an excellent option.

When the decision is to use OER at either level 1 or level 2, keep communication flowing, and be as proactive as possible; anticipate there will be some glitches, and remember that everyone adapts to technology at a different pace. The concept of libraries championing access is as old as antiquity, but as a delivery system, OER is still very new and evolving for all of us.

OER Level 1: Increasing Faculty Awareness and Encouraging Adoption

Advantages

Increasing faculty awareness of providing OER textbook access through OpenStax or other providers can definitely make a difference for our students. These resources can work well for introductory classes, and this approach is generally the first application of OER. In addition to OpenStax, OER Commons, MERLOT, and Open Library Network are presently potential sources of OER full-content textbooks. OpenStax has an Institutional Partner Program, which offers training on OER adoption.

Many of the OER textbooks are particularly well suited for introductory courses—thus, providing students with substantial savings early in their educational endeavors. Mitigating stress early in the student's experience relates to student persistence (Tinto 2016). The "Open 101: An Action Plan for Affordable Textbooks" (Vitez 2018) report, referenced at the beginning of this chapter, makes a powerful case for generating significant savings for students when OER textbooks are used. To illustrate, they reviewed and compared textbook options for 10 introductory courses at 40 institutions of higher education. The 10 courses were College Algebra, Anatomy and Physiology I, General Biology I, Chemistry I, English Composition I, U.S. History I, U.S. Government and Politics, General Psychology, Introductory Sociology, and Elementary Statistics.

Prices for appropriate course texts for these 10 introductory courses were compared as:

- **Bundled** (the student had to purchase the text at the bookstore in order to obtain the access code for quizzes and related materials);

- **Solo title**, meaning the student could purchase the book new or used either at the bookstore or online; and
- **OER** textbook, typically free online.

The survey (Vitez 2018) revealed that using OER textbooks for **just these 10 introductory courses** would result in a **nationwide savings of $1.5 billion per year in course textbook costs** because open textbooks are already available in each of these subjects from OpenStax as well as other open textbook publishers.

Considerations

Although faculty are becoming increasingly aware of the burden of textbook costs and may factor that into their textbook selections, not all faculty are amenable to using OER textbooks. Research (Jung, Bauer, and Heaps 2017) has indicated some mixed results in terms of faculty satisfaction with OER textbooks, citing a perception of poor editing of the open textbooks, finding factual errors in the texts, and broken links as problems they have encountered. On the other hand, a larger percentage of faculty in the same survey (Jung, Bauer, and Heaps 2017) reported higher student exam scores, which they attributed to students having the text in time for the first class, due to students not having to wait for their financial aid disbursements to purchase their textbook. Of those surveyed faculty members, 62 percent thought open textbooks were about the same quality as traditional textbooks, and 91 percent indicated a willingness to adopt open textbooks when quality was at least equivalent to traditional textbooks. (Jung, Bauer, and Heaps 2017)

As is true of most of us when it comes to embracing change, some faculty will be early adopters of OER, and some others will likely come around to it later. As OER is a constantly emerging and evolving field, issues that presently create roadblocks and dissuade some faculty from considering adopting an OER text may well be resolved in the near future. Additional considerations are whether your institution will provide funding for incentives for faculty to adopt an OER textbook, which acknowledges the additional time commitment involved. Your institutional culture and the decision-makers with respect to textbooks are also factors. For instance, at some institutions, departmental deans may require that all classes in particular courses use the same text. Another important consideration concerns access to the OER textbook. Find out early if the textbook source under consideration will be compatible with the learning management system (LMS) at your institution, whether as a PDF embedded in the LMS or as a web-based permalink, as this information is essential.

OER Level 2: Building with Openly Sourced Materials

OER Level 2 involves combing freely sourced materials to support the learning outcomes of the class. These materials may consist of information, maps, images, graphs, and other learning tools that users assemble from numerous sources to support the learning outcomes appropriate to their course and adapt these as needed. "Reuse, revise, and remix" are the operative words with OER, so this is not simply an exercise in creating new material from an online repository. It quickly becomes apparent that this approach will take significant time, from design to implementation, which your faculty, librarians and e-learning staff may not have, and at this level of OER deployment, all those departments will absolutely need to be in play.

At present, there is not one single overarching repository of all OER sources. When faculty want to pursue this option and understand both the longer timeline to implementation as well as the need to involve and coordinate with various departments to ensure the material is vetted, compliant, and can be made fully accessible to disabled students (i.e., adding audio or closed-captioning), this approach can result in customized and highly effective course material.

Advantages

There is potential to save students significant money on textbook expenditures, which in theory has tremendous appeal, and the ability to create customized material perfectly suited to the learning outcomes of a class.

Considerations

While there is not a *cost* to the student, or at least perhaps only a nominal cost, there is certainly a *price* involved when taking OER to this level because of the amount of faculty and staff time needed to locate, then revise and reuse, copyright compliant, openly accessible course materials. In this situation, other departmental initiatives may have to be reprioritized; therefore, this level of involvement certainly comes at a *price*, if not at a direct *cost*.

Real World Scenario: University of Central Florida and OER through Collaboration

Two librarians from the University of Central Florida (Avila and Wray 2018) described their experience in helping a faculty member locate OER sources, an opportunity which came about when the faculty member initiated contact with Avila, the university's science subject librarian, for assistance regarding a textbook that was no longer in print. Although the initial request was to locate a replacement textbook, with sufficient advance time as well as support from instructional designers, this collaboration ultimately led to the development of all new course content with revised modules, updated readings, and links to library e-book chapters.

Avila and Wray (2018) shared their replicable steps, noting that regular open communication with faculty about how a textbook initiative can support students and institutional priorities is essential to achieving faculty buy-in, as is creating and building upon librarian/faculty relationships, particularly with subject liaison librarians. Other essential steps for librarians include identifying faculty goals and reviewing their course syllabus and learning objectives before the initial meeting with the faculty member, identifying and agreeing upon a reasonable timeline, and ensuring that licensed materials selected are DRM-free or have adequate seat licenses when possible. To aid faculty in locating appropriate resources, the faculty member was given access to search (but not purchase) via the library's acquisitions software as well as the ability to save titles of interest to a folder in the acquisitions software. Avila and Wray (2018) stressed the importance of keeping communication open, asking questions, providing timely feedback, and meeting deadlines for a successful outcome.

OER: A Few Final Words about a Massive Subject

While faculty awareness of the textbook cost crisis has grown significantly, it is imperative to understand that faculty may also have concerns about OER sources, particularly for OER Level 2. These include difficulties in locating sources, concerns about the authority of a source, and the amount of time needed to implement OER. As referenced previously, traditional textbooks include convenient supporting materials and assessments directly related to class content, which is suitable for immediate use—thereby, appealing to busy faculty. Understandably, faculty are highly invested in their students' learning outcomes, and principles of academic freedom certainly support them in their choice of textbook. The advantages and considerations for various textbook affordability initiatives are summarized in Table 9.1.

Table 9.1   Textbook Affordability Initiatives at a Glance

Initiative	Advantages	Considerations
Purchasing print textbooks or e-textbooks	Community college transfers are accustomed to having reserve textbooks in the library Initiative can be deployed relatively quickly	Initial cost of purchase Ongoing cost for new editions Print reserves (i.e., "Library use only") will be accessible only during operating hours

Initiative	Advantages	Considerations
OER Level 1	Savings for students Often well suited to general education course texts	Significant faculty time commitment LMS compatibility
OER Level 2	Savings for students Potential for a class to be entirely customized to support learning outcomes	Significant time investment for faculty, librarians, and e-learning personnel There is a *cost* even if there is not a *price*

Textbook Affordability Initiatives at a Glance

Now that we have discussed various options available, as well as advantages and considerations for each, we will consider steps involved in starting a textbook initiative.

Textbook Affordability Initiative: Getting Started

Taking an Environmental Scan

It is wise to begin a textbook affordability initiative by gathering information. We suggest you start by determining who your stakeholders are and what level of textbook affordability initiative works best at your institution. Stakeholders include enrollment services, student academic success departments, faculty, provosts, deans, and other administrators. Once defined, work toward turning stakeholders into partners. Every student support unit and teaching unit can play a role (Beile 2019).

Two major reasons to undertake a textbook initiative are supporting all students' success, including transfer student success, and supporting institutional goals and/or institutional metrics. It would be useful to learn what percentage of your student body receives financial assistance as well as whether your institutional funding will be determined by performance-based metrics, and if so (which is likely the case, given the growth in the performance-based funding trend), specifically which metrics your institution is prioritizing. This information will help you align the need for a textbook initiative with a specific metric, such as student retention or graduation rates. The financial aid information is beneficial data because a student's financial aid applies to their tuition and fees first, and the remaining balance, if there is one, will go toward the student's living expenses and books. If a large percentage of students receive financial aid, logically, at a minimum, that same percentage of students will be adversely affected by textbook costs.

Various studies support that high textbook costs create a negative situation for our students. The "Open 101" report referenced earlier in this chapter (Vitez 2018), noted that 65 percent of students skipped purchasing a course text due to cost, which limits them from fully participating in the class. A 2018 survey conducted by the Florida Virtual Campus, lists a number of negative impacts stemming from the high cost of textbooks. These include students not purchasing the required textbook (64.2%), students taking fewer courses (42.8%), students not registering for a specific course (40.5%), students earning a poor grade (35.6%), and students dropping a course (22.9%). When students take fewer classes or they complete fewer classes per semester due to the high cost of textbooks, this delayed progression manifests itself in graduation rates. Although textbooks, viewed through an educator's lens are essential, based on a student's hierarchy of educational expenses (Figure 9.1), textbooks are, of financial necessity, the last thing they are able to purchase with whatever financial assistance or personal funds remain to them.

Review Contracts and Policies

What seems a logical starting point in starting a textbook affordability initiative is to obtain lists of textbooks from your campus bookstore and check those titles against library holdings; however, this may prove easier said than done. Thus, it is wise to review your current bookstore contract early in the information gathering process. For example, does the contract contain any language about textbook affordability? At the University of Central Florida (Beile 2019), a textbook affordability initiative came about because a student-minded librarian designed a LibGuide featuring less expensive sources for textbooks other than the campus bookstore. The bookstore regarded that as a violation of the "non-compete" clause in their contract, which complicated the library/bookstore relationship early in the process. Thanks to a more proactive review of the bookstore contract at renewal time, the bookstore now price-matches and makes materials available to students unbundled (Beile 2019).

Similarly, it would be wise to review library policies and procedures in advance of rolling out a textbook affordability endeavor, as some policies and processes will likely require revision. Regular communication and genuine buy-in by librarians and support staff will be essential to the success of the initiative. The value of transparency in fostering informed participation of the staff members who work with these processes daily cannot be overstated.

Additional Considerations

Even if your library had a "no textbooks" provision in the collection development policy, comparing the bookstore's list of textbooks and required readings with your holdings will likely reveal some overlap. In addition, reviewing interlibrary loan requests for textbooks, whether those requests were filled or not, will reveal potentially important unmet needs.

Once it is determined which titles the library can and should purchase, either in print or as e-books, do not be surprised, as students often are, at just how quickly that budget will tap out. As an example, the initial funds designated for purchasing textbooks at the University of Central Florida Libraries totaled **$10,000.00**, which purchased **57 textbooks** (Beile 2019).

Despite how compelling a textbook affordability initiative seems, there may still be hurdles to overcome. So keep in mind what we are calling the *Four Ps to Success:*

- Preview the institutional landscape for stakeholders,
- Build partnerships,
- Develop a plan, and
- Persevere.

Real World Scenario: Robert Morris University and Textbook Reserves

The following example of a successful reserve textbook initiative illustrates some of the concepts in this chapter. Robert Morris University, Pittsburgh, Pennsylvania, is a private, not-for-profit suburban institution with an enrollment of approximately 5,000 students in undergraduate, graduate, and doctoral programs. In 2012, the university library rolled out a textbook initiative, based in part on the work of an honors class tasked with analyzing factors in student retention of which one was the cost of textbooks. That finding led to additional research, including a library survey of students and faculty. The survey revealed that a majority of students believed the cost of textbooks was not always worth the personal investment, while faculty believed textbooks were essential to teaching (Schlak and Johnston 2018).

Over 90 percent of the students surveyed expressed a strong preference for print texts over electronic versions, and 14 percent of the students surveyed were aware of students who were unable to continue their studies due to the cost of textbooks. This resulted in the development of a textbook reserve program at the university library. A pilot program included acquisition, processing, and reserve placement of all required textbooks for approximately 35 university-wide core curricular courses. The library developed a collaborative partnership with the university's Office of Student Life both for funding purposes to share the textbook cost evenly and as the best means of informing students of this new service.

At the two-year mark, the library initiated a student survey of the textbook reserve program users, specifically to assess whether the affordability aspect and justification for the program was making the intended difference.

They learned that students believed the program helped them with budgeting for expenses and that nearly 70 percent of the students surveyed reported using the reserve textbooks regularly, with nearly a third of respondents using the program multiple times per week. Interestingly, although the library faced some initial opposition from the university bookstore, that was overcome when the bookstore staff realized the library would be purchasing from them each semester. The bookstore now views the library staff as partners rather than competitors. The program does not provide access to all textbooks but does focus on texts for core courses and invites the teaching faculty to make up the difference. The library is presently exploring expanding access with OER resources (Schlak and Johnston 2018).

From this example and related information, it is apparent that much needs to happen behind the scenes prior to initiating a textbook affordability initiative, and much of that involves communication and collaboration. From administrators to the campus bookstore, frontline library staff to behind-the-scenes library staff, and everywhere in between, there are perspectives to appreciate, processes to understand, and viewpoints to share. Providing some level of relief, enabling students to continue their academic progression without textbook costs creating an insurmountable barrier, is a cause that is easy to support in theory; in reality, however, it will take communication, collaboration, and buy-in for a successful initiative. Take the time to communicate, collaborate, and build—or build upon—relationships for the best outcome.

Interlibrary Loan for Textbooks—Troublesome or Tractable?

Admittedly, the very concept of using interlibrary loans for textbooks seems problematic from the start. Whatever textbooks a library has will likely be on reserve, meaning they are not available for outside loan, and even if they were, loan periods are typically three to four weeks, and not a full semester. Nevertheless, some interesting research sheds light on the validity of an interlibrary loan option, at least in some situations. Consider important takeaways from the following scenario.

Real World Scenario: University of Connecticut and ILL Requests for Textbooks

Librarians at the University of Connecticut, Storrs, Connecticut, experienced the value of staff involvement when they found themselves in a dilemma with respect to interlibrary loan requests for textbooks (McNeil 2017). The university is a large research institution with a high document delivery and interlibrary loan volume. At times, unmediated interlibrary loan requests for textbooks were filled by the lending institutions but cancelled upon receipt by the university library since library policy prohibited the use of interlibrary loans for textbooks. Students could see that their request had been filled and then cancelled, leading to significant dissatisfaction. Mediated requests for textbooks were not processed, but staff struggled with determining what was or was not a "textbook," so the cancellations felt capricious.

Thus, tremendous staff time went into enforcing a policy that was ambiguous, particularly since "textbook" is not well defined; not consistently included in a MARC record; and, like art, is often in the eye of the beholder. When textbook loans were cancelled or not processed, frontline staff had to deal with dissatisfied patrons face-to-face. In the midst of these challenges, a staff member suggested "Rapid," a resource sharing system that could be used to take the guesswork out of which requests met the definition of "textbook," and the library clarified their interlibrary loan policy to remove the word "textbook" from titles that would not be processed and substituted "course-adopted text." Thanks to these measures, negative feedback all but disappeared, because a staff member's participation in the discussion led to a decision informed by actual data rather than staff-mediated judgment calls (McNeil 2017).

Real World Scenario: Northwestern University and Interlibrary Loans for Textbooks

In other research, Librarians at Northwestern University, Evanston, Illinois, initiated a student survey to explore the issue of interlibrary loans for textbooks (Munson and Savage 2013). Of necessity, their research made some reasonable assumptions of unmediated interlibrary loan requests for books that appeared to be for class use (i.e., if the book is a seventh or eighth edition, if the title includes "Introduction to . . ." or "Fundamentals of . . .") and similar flags. They learned that the student's request for what was apparently a textbook was filled 56 percent of the time and that the average loan period was for eight weeks. This would indicate that the student had the book for the initial loan period plus one renewal. Almost 49 percent of the time, students were flexible about accepting an earlier edition of the book, and interestingly, survey comments revealed instances where students used an interlibrary loan as an opportunity to review the book thoroughly, and if they found it very useful, they would purchase it. Munson and Savage (2013) note that given the cost of textbooks, it is not surprising that students would want to evaluate their return on a potential investment prior to purchasing it, and there are few other options for a student to use a book for free, making borrowing the book from a library their best option.

Munson and Savage (2013) posited that based upon the results of their study, interlibrary loans *can* provide an effective way for students to acquire their textbooks, but its effectiveness is highly dependent on the particulars of the requested item. In general, they found interlibrary loans for textbooks to be less effective than overall interlibrary loan requests due to a lower fill rate, shorter loan periods, and fewer options for renewals. Nevertheless, they found students could reasonably expect to acquire a textbook through an interlibrary loan, and the students' previous overall success acquiring materials via an interlibrary loan led them to use this service for textbooks as well. They concluded that an interlibrary loan satisfies their customers' expectations for textbooks.

ILL for Textbooks: Considerations

Additional research conducted around the same time as the work of Munson and Savage (2013) addresses the issue of interlibrary loan for textbooks. In 2013, Blackburn and Tiemeyer reviewed the web pages of 125 Association of Research Libraries (ARL) institutions for their interlibrary loan policies and textbook collection information, ultimately examining the web pages of 101 ARL libraries. Of this number, 50 institutions clearly indicated either on their FAQ or library services web page that their interlibrary loan services would not order textbooks; 30 institutions did not address interlibrary loan for textbooks; and several institutions either did not provide online access to their interlibrary loan policies or required authentication for access to those policies. Fourteen academic libraries of the 101 reviewed indicated they would attempt to fill a textbook request, although 11 of those 14 included a disclaimer noting that a lending institution might not fill the request.

While we are not suggesting interlibrary loans be part of a textbook affordability initiative, it does appear from these research articles that students may be able to obtain, if not the most current edition of a textbook via interlibrary loans, at least something close, and do so more often than not. For the student, this is far better than having no course text at all, and for the librarian, at a minimum, it is certainly good to be aware of this practice and general likelihood of the student successfully obtaining the requested item.

Further, it is important to address the issue Munson and Savage (2013), Blackburn and Tiemeyer (2013), and McNeil (2017) pointed out with respect to cancelling mediated interlibrary loans for what appear to be textbooks. As noted in the scenario referenced earlier in this chapter, McNeil (2017) described cancelling requests as at times "capricious." Munson and Savage (2013) describe this process as "haphazard and subjective" and noted that prohibiting the borrowing of textbooks via policy is difficult to enforce for unmediated interlibrary loan requests. Thus, at a minimum, determining which books are in fact "course-adopted texts" at your institution may be a worthwhile endeavor to remove guesswork from this process, thereby improving customer service and supporting student needs.

Scaling for Success

As is true of most challenges, opportunities often lie hidden within. Clearly, the opportunity here is for librarians to support the academic success of transfer, and *all* students, by helping make textbooks affordably accessible. While there is not just one clear road to resolution, there is certainly a clear and documented need. We hope we have at least cut through some of the thorny brush to either help you carve out your own path or build upon an existing endeavor.

Whichever direction you decide to take concerning textbook affordability, be certain to document your results in terms of actual dollar savings passed on to students, as well as the positive impact your initiative has on student enrollment and grades. In this way, the demonstrable value your library brings to supporting the academic success of all students, including transfer students, as well as supporting your institutional mission, is neither overlooked nor underestimated.

The following are some real-world tested opportunities to build your successful initiative:

- Host a public-facing website at the institutional level, and identify textbook affordability as a college or university initiative.

- Create a textbook affordability committee with representation from campus-wide stakeholders.

- Provide funding for faculty incentives and grants to create or transition to no- or low-cost course materials.

- Draft a statement in support of affordable textbooks and disseminate to faculty.

- Create dedicated positions to work directly with faculty.

- Fund a print textbook reserve collection for high enrollment general education program courses and gateway courses.

- Join the OpenStax Institutional Partner Program. (Beile 2019)

Practical Applications of Chapter 9

- The increasing costs of textbooks impact all students, but transfer students may be particularly disadvantaged.

- Research shows that the skyrocketing cost of textbooks can cause students to take fewer classes or select classes with less expensive textbooks, thereby negatively affecting graduation timelines. Students may also forego purchasing a text altogether, potentially affecting their grades. Both of these very real scenarios have the potential for a negative impact on institutional metrics regarding graduation timelines and student GPAs. Metrics may be tied to institutional funding—hence, the importance of library involvement in a textbook affordability initiative to support student success, thereby supporting institutional initiatives is clear.

- Textbook initiatives can include print textbook and/or e-textbook purchases and open educational resources (OER). For ease of understanding, we have divided OER into two levels: level 1 is adoption of an OER textbook, generally best suited to foundational courses; and level 2 is creation of all course content from openly sourced materials.

- **Four Ps** to help build a successful textbook affordability initiative: **Preview** the institutional landscape for stakeholders, build **partnerships**, develop a **plan**, and **persevere**.

References

Avila, Sandra, and Christina C. Wray. 2018. "To Infinity and Beyond: Reducing Textbook Costs through Librarian/Faculty Collaborations." *Journal of Library & Information Services in Distance Learning* 12(3–4): 90–100. doi:1 0.1080/1533290X.2018.1498618.

Blackburn, Gemma, and Robyn Tiemeyer. 2013. "Textbooks and Interlibrary Loan." *Journal of Interlibrary Loan, Document Delivery & Electronic Reserve* 23(1): 5–18. doi:10.1080/1072303X.2013.769040.

Brown University. 2019. "Brown to Cover Textbook Costs for More than 1,100 Students." Accessed September 24, 2019. https://www.brown.edu/news /2019-04-03/textbooks.

Bureau of Labor Statistics, United States Department of Labor. 2016. "College Tuition and Fees Increase 63 Percent Since January 2006." *TED: The Economics Daily.* August 30, 2016. Accessed September 29, 2019. https:// www.bls.gov/opub/ted/2016/college-tuition-and-fees-increase-63-per cent-since-january-2006.htm.

Colvard, Nicholas C., Edward Watson, and Hyojin Park. 2018. "The Impact of Open Educational Resources on Various Student Success Metrics." *International Journal of Teaching and Learning in Higher Education* 30(2): 262.

Florida Virtual Campus, Office of Distance Learning and Student Services. 2018. "2018 Student Textbook and Course Materials Survey." December 20, 2018. https://dlss.flvc.org/documents/210036/1314923/2018+Student+Text book+and+Course+Materials+Survey+-+Executive+Summary.pdf/3c097 0b0-ea4b-9407-7119-0477f7290a8b.

Jung, Eulho, Christine Bauer, and Allan Heaps. 2017. "Higher Education Faculty Perceptions of Open Textbook Adoption." *International Review of Research in Open and Distributed Learning* 18(4). doi:10.19173/irrodl.v18i4.3120. https://search.proquest.com/docview/1934162809.

McNeil, Erika Hanson. 2017. "ILLiad, Rapid, and an Unmediated Solution to the Interlibrary Loan Textbook Dilemma." *Journal of Access Services* 14(2): 68–79. doi:10.1080/15367967.2017.1299579.

Munson, Kurt I., and Devin Savage. 2013. "Interlibrary Loan's Efficacy in Meeting Students' Expectations to Acquire Textbooks: Results from a Study Conducted in a Large Research Library." *Journal of Interlibrary Loan, Document Delivery & Electronic Reserve* 23(4–5): 191–200. doi:10.1080/1072303X.2014.890151.

Perry, Andre. 2018. "Nothing Says 'Welcome to College' Like Exorbitant Textbook Prices." *The Nation.* Accessed June 6, 2019. https://www.thenation.com/article/nothing-says-welcome-to-college-like-exorbitant-textbook-prices/.

Schlak, Timothy M., and Bruce Johnston. 2018. "A Case Study and Analysis of a Successful and Collaborative Student-Centered Textbook Reserve Program in a Mid-Size Academic Library." *Public Services Quarterly* 14(1): 22–35. doi:10.1080/15228959.2017.1359136.

Senack, Ethan. 2014. *Fixing the Broken Textbook Market: How Students Respond to High Textbook Costs and Demand Alternatives.* Washington, DC: Center for Public Interest Research.

Supiano, Beckie. 2019. "Low-Income Students Told Brown U. That Textbook Prices Limited their Choices. Here's What the University Is Doing about It." *Chronicle of Higher Education*, April 11, 2019. https://www.chronicle.com/article/Low-Income-Students-Told-Brown/246104.

Tinto, Vincent. 2016. "From Retention to Persistence." *Inside Higher Ed.* Accessed September 17, 2019. https://www.insidehighered.com/views/2016/09/26/how-improve-student-persistence-and-completion-essay.

UNESCO. 2002. "UNESCO Forum on the Impact of Open Courseware for Higher Education in Developing Countries, Final Report." https://unesdoc.unesco.org/ark:/48223/pf0000128515.

Vitez, Kaitlyn. 2018. "Open 101: An Action Plan for Affordable Textbooks." Student Public Interest Research Group (PIRGs). Accessed September 29, 2019. https://studentpirgs.org/2018/01/25/open-101-action-plan-affordable-textbooks/

"Which Colleges have the Largest Endowments?" 2019. *Chronicle of Higher Education*, January 31, 2019. https://www.chronicle.com/article/Which-Colleges-Have-the/245587.

CHAPTER 10

Holistically Supporting Transfer Student Success: The Essential Role of Libraries

Quit wishing for a different kind of student. We want to be the right college for the students we have.

—Dr. D. Russell Lowery-Hart, president,
Amarillo College

In order for libraries to support our transfer students holistically, we must first seek to understand them, including their educational, familial, and cultural backgrounds as well as the particular struggles they may face as students who are also combining educational goals with outside lives and experiences, including their roles as employees, veterans, spouses, and parents. This understanding, which will be unique to each of our campuses, should be evident in our library operations, services, and initiatives. We must also consider whether broader institutional policies or practices, although well intended, in practice serve to further marginalize these students. However, as Alicia Abney (2018) observed, there is one commonality among all transfer students: they all arrive at their new institution with uncertainties.

In one way or another, the transfer experience is fraught with uncertainty. We have established that transfer students face significant stressors, affecting their ability to persist and complete their educational goals. These stressors include how their credits will transfer, whether they will run out of financial aid before completing their degree requirements, challenges in fitting into a new institution when it seems everyone else has already made a connection, and navigating a larger campus—with more services—but being unsure of how to make effective use of those services. These challenges are significant but are generally considered as part of the "standard" transfer student experience. However, for many transfer students, the delicate balancing act of meeting work and/or family responsibilities compounds the "standard" challenges of transferring to a new institution; and perhaps most worrisome of all is a heightened awareness of the numbers of our students who are lacking bare-bones essentials, with food and housing insecurity becoming increasingly prevalent.

Hunger on Our Campuses

A recent *Chronicle of Higher Education* article summarizes the factors squeezing *all* students nationwide and noted that increasing tuition rates have dropped the purchasing power of the Pell Grant (Mangan and Schmalz 2019). The *Chronicle* article references a recent Government Accountability Office (GAO) report that found that the average Pell Grant, which is about $6,000 per year, covers only 37 percent of students' two-year college expenses. Since Pell monies apply toward tuition and fees first before any remaining balance is refunded for other "cost of education" expenses such as food and housing, gaps in students' remaining financial assistance funds can lead to textbook affordability issues (chapter 9). For some of our students, however, these gaps are far more concerning, because they extend to food and housing insecurity.

The U.S. Department of Agriculture (2019) developed ranges to describe food insecurity and defining characteristics. These include:

- the fear of food running out before there was money to buy more,
- an inability to afford balanced meals, and
- being hungry and/or losing weight as the result of an inability to purchase sufficient food.

Although many college students are not eligible for food stamp assistance through the Supplemental Nutrition Assistance Program (SNAP), the GAO report states that based on their review of U.S. Department of Education data, 2 million students **were potentially eligible** to participate in the SNAP program but did not report receiving SNAP benefits in 2016. At nine of the 14 colleges the GAO contacted for this study, college officials and students alike said they were unfamiliar with or did not understand the SNAP program eligibility requirements (United States Government Accountability Office 2019).

A 2019 student protest and hunger strike at the University of Kentucky (Lexington, Kentucky) brought food insecurity and other issues to the fore at that institution, which resulted in the establishment of a $1 per meal student café, open to **all** students with a valid ID card. Determining that the café should be available to all students reduced any stigma that students might associate with dining there (Fink 2019). The protest also resulted in better coordination of food and housing support through the addition of a one-stop "Basic Needs Center" to include funding and staffing to support that center. A student survey found that 43 percent of the University of Kentucky student respondents were food insecure in some way (Patel 2019).

Food pantries are also becoming increasingly common on our campuses, and this is not just within the United States. The 2016 report "Hungry for Knowledge: Assessing the Prevalence of Student Food Insecurity on Five Canadian Campuses" provides evidence based on student surveys from five Canadian universities spread across the country that two out of five surveyed students are indeed suffering from some degree of food insecurity, with 8.3 percent of surveyed students reporting severe food insecurity (Silverthorn 2016). Nearly half all respondents (49.5%) reported that they had to sacrifice purchasing healthy food in order to pay for essential expenses such as rent, tuition, and textbooks. The report also revealed that 656 of the students surveyed, or 15.6 percent of those surveyed, thought about going to a food bank but felt too ashamed to do so. In a related article (Lorinc 2016), a campus food bank coordinator at Ryerson University, one of the five Canadian institutions surveyed, acknowledged that some food bank users ask staff to cover their food donation boxes with bags so that other students in the student center will not know they have visited the food bank (Lorinc 2016). According to the "Hungry for Knowledge" report (2016), almost a third of Ryerson's surveyed students (30.9%) reported moderate food insecurity (p. 15).

A recent article in *American Libraries* noted that some academic libraries are now providing space for campus food pantries, including Fort Hays State University in Hays, Kansas (Udell 2019). One student who has made use of that pantry, a senior who is working two jobs, said he uses the service to supplement his diet with healthier choices or when "crunched" by bills. The student noted that although the library location may seem unusual for a food pantry, it is actually ideal because of the library's proximity to the quad and residence halls and because it is a place the students frequent. Another library pantry mentioned in the same article is Mason Library at Keene State College, New Hampshire. Mason Library partners with the campus food pantry to offer bags of food students can pick up at the circulation desk, an idea that stemmed from the food pantry's limited hours of operation. Elizabeth Dill, director of library services at Troy University in Dothan, Alabama, is working with Troy's student government and administration, a local food bank, and other stakeholders on the issue of food insecurity on campus with the intent of generating support for a library-based initiative. "Do what you can, even if you can't start a pantry," Dill encourages. "You can do an exhibit, you can do a LibGuide, you can bring in speakers, someone on your faculty can speak. There are a lot of ways libraries can participate" (Udell 2019).

Issues of food insecurity are not limited to schools enrolling large numbers of lower-income students, however. As a number of elite institutions have sought to increase diversity through a "need blind" application process, in which a students' ability to pay is reviewed only after the student has been accepted based on their GPA, standardized test scores, extracurricular activities, and other factors (West 2016), unintended negative outcomes may occur, as Anthony Abraham Jack learned in his research. Jack, an assistant professor at Harvard University's Graduate School of Education, is bringing increased understanding to challenges facing financially disadvantaged students who are accepted at prestigious colleges and universities. His book, *The Privileged Poor: How Elite Colleges Are Failing Disadvantaged Students* helps readers appreciate how initiatives to increase diversity at prestigious institutions can fall far short of good intentions. Jack separates students who are from financially strapped families into two groups: the "Privileged Poor"— students from underprivileged situations who received the opportunity to attend a private, charter, or boarding school prior to attending the university; and the "Doubly Disadvantaged"—students from the same underprivileged backgrounds, but who had no educational options beyond attending an often underfunded public high school, frequently located in a crime-ridden neighborhood, until they were accepted by a prestigious university. Jack's research involves interviews with a number of "Privileged Poor" and "Doubly Disadvantaged" students at an actual prestigious institution, which he anonymized as Renowned University. Perhaps most troubling—and ironic—was that issues of food insecurity even occurred at this anonymized prestigious institution. When the campus food services closed down during spring break week, assuming all students would be either embarking on vacations or returning home, the students without financial resources to travel—or even sufficient funds for off-campus restaurant meals for a week—indeed suffered from hunger. Jack (2019) notes, "Both the Doubly Disadvantaged and the Privileged Poor talked about something more basic: surviving. They described how they scrounged for sustenance. They recounted how they rationed their provisions. They narrated how they effectively starved themselves as they tried to stretch every morsel of food they could get their hands on. . . . An empty pocket meant an empty stomach."

In July 2019, legislation sponsored by Senator Elizabeth Warren (D-MA) was introduced to address the issue of campus hunger. The College Student Hunger Act, S.2143, aims to amend the Food and Nutrition Act of 2008 and make SNAP benefits more accessible to students. The proposed legislation expands eligibility in several ways, including extending SNAP eligibility to students who receive the maximum Pell Grant award as well to as students who are determined to meet federal financial aid criteria to be evaluated as financially independent students. If passed as introduced, the potential impact of this legislation could be significant.

A Deliberate Strategy of Support

According to the American Association of Community Colleges, over 12 million students are currently enrolled at a community college, many of whom aspire to obtain a bachelor's degree (Bumphus 2019). Given the general demographics of our transfer student population: often starting at a community college, often low income, first generation in college, frequently older, and may be balancing work and family responsibilities, it is essential for all faculty and staff to support the success of these students as much as possible. Let us examine additional research-informed ways to help us accomplish this.

Although a "one-size-fits-all" approach often does not serve students, or anyone, for that matter, especially well, we do have some information about transfer students in general that can inform us in building a deliberate strategy of support. For example, we know (chapter 2) that *academically* and *socially* engaged students, whether they are transfer students or not, tend to persist, and persistence leads to retention and graduation (Engle and Tinto 2008).

We also have some interesting research on transfer students and orientations to consider. In a focus group study of successful community college transfer students, the transfer students found *orientations specifically for transfer students* to be more helpful, and when there was a fee to attend the orientation, the students in the focus group did not attend because of the expense (Ellis 2012).

In a separate study (Mayhew, Stipeck, and Dorow 2011), transfer students were significantly more likely than new incoming freshmen to agree that the orientation program helped them develop effective study skills, improve time management, adjust to the academic demands of college, and have a better understanding of professors' expectations. Thus, transfer students in this particular study found that orientations supported them *academically*, while the new first-year students in this study felt that orientation programming was a successful means to help them develop friendships and adjust to the *social* aspects of college. On this basis, the authors suggested that transfer students overall might view orientations more as a means to adjust academically rather than as an introduction to a new social network.

Arranging for librarians to be included in these orientations, even if it is just a brief introduction, accompanied by dissemination of a transfer-specific library handout, is an important early link in transfer student success. Because academic libraries often differ in procedures with respect to how students access services and resources, such as computers, reserve textbooks and study rooms, providing transfer students with information specific to the institution at the outset can reduce "transfer fog." "Transfer fog," defined as a gap in knowledge contributing to transfer student anxiety, unease, and frustration is due to students feeling uninformed on their new campus (Harrick and Fullington 2019). Harrick and Fullington (2019) conducted focus groups of new transfer students to Brooklyn College, New York, honing in student experiences with the college library. Their results supported the need for the library to intervene proactively in order to reduce students' feelings of being overwhelmed and confused. One focus group participant shared, "If there was a tour to the library, then I wouldn't have been confused. I literally roamed around the second floor for a good half hour looking for a space." Another student in the focus group stated she would like to meet librarians at the orientation, because she "would have wanted to see a familiar face. Then you would feel comfortable going back to them for more questions."

If we do not take the initiative to make a connection early in the student's transfer experience, then students will likely apply information on services and procedures from the library at their *previous* institution, resulting in time lost and frustration (Harrick and Fullington 2019). Similarly, given the decreasing presence of libraries and librarians in public schools, new dual-enrolled high school students could even misapply information from the services and resources of their *public library*—for example, expecting to find all biographies shelved together.

If inclusion in an existing transfer student orientation is not possible, perhaps because one does not yet exist, creating a separate library orientation of some sort, such as a tour specifically designed for transfer students, and not combining this for freshmen and transfer students, is another avenue. Informed by the understanding that transfer students may have already had some type of information literacy instruction, Harrick and Fullington (2019) suggest framing the tour as a way to learn "insider tips for success," subtly acknowledging students' previous experience. This approach may increase participation.

Lester, Leonard, and Mathias (2013) suggest that students who transfer from community colleges correlate social *and* academic engagement with a classroom setting, which aligns with their initial educational experience at community colleges, which are typically nonresidential campuses. Additionally, the community college transfer students in this study viewed *social engagement* in a broad sense, extending to their family, mentors, colleagues, and friends within their churches and community-based groups. Because transfer students may be older, and may have family and work obligations,

Lester, Leonard and Mathias (2013) noted that when these family and work obligations became support structures, students felt empowered to succeed academically. Thus, transfer students correlated these positive interactions with individuals *outside the immediate campus community as social engagement* (italics ours), as in this interview response from a 27-year-old junior:

> But my wife and my family are very supportive and even my in-laws are very supportive. . . . [S]ometimes I have to sacrifice things in order to study or to go to a program or whatever and they understand that, they get that, so they're very supportive of that. (Lester, Leonard, and Mathias 2013)

Lester, Leonard, and Mathias (2013) acknowledge that some transfer students also participated in traditional avenues for social engagement, including Greek life and the national transfer student honor society, Tau Sigma (http://www.tausigmanhs.org/), but the students in this study did not view traditional campus-based social engagement as essential to their transition or academic success. Because these students made a strong connection between academic engagement and a sense of belonging, the students who felt academically integrated also felt socially integrated. The students also reported a heightened sense of engagement when faculty members created opportunities for deeper interactions, including when faculty provided extensive feedback on their assignments or paid particular attention to the students' progress.

A recent focus group study of vertical transfers by Shaw and Chin-Newman (2017) explored the relationships and resources students found supportive during their transition. They found three areas of support they termed: *emotional support, practical support,* and *campus capital*. While *emotional* and *practical support* often came from the students' friends and families and ranged from verbal encouragement (emotional support) to family members offering the student a place to stay nearer to campus or spouses taking on more household and meal preparation responsibilities (practical support), campus personnel also provided students with emotional and practical support. One focus group participant admitted to being very nervous about making application to the university and shared how a **campus staff member**, in reviewing her transcript said, "You know what? You're ready to apply, there is no doubt in my mind . . . you will be accepted." This seemingly small bit of encouragement enabled the student to push past her anxiety and apply. She was accepted (Shaw and Chin-Newman 2017).

Another transfer student and focus group participant (Shaw and Chin-Newman 2017) in her 50s said the person who helped her the most was a **departmental secretary** who gave her a five-minute tutorial on how to use Blackboard (Learning Management System). Additionally, a traditional-aged transfer student found her **work-study supervisor** to be a highly valued campus resource. The student noted that other transfer students often do not know the answers to needed information themselves; however, her supervisor, who had both knowledge and more time than the student perceived her instructor had to help her navigate the campus, was a highly valued source of support (Shaw and Chin-Newman 2017). Certainly, there is a role here for librarians and well-trained library support staff to provide campus capital. This can include proactively approaching any student who appears to need assistance, and as Harrick and Fullington (2019) point out, "Library managers need to remind public services staff to treat every semester as each student's first, and to be gentle and helpful to everyone." The title of their article "'Don't Make Me Feel Dumb'": Transfer Students, the Library and Acclimating to a New Campus" says it all.

As Shaw and Chin-Newman (2017) pointed out, the faculty and staff of the institution are in the best position to provide *campus capital*, thereby equipping students to navigate their new institutions successfully. Research by Hyatt and Smith (2019) further emphasizes the importance of connecting faculty and transfer students. Their research supports that community college students may be hesitant to approach faculty, as well as an uncomfortable truth: in some cases faculty have been reluctant to bridge this gap, in part due to a perception of community college students as underprepared and the faculty's lack of understanding of the transfer process. Therefore, Hyatt and Smith (2019) advocate for programs to connect students with faculty such as through an assigned advisor and for workshops for faculty to receive training on how they may assist transfer students in navigating the college to university transition. Librarians who have collaborated with their feeder college or destination university counterparts to improve transfer student success could be important contributors to, or even initiators of, this conversation.

The University at Albany, State University of New York, developed a deliberate strategy of support in the form of a multifaceted approach to transfer student retention, with specific initiatives for transfer students (Jacobson et al. 2017). Institutional data was examined to determine characteristics of students transferring *to* the University at Albany as well as characteristics of first-time, full-time students who transferred *out*. Library involvement in this endeavor was evident from the outset with the inclusion of a librarian as cochair of an Enhancing Student Experience (ESE) Working Group. The university's strategy included support of transfer students through enhanced *academic support* as well as development of enhanced *engagement activities*. While the library was often a partner in Albany's transfer student initiatives, they managed a specific initiative, involving emailing "at risk" transfer students, defined as students with a GPA below 2.0, at various times during the semester to share graphically appealing messages on various library services and resources. Additionally, the library worked with transfer transition leaders (TTLs), peer-mentor students who are recruited primarily through the university's Tau Sigma chapter. Librarians helped to prepare the TTLs for their support role through interactive sessions, which included discussions of library resources and services, a library tour, an overview of the top 11 things new transfer students need to know about the library, and a challenge for the TTLs to come up with true and false questions to ask each other at the end of the sessions. This interactive challenge allows librarians to check informally to ensure the TTLs have a clear understanding of library services and resources themselves. Perhaps most importantly, through this university initiative, the library was recognized as a partner in improving transfer student success and, as a result, gained valuable insights into campus projects, initiatives, and key players. This helped the library create new initiatives as well as refine their existing services (Jacobson et al. 2017).

As stressed throughout this book, the power of collaboration and partnership cannot be overstated.

Informed Support of "The Students We Have"

Cultural and ethnic diversity is also a consideration with respect to supporting our transfer students holistically. According to the American Association of Community Colleges website, https://www.aacc.nche.edu/, the demographics of students enrolled for credit at U.S. community colleges are currently represented as:

Hispanic	25%
Black	13%
White	46%
Asian/Pacific Islander	6%
Native American	1%

As noted in chapter 1, historically, the primary role of community colleges has been to facilitate student transfer to a four-year institution; therefore a review of recent research coupled with knowledge of the student demographics at our institution, whether it is a college or university, can inform us as we examine our library resources and services. The following is a very brief overview of student populations on our campuses, presented in alphabetical order.

Adult Students

Because transfer students are often older than the traditional college age range of 18–22 years of age, it is important for librarians to consider a brief summary of information on how adults learn. In adult education theory, the term "andragogy" literally means "leader of man" as opposed to pedagogy, which means "leader of children" (Ludovico 2017). This term acknowledges a clear distinction in learning styles based on students' age and life experience. Although our educational endeavors are primarily geared toward an "adult" population, at least in the legal sense of the word (dual-enrolled high school students are likely exceptions), nevertheless, we do refer to teaching at the college or university level as "pedagogy." Adult education authority Malcolm Knowles (1913–1997) was widely quoted and cited for his work on adult learning, and he focused on equipping professional practitioners to be more enlightened about, and effective and flexible with, adult learning styles ("Malcolm Shepherd Knowles" 2019).

Knowles's hypothesis was that adults differ from children in their learning in several significant ways, including having a different orientation to and motivation for learning, as well as a need to know *why* they need to know something before they work to learn it. Embedded within this theory is a strong emphasis on the need for practitioners to consider the life experiences and roles of the adult student and the adult learner's immediate needs in these contexts (Ludovico 2017).

Applying Knowles's work helps us better appreciate that adult students are more likely motivated for personal reasons, whether to obtain a promotion at their place of employment or to be qualified to obtain an altogether different type of employment, in order to build better lives for themselves and perhaps also their families. They seek out institutions of higher learning not as empty vessels to be filled with knowledge, but rather as individuals who have been shaped by life experiences. Alicia Abney (2017) puts it this way: the difference between a younger student and an adult student is not age based; it is about life experience, and the adult student has experienced something that made them grow up and accept responsibility.

As librarians, many of us have embraced our vocation as a second career and returned to the university as adult learners ourselves. Our own experience may provide us a deeper and more empathetic understanding of how adult students, goal oriented and informed by life experience, approach learning. With respect to being goal oriented, one of the authors of this book, Peggy Nuhn, well recalls leaving work early every Tuesday one summer in order to drive over an hour to the University of South Florida for a 6:00 p.m. required class, returning home after 11:00 p.m., and being back at work by 8:00 a.m. the next morning. "After the first class, I made numbered sticky notes, one for each of the remaining weeks of the term, and stuck them to the side of my desk, so that each Wednesday morning I could pull one off and visualize my progress through this challenging schedule."

Our responsibility to acknowledge the life experience of adult students in our teaching has particular application to our transfer student population. Makiba Foster and Kris Helbling (2015) considered this when they applied adult education theory to developing a one-credit course for underserved adult students at Washington University in St. Louis, Missouri. "Mastering Research in Today's Academic Library" debuted in the spring 2013 university catalog and was marketed primarily to working adult students. They noted, "In our research, we encountered some useful principles of Adult Learning Theory: adult learning is filtered through the lens of their established knowledge and life experiences and adult learners are highly practical and goal-oriented. Throughout the semester, we tried to be deliberate in practicing these principles, which guided our scheduling, lecture style and assignments. Thus, we emphasized that this course would not only help toward their ultimate goal of a college degree but also help them gain transferable skills useful in the workplace" (Foster and Helbling 2017).

Asian American Students

According to the American Association of Community Colleges "Fast Facts" (2020), referenced earlier in this chapter, demographic data shows that Asian Americans make up approximately 6 percent of community college students. A recent article in the *Community College Review* (Park and Assalone 2019), states that Asian Americans have higher rates of transfer to four-year institutions than other racial or ethnic groups, but little is known about the conditions affecting college access that might in turn affect transfer. The report (Park and Assalone 2019) notes that Asian American students are frequently influenced by family and a desire to stay close to home to pursue their educational goals and that **reverse transfer** (chapter 1) may occur more within this group of students. Park and Assalone (2019) referenced studies that indicated Asian American male students viewed college as an opportunity to gain specific job-related skills, while female students viewed college more as an opportunity for self-discovery and self-reflection.

This information has particular implications for college librarians, given the potential for more Asian American students to take the reverse transfer pathway. Consider that reverse transfer students are likely to need information literacy instruction and supports *specific to the resources at their new institution*, and college resources generally vary significantly from those at the university the student previously attended. Additionally, Kim et al. (2019) shed additional light on the Asian and Asian American student experience. They note that Asian and Asian American students face unique experiences as a nonbinary (i.e., White/Black) minority in the United States, driven by assumptions and stereotypes depicting them as the "model minority." As such, Asian and Asian American students are often viewed as academically strong role models for other students, despite having many of the same academic challenges. This places significant pressure on the students. Additionally, Asian and Asian American students, per Kim et al. (2019) are often reluctant to seek assistance, which may lead them to delay seeking help until the problem has become significant.

Placing this information in a library context, we can easily envision a familiar scenario: the frustrated student who seeks librarian assistance for an assignment that is due the next day—or even later that same day. We all have had this experience with students from all demographics; however, with this increased awareness, we can better appreciate the importance of framing these interactions in the most positive light possible so that we do not unwittingly add to the student's mounting pressure. Graciously directing the student to easily accessible library resources—for example, databases and print materials currently on the shelf at our location—as well as offering practical suggestions suitable to the immediacy of the situation may lead the student to seek us out sooner the next time.

Black Students

According to the "State of Higher Education in California" (2015) by the Campaign for College Opportunity, California is home to the fifth largest Black population in the United States. With respect to transfer students, the California report notes a shift in enrollment patterns, with decreasing numbers of students transferring to a state university, and increasing numbers of Black students enrolling in private, nonprofit, or private for-profit institutions, following their community college graduation. Additionally, the *Chronicle of Higher Education* (Brown 2019) notes the gender gap for Black students is wider than it is for any other group, as nearly two-thirds of Black undergraduates, and more than two-thirds of Black graduate students, are women. According to the *Chronicle* article, Black male students pursuing bachelor's degrees were the most likely among any demographic group to drop out after their freshman year.

Stewart, Ju, and Kendrick (2019) conducted a survey of 160 Black students who identified as high-frequency library users to learn whether students identified academic libraries as welcoming spaces and to determine how students gauge "welcomeness," defined as the student's perception of being "gladly received." The surveyed students were attending non-historically Black colleges and universities in 35 states and the District of Columbia. Overall, the quantitative results revealed that the majority of survey participants felt welcome; however, some students also identified instances of feeling unwelcome during an academic library visit. Areas of concern included friendliness, nonverbal communication (i.e., body language), and whether their information needs were met. Research by Elteto, Jackson, and Lim (2008) on whether the campus library is perceived as a welcoming space mentioned several factors for our consideration, particularly the importance of a diverse library staff. Among student survey responses, the following are significant for us. "Sometimes the staff's facial expressions do not seem "welcoming," and "Have a more diverse group of people working so that others will feel more comfortable speaking with them" (Elteto, Jackson, and Lim 2008).

International Transfer Students

As noted in chapter 3, the transfer experience can make U.S. students feel like an immigrant to a new country, and in recognition of the challenges of transfer students' assimilation to a new campus, it has been suggested that the term "transfer shock" would probably be more appropriately replaced by "culture shock" (Whang et al. 2017). Therefore, it stands to reason that students transferring to our institutions as international transfer students would truly experience a sense of culture shock. According to the Migration Policy Institute, the United States remains the country of choice for the largest number of international students, hosting about 1.1 million of the 4.6 million enrolled worldwide in 2017 (Zong and Batalova 2018).

Library outreach to international students can be challenging, just as it can be for our domestic transfer students, based upon Rosenzweig and Meade's (2017) article on the challenges in, and the importance of, library outreach specific to short-term international students and the importance of institutional partnerships to accomplish this. Rosenzweig and Meade (2017) note, "The clearest finding that is evident from the first year of this outreach program is the *critical importance of a close partnership with program faculty and staff* (italics ours). Every time a cohort leaves and a new one arrives, the library's reputation with the short-term students is reset and outreach efforts must begin again. But, the *program faculty and staff remain in place, allowing the library to build closer relationships with them, and then rely on them to help represent the importance of the library to their students.* Furthermore, the relationship of that partnership to the outreach program's success is very evident."

While most international students will experience some degree of stress or anxiety with respect to navigating a new college or university in an unfamiliar country, many will also be accustomed to library systems that have some similarities, although classification systems and specific services will vary, as will student access to open stacks. Aaronberg (2017) and Mu (2007) provide us with some very useful information to support East Asian students (Japan, China, Vietnam, Korea, and Thailand), much of which can inform our support of international transfer students. Both Aaronberg and Mu point out that educational styles differ significantly between U.S. and East Asian cultures, and Aaronberg (2017) specifically notes that Asian students may encounter difficulties with essay-type assignments and critical thinking.

In addition, Aaronberg and Mu both note that East Asian students are unfamiliar with the need to cite sources as well as the concept of plagiarism. Another consideration is that the role of the librarian is different between the two cultures, with librarians in East Asia not required to hold MLIS degrees (Aaronberg 2017). Therefore, East Asian students may not be inclined to seek out a librarian for reference assistance, with Mu (2007) noting that students tend to view the library more as a place to study and that they think of librarians more as bookkeepers rather than information providers.

Datig (2014) provides additional insights on how international students view libraries, based upon their previous experience in their country of origin. Datig designed a survey of students attending New York University in Abu Dhabi, which is a hub of New York University's global network. The surveyed students were from a number of countries, including Mexico, Pakistan, New Zealand, Hungary, and Russia. Major takeaways from the survey include the students' primarily equating a library with *books* and as a place for *quiet study* and *aligning the role of the librarian with those books*, making the librarian primarily responsible for organizing and circulating books. Datig (2014) noted, "Regarding librarians, it is clear from this study that students do not have a full sense of what we do. Even students who worked in libraries as assistants were often only exposed to the librarians' circulation activities. Therefore, when students are introduced to the academic library, *the role of librarians should be emphasized*" (italics ours). Datig (2014) noted that international students need to know more about librarians' research expertise, their subject specialties and technological experience, and librarians' contributions to academic knowledge. Datig (2014) emphasized that students also need to know that librarians are capable of answering questions beyond, "Where is this book?" Furthermore, Datig noted that students are receptive to having positive relationships with librarians, so librarians should be friendly, engaged, and ready to interact with the students; in fact students with the largest number of positive interactions with librarians had a greater sense of the scope of librarians' responsibility and felt more positively toward libraries in general. Datig (2014) concluded that our everyday interactions with students, no matter how small, could have a large effect on how students view the library.

Latina/o Students

According to Peña and Rhoads (2019), Latino males are vastly overrepresented at community colleges, with estimates that over 70 percent of Latino males begin their higher education journey at a community college. The authors note that although Latinos enroll at community college in great numbers, their enrollment rates are not synonymous with degree completion and successful transfer to four-year institutions, adding that Latinos attending community colleges are *among the least likely* to transfer to four-year institutions. Peña and Rhoads put these numbers in context, noting that although 85 percent of Latinos who attend community colleges aspire to transfer to a four-year institution, only 14.6 percent graduate from a community college in three years, compared to 22 percent for White males and 24 percent for Asian males.

Peña and Rhoads interviewed 16 Latino males attending two different California community colleges, both with significant Latino populations. Admittedly, their sample size was small, but their results warrant sharing to increase our understanding. Of specific interest is that that the majority of Latino males surveyed reported a reluctance to seek help due to their perception of masculinity, which suggests that strong men can succeed on their own. While the Peña and Rhoads survey did not specifically inquire about academic library services, it is clear that there are implications for us, particularly given that the vast majority of librarians are women.

Interestingly, a program counselor at one of the colleges participating in the Peña and Rhoads survey noted that such perceptions may negatively impact matriculation for Latinos stating, "When Latino males come into the community college not a lot of them are taking advantage of programs like Summer Bridge . . . But the Latinas are! They [Latinas] are heavily enrolled in them. So, the Latino males . . . take a little bit longer to matriculate, to get the steps completed" (Peña and Rhoads 2019). Another counselor concurred with this observation, adding, "I've noticed that a lot of times men of color don't necessarily seek out help, because that's something they haven't learned how to do. They're more hesitant to ask for help when they need it when compared to women of color." As a result, the First Year Experience staff recognized it was *their* responsibility to reach out to Latino students. Perhaps the same may be said of librarians, for example, by considering whether our expectation that all students would be comfortable approaching a traditional reference desk is correct and whether that physical arrangement is perceived as imposing, potentially deterring students who are already reluctant to seek help.

An awareness of our libraries as a space is important. One research study (Andrade 2018) explored Latina/o student perceptions of physical spaces on campus. The sample group comprised Latina/o students who had transferred from a California community college either to a California State University (CSU) campus or to a University of California (UC) campus. All the surveyed students were either in their second semester at a CSU campus or third trimester at a UC campus.

The survey identified three spaces of socioacademic integration (Andrade 2018): (1) spaces to connect with other Latina/o students, (2) spaces to be alone, and (3) spaces to benefit from others in their majors. The most prevalent theme that emerged was that students navigated toward spaces where they could connect with other Latina/os, and *the most common place they visited to meet other Latina/os was the library*. Students also identified the library as a space to be alone. One student preferred the library because "everyone is quiet minding their own business," and the library was where she could "get away from people." Andrade (2018) posited that the physical makeup of these spaces: offering sofas and comfortable homelike seating, tables to work, and open space actually contributes to students' socioacademic integration.

Student Veterans

Although the maturity and experience of veterans should serve them well in their academic pursuits, this group of students is not without challenges, as noted by Dillard and Yu (2016). Dillard and Yu posit that veterans' diverse set of characteristics, such as being older and having real-world experience as well as specialized knowledge may cause them to perceive college as simply a means for greater career advancement, potentially causing them to underestimate the rigors of academic life. Retention and graduation rates for veterans support this finding, with graduation rates at about 52 percent (Dillard and Yu 2016).

As noted earlier in this book, for many students "transfer shock" may be synonymous with "culture shock." The same may be true for our student veterans. Dillard and Yu provide insights into how culture shock for transitioning veteran students occurs, by noting that the initial introduction to military life, in the form of basic training, wears down instincts of individualism and trains recruits to think and act as part of a unit, because mission success and limiting losses demand strict obedience to team goals. Therefore, Dillard and Yu note that when transitioning to a college or university environment fostering individual development and critical thinking, student veterans contend with a dramatic shift in culture. In higher education, students ask questions and challenge the status quo; there is less structure, with much learning occurring outside the classroom and more focus on developing the individual rather than a team-centric culture. This shift can create challenges for student veterans, particularly if their previous academic frame of reference was high school, which also tends to be highly regimented. The military-to-academic transition, perhaps coupled with increased and unanticipated academic rigor, intensifies the culture shock for veterans, and when additional potential obstacles including post-traumatic stress disorder (PTSD), traumatic brain injury (TBI), and/or family and employment concerns compound the mix, veterans may find themselves feeling isolated and confused.

In other research (Sorensen 2018), female veterans were interviewed about their transition to college. Sorensen states, "One of the biggest findings that contradicted my prior beliefs/assumptions was the high number of participants who felt self-doubt. The majority of the participants mentioned they were daunted, or terrified, or intimidated by their experiences with instructors, other students, or going to college. These women are strong. They are women warriors. It did not occur to me they would be self-conscious or insecure."

Dillard and Yu recommend founding and maintaining student veteran groups to provide social support, coupled with faculty and staff education workshops about military life and culture, preferably led by a faculty member in order to increase faculty participation. These workshops (Dillard and Yu 2016) can inform campus faculty and staff on military-related topics such as deployments, PTSD, TBI, challenges to veterans' academic transitions, and provide information on campus resources. Furthermore, Dillard and Yu recommend identifying offices where staff have attended these informative workshops either on the institution's website or with a sticker designating the area as a "Green Zone." In military terminology, a "Green Zone" signifies a secure safe haven. This would send a strong message to student veterans that there are faculty and staff, including faculty and staff at the library, who are willing to help, and create what Dillard and Yu call a "veteran-friendly campus."

"No Excuses"

To be clear, the authors of this book are not advocating for all students to take a lockstep, full-time enrollment march to a baccalaureate degree. On the contrary, transfer students in particular may have many valid reasons for part-time enrollment as well as periods of non-enrollment based on their family and work responsibilities. For some students, a few classes in a particular course of study may be exactly what they need to advance their careers, and if those few classes taken over a few semesters meets their need, we are pleased to have been a part of their abbreviated educational journey. However, the authors of this book, and all educators, want to be certain that to the best of our ability, all students receive sufficient support to succeed, and their academic success is not hindered by circumstances we can ameliorate.

Under the leadership of President Russell D. Lowery-Hart, Amarillo College, Texas, takes student support to new levels. This community college enrolls approximately 10,000 students and offers AA and AS degrees as well as certificates. Their "No Excuses" policy aims to remove financial roadblocks to student success, and that policy extends to providing students support with rent, transportation and childcare as needed (Bombardieri 2018). Amarillo's emergency fund can cut a check within hours to cover a student's car repair or utility bill, a relatively small financial setback for some, but which could push a cash-strapped student to drop a class or withdraw from school entirely. What separates Amarillo College from most other colleges is how much they focus on mitigating the effects of poverty. For that reason, Amarillo College and President Lowery-Hart are "being watched by college leaders all over the U.S., because finding realistic solutions for student poverty could be transformative for the U.S. higher education system" (Bombardieri 2018).

In all likelihood, we do not work at an institution with a student support structure comparable to Amarillo College (although it certainly provides an aspirational model). However, as librarians, we *can* take deliberate steps to support transfer students in many ways including the following:

- By being sensitive to any indications that the student is having difficulty in school or at home and by making appropriate referrals to campus resources, such as the counseling center, the campus veteran's services office, the campus food pantry, or the financial aid office.

- By taking a page from the book of our colleagues in public libraries by helping students find resources on local, state, and/or federal support such as local food banks as well as the SNAP program website: https://www.fns.usda.gov/snap/student.

- By making proactive and appropriate campus referrals. Referrals often work best when we have a specific contact person in a department, so having, or building, collaborative relationships with personnel in student services, the writing center, the veteran's services office, and other departments will help us serve our students holistically.

- By proactively alleviating library anxiety.

- By reflecting diversity in library staffing, including staffing of student assistants, and by celebrating diversity in our collections, exhibits, and displays.

- To increase the comfort level of demographic groups reluctant to seek assistance (i.e., Asian and Asian American students, Latino males), consider giving student assistants who represent diverse populations more of a front facing role, at least on occasion. Granted, their work assignment may be in a nonpublic area, such as technical services or interlibrary loans; but for a portion of their work assignment, consider their potential as library ambassadors.

- By identifying the library staff members who speak other languages, perhaps by wearing a badge ("Wo shuo zhongwen" or "I speak Chinese") and/or listing these individuals on the library website to facilitate assistance for English as a second language students. Few gestures surpass making a person feel respected and welcomed more than a few words in their native tongue.

- By providing transfer-specific library orientations or information literacy sessions, a transfer-specific page on the library website, and/or a transfer-specific LibGuide.
- By beginning to scaffold our information literacy instruction, particularly if we are at an established feeder college, acknowledging that many of these same databases will be needed for their university research.
- By working collaboratively with the librarians at the established feeder colleges for our institution **or** by working collaboratively with the librarians at the four-year institutions our students primarily matriculate to.
- By promoting our study rooms as safe, neutral places to meet with group partners or to study solo without distraction.
- By fostering student connections with faculty as appropriate; for example, by encouraging students to take specific assignment-related questions to their faculty member.
- By engaging in institution-wide initiatives for transfer students.
- By working collaboratively with other campus partners to support transfer student success.
- By helping students to understand that using library resources effectively can actually save them time.

We can start with simple steps. The important thing is simply to start.

Real Life Scenario: Instruction

For years, one of the authors of this book, Peggy Nuhn, realized that students at a large feeder college often believed that Google or Google Scholar would meet all their academic research needs and, as a result, may not be fully engaged for the obligatory English Composition "library instruction class." Nuhn explains, "As a university librarian physically located at one of our larger DirectConnect partner colleges, I understood that my unique vantage point and position, which included teaching information literacy for the partner college students, allowed me to make an early connection to support future vertical transfer students. I also realized from previous research that students tend to overestimate their research abilities, which can make holding their attention for an instruction class more challenging. Therefore, I begin my information literacy classes by finding out more about the students and sharing a bit about myself. Asking for a show of hands, I would inquire how many of the students were combining school with employment, then ask whether it was full-time or part-time employment, or perhaps they were juggling multiple jobs. Consistently, most of the hands went up as full-time employees. I also asked about whether the students had family responsibilities of some sort or other, perhaps with their own children, or perhaps they have the responsibility for helping with younger siblings or for helping a grandparent with errands. Many of the same students again raised their hands. I never failed to be impressed by how much these students were taking on, and I acknowledged their busy lives, and thanked them for allowing us to be part of their journey. Lastly, I would inquire how many of the students planned to transfer to a university, perhaps through DirectConnect, or perhaps elsewhere. By this point, the students were fully engaged in the class, and this clear demonstration of just how much our students are taking on has never been lost on the classroom professor. At that point, I would share that I had obtained my B.S. as a full-time employee and part-time student; my Master's as a full-time employee, part-time student and by then a single parent. I would acknowledge that combining work, school and family is not the easiest path to a degree, but clearly it can be done, and from my experience, the best way to succeed in college while juggling multiple additional responsibilities is to learn time saving tools and take advantage of small snippets of time to work on assignments.

"I then framed my instruction on how to use library resources efficiently and make use of database features such as folders, permalinks and email, and acknowledge that many of the same databases the college uses, and more besides, would be some of the students' primary research tools upon transfer to the university. In other words, I hoped to instill that familiarity with database searching isn't a 'one off' just for their upcoming assignment; mastering it is worth the time investment. This was a small step into scaffolding for information literacy instruction to come. I also encouraged students to explore the databases outside the scope of their assignments, perhaps by looking up articles on any topics of personal interest such as music, fitness or health, to experiment with how keywords and Boolean operators worked on subjects familiar to them.

"In addition, I used real life scenarios for example, by suggesting that perhaps on the student's lunch break they might be able to use their work computer for personal reasons. If so, I showed them what they might do with 20 minutes of available time, demonstrating how to set up a search, review the abstract, and email three to five promising articles to read in-depth later. Another example was how one might work on an assignment while sitting in a doctor's or dentist's waiting room, such as reading through one of those emailed articles from their phone, rather than browsing an outdated magazine. I emphasized the importance of working ahead on assignments as often as possible because life happens. Laying the basic foundation for the 'Research is Inquiry' frame, I also acknowledged that research is a process, which unfolds over time; that the best research paper is not written the weekend before it is due; and that research is not a scavenger hunt for 'the perfect article' which summarizes all aspects of a topic. I also noted that some trial and error and perhaps a bit of frustration along the way is to be expected, however, over the course of a research assignment which is broken into manageable bits in chunks of time, the students will become more and more familiar with their topic as well as the keywords related to that topic. After allowing time for questions or time to repeat steps, I warmly encouraged the students to seek librarian assistance whenever they needed support in locating resources, and had my business cards available."

Real Life Scenario: Reference

Something to consider is whether we really listen to what students reveal to us in a reference consultation. Granted, we are often busy and may be understaffed. However, when we listen closely, we will find that often students will share a bit about their lives or challenges, academic and otherwise. Perhaps because librarians are generally not the faculty member who is grading their research paper, students may be more open with us. If so, at a minimum, we need to take the time to listen, to suggest available supports, and ask the student to circle back to us with how the suggested referral worked out.

For many years, the authors of this book worked at a single-service point information services desk (ISD) that combined circulation and reference. Between students asking for study room keys, headphones, and other items housed at the ISD, as well as circulation functions, it was a busy and frequently noisy place. A single-service point was, and still is, a trend and can work well; however at our location, invariably, the student needing in-depth reference assistance would be interrupted by a student asking for a pen or to use the stapler; then, once the student's train of thought was derailed, they would gather their books and say, "Oh, you're busy. It's okay." It was *not* okay. Finally, we requested permission to staff a research desk on the "Quiet Study" second floor of the library as a stand-alone research-service point. It was not an easy sell because the first-floor staff was accustomed to having librarians immediately at hand. However, from the new second floor research desk students needing reference assistance were not rushed, were not overheard, and were not interrupted. They relaxed. In that environment, true learning can occur. Clearly, our change supported student learning. After all, who wants to admit utter confusion over what an annotated bibliography entails in front of four other people? It was in this second-floor stand-alone service-point setting that the student who had been so reluctant to seek assistance realized just how much a librarian could help her succeed academically. Usage statistics support that the second-floor research desk fulfills a need and is now an accepted service point. (Reminder: Whatever your initiative is, never forget to collect data.)

We share these examples to demonstrate that some adjustments, such as acknowledging our students' busy lives can be easily incorporated into an instruction session, while other adjustments may call for persistence. We suggest that all library instruction, outreach, services, and policies require an examination in order to ensure we are supporting transfer students, and all students, by alleviating their stress to the extent we can at our respective campuses.

In summary, how do we holistically support transfer student success? By meeting students at their point of need, by ensuring they understand how to access library resources and connect with librarians, by honoring and respecting their academic and life experiences and struggles, by actively listening so that we may help facilitate their connection with additional campus or local/state/federal resources. We support them by building partnerships inside and outside our institutions and by being collaborative. We support them through our involvement in and support of student success initiatives on our respective campuses and by having a place at the table when *any* campus initiative connected to student success is the topic. We support their attainment of information literacy competencies so that they can succeed academically now, and later as employees and as our neighbors. We support them individually and one student at a time, not as "underprepared transfer students," but as individuals who are determined, often against great odds, to build a better life for themselves and their families.

We do this because libraries have an essential role in supporting transfer student success.

Practical Applications of Chapter 10

- Participate in—or initiate—a transfer-specific new student orientation.
- Offer a transfer-specific library tour or workshop early each semester, framed as "insider tips" to subtly acknowledge transfer students' previous academic experience.
- Consider how information literacy classes can best support adult learners: andragogy over pedagogy.
- Reflect the diversity of your campus through library exhibits, artwork, and collection development.
- Take a fresh look at library services and operating hours through the lens of working adults.
- Develop or build upon relationships between librarians at known feeder colleges and universities to explore whether some alignment of information literacy instruction is possible.
- Be proactive in making appropriate referrals; referrals work best when you know your colleagues in other departments.
- Consider how the library can be involved in supporting a campus food pantry initiative—or start one!

- Increase awareness of specific challenges among demographic groups, including a reluctance to seek help, and incorporate this knowledge into all interactions.
- Build or expand campus relationships to enhance referrals.
- Be proactive to be involved in campus initiatives to support student success.
- Support the students you have!

References

Aaronberg, Melissa. 2017. "A Cross Cultural Framework: Implications for Improving the Academic Library Experience for East Asian Students." *Endnotes: The Journal of the New Members Round Table* 8(1): 36–45.

Abney, Alicia. 2018. "The Complexities of Transfer Students." *EvoLLLution.* Accessed September 29, 2019. https://evolllution.com/attracting-students/accessibility/the-complexities-of-transfer-students/.

American Association of Community Colleges (AACC). 2020. "Fast Facts." Accessed September 4, 2019. https://www.aacc.nche.edu/research-trends/fast-facts/.

Andrade, Luis M. 2018. "Latina/o Transfer Students' Selective Integration and Spatial Awareness of University Spaces." *Journal of Hispanic Higher Education* 17(4): 347–74. doi:10.1177/1538192717701252.

Bombardieri, Marcella. 2018. "Colleges Are no Match for American Poverty." *Atlantic,* May 30, 2018. https://www.theatlantic.com/education/archive/2018/05/college-poor-students/560972/.

Brown, Sarah. 2019. "Nearly Half of Undergraduates Are Students of Color. But Black Students Lag Behind." *Chronicle of Higher Education*, February 14, 2019. https://www.chronicle.com/article/Nearly-Half-of-Undergraduates/245692.

Bumphus, Walter G. 2019. "Message from the President." AACC. Accessed September 25, 2019. https://www.aacc.nche.edu/about-us/message-from-president/.

Datig, Ilka. 2014. "What Is a Library? International College Students' Perceptions of Libraries." *Journal of Academic Librarianship* 40(3–4): 350–56. doi:10.1016/j.acalib.2014.05.001. https://www.sciencedirect.com/science/article/abs/pii/S0099133314000676.

Dillard, Robert J., and Helen H. Yu. 2016. "Best Practices in Student Veteran Education: Making a 'Veteran-Friendly' Institution." *Journal of Continuing Higher Education* 64(3): 181–86. doi:10.1080/07377363.2016.1229106.

Ellis, Martha M. 2012. "Successful Community College Transfer Students Speak Out." *Community College Journal of Research and Practice* 37(2): 73–84. doi:10.1080/10668920903304914.

Elteto, Sharon, Rose M. Jackson, and Adriene Lim. 2008. "Is the Library a 'Welcoming Space'? An Urban Academic Library and Diverse Student Experiences." *Portal: Libraries and the Academy* 8(3): 325–37. https://search .proquest.com/docview/216166877.

Engle, J., and Vincent Tinto. 2008. "Moving Beyond Access: College Success for Low-Income, First Generation Students." The Pell Institute. https://files .eric.ed.gov/fulltext/ED504448.pdf.

Fink, Jenni. 2019. "University of Kentucky Offering $1 Lunches after Students Go on Hunger Strike for Basic Needs." *Newsweek*. April 9, 2019. https:// www.newsweek.com/university-kentucky-lunches-students-hunger -strike-basic-needs-1391001.

Foster, Makiba, and Kris Helbling. 2015. "Is Your Library Serving Adult Learners?" *Library Journal* 140(11):18–19.

Harrick, Matthew, and Lee Ann Fullington. 2019. "'Don't Make Me Feel Dumb': Transfer Students, the Library and Acclimating to a New Campus." *Evidence Based Library and Information Practice* 14(3): 77–91. doi:10.18438/ eblip29512.

Hyatt, Sally E., and Douglas A. Smith. 2019. "Faculty Perceptions of Community College Transfer Students: The Private University Experience." *Community College Journal of Research and Practice*. doi:10.1080/10668926.2019.1 610673.

Jack, Anthony Abraham. 2019. *The Privileged Poor: How Elite Colleges Are Failing Disadvantaged Students* Cambridge, MA: Harvard University Press.

Jacobson, Trudi, John Delano, Linda Krzykowski, Laurie Garafola, Meghan Nyman, and Holly Barker-Flynn. 2017. "Transfer Student Analysis and Retention: A Collaborative Endeavor." *Reference Services Review* 45(3): 421–39. http://www.emeraldinsight.com/doi/abs/10.1108/RSR-10-2016-0069.

Kim, Suk-hee, James Canfield, Patricia Desrosiers, Dana Harley, and Vanessa Hunn. 2019. "Embracing Inclusive Excellence: Asian and Asian American College Students." *Journal of Human Behaviour in the Social Environment* 29(8): 1015–25. doi:10.1080/10911359.2019.1647907.

Lester, Jaime, Jeannie Brown Leonard, and David Mathias. 2013. "Transfer Student Engagement: Blurring of Social and Academic Engagement." *Community College Review* 41(3): 202–22. doi:10.1177/0091552113496141.

Lorinc, Jacob. 2016. "Four in Ten University Students Lack Food Security as Education Costs Skyrocket." *Macleans*, October 26, 2016. Accessed August 30, 2019. https://www.macleans.ca/education/four-in-ten-university-students -lack-food-security-as-education-costs-skyrocket/.

Ludovico, Carrie. 2017. "Seeing the World through Adult Eyes." *College & Research Libraries News* 78(5): 250. doi:10.5860/crln.78.5.250.

"Malcolm Shepherd Knowles." 2019. *Encyclopedia of World Biography Online*. Gale in Context: Biography. Accessed September 29, 2019.

Mangan, Katherine, and Julia Schmalz. 2019. "Food, Child Care, Rent: This College Goes the Extra Mile to Serve Low-Income Students." *Chronicle of*

Higher Education, April 3, 2019. Accessed September 25, 2019. https://www.chronicle.com/interactives/20190403-amarillo.

Mayhew, Matthew J., Christopher J. Stipeck, and Andrea J. Dorow. 2011. "The Effects of Orientation Programming on Learning Outcomes Related to Academic and Social Adjustment with Implications for Transfers and Students of Color." *Journal of the First-Year Experience & Students in Transition* 23(2): 53–73.

Mu, Cuiying. 2007. "Marketing Academic Library Resources and Information Services to International Students from Asia." *Reference Services Review* 35(4): 571–83. doi:10.1108/00907320710838390.

Park, Julie J., and Amanda Assalone. 2019. "Over 40%: Asian Americans and the Road(s) to Community Colleges." *Community College Review,* 47(3): 274–94. doi:10.1177/F0091552119852161.

Patel, Vimal. 2019. "In Kentucky, a Hunger Strike for Basic Support Forces a President's Hand." *Chronicle of Higher Education* April 3, 2019. https://www.chronicle.com/article/In-Kentucky-a-Hunger-Strike/246054.

Peña, Mauro Ivan, and Robert A. Rhoads. 2019. "The Role of Community College First-Year Experience Programs in Promoting Transfer among Latino Male Students." *Community College Journal of Research and Practice* 43(3): 186–200. doi:10.1080/10668926.2018.1453393.

Rosenzweig, James W., and Qing H. Meade. 2017. "Checking Out the Library: Partnering for Outreach to Short-Term International Students." *Journal of Library Administration* 57(4): 375–88. doi:10.1080/01930826.2017.1291180.

Shaw, Stacy T., and Christina S. Chin-Newman. 2017. " 'You can do it!' Social Support for Transfer Students during the Transition from Community College to a Four-Year University." *Journal of the First-Year Experience & Students in Transition* 29(2): 65–78.

Silverthorn, Drew. 2016. "Hungry for Knowledge: Assessing the Prevalence of Student Food Insecurity on Five Canadian Campuses." Toronto Meal Exchange. https://www.mealexchange.com/.

Sorensen, Alma Margaret. 2018. "Warrior Women: A Phenomenological Study of Female Veterans Transitioning into and through College." ERIC. https://files.eric.ed.gov/fulltext/ED588089.pdf.

State of Higher Education in California. 2015. Campaign for College Opportunity. https://collegecampaign.org/wp-content/uploads/2015/05/2015-State-of-Higher-Education_Blacks.pdf.

Stewart, Brenton, Boryung Ju, and Kaetrena Davis Kendrick. 2019. "Racial Climate and Inclusiveness in Academic Libraries: Perceptions of Welcomeness among Black College Students." *Library Quarterly* 89(1): 16–33. doi:10.1086/700661.

Udell, Emily. 2019. "Food for Thought: Academic Libraries Are Fighting Campus Food Insecurity with Onsite Pantries." *American Libraries,* May 2019. https://americanlibrariesmagazine.org/2019/05/01/library-campus-food-insecurity-food-for-thought/.

United States Department of Agriculture, Economic Research Service. 2019. "Definitions of Food Security." Accessed July 7, 2019. https://www.ers.usda.gov/topics/food-nutrition-assistance/food-security-in-the-us/definitions-of-food-security.aspx.

United States Government Accountability Office. 2019. "Food Insecurity: Better Information Could Help Eligible College Students Access Federal Food Assistance Benefits." https://www.gao.gov/products/GAO-19-95.

West, Kate. 2016. "Leading with Need-Blind: A Closer Look at Diversity Goals and Other Factors Driving Need-Blind Admissions and How Campus Administrators Are Making These Policies Work." *University Business* 19(7): 53–55.

Whang, Linda, Christine Tawatao, John Danneker, Jackie Belanger, Stephen Edward Weber, Linda Garcia, and Amelia Klaus. 2017. "Understanding the Transfer Student Experience Using Design Thinking." *Reference Services Review* 45(2): 298–313. doi:10.1108/RSR-10–2016–0073.

Zong, Jie, and Jeanne Batalova. 2018. "International Students in the United States." Migration Policy Institute. Accessed September 4, 2019. https://www.migrationpolicy.org/article/international-students-united-states.

Index

Academic engagement: "campus capital," 157–58; equates to social engagement, 157; faculty interactions, 157; library support of, 158–59; workshops, 159

Academic libraries, 3, 8, 10–11, 42, 44, 49–51, 51–55, 63–64, 76–80, 92–95, 103, 121, 156, 162; collaborative work, 42, 75; contributing to institutional mission, 10–11; i-School(s), 77–80; partner-collaborator, 103; perceived "welcomeness" of, 162; transfer students, 8, 48, 49–51, 51–55, 92–95, 121, 156. *See also* Food insecurity; Information literacy; Marketing to transfer students; Niche library initiatives; Online library tools; Partnership(s); Textbooks

Access, accessibility, 8–9, 17, 20, 44, 49, 57, 105, 107–13, 117, 125–27, 132, 134, 136, 137, 139, 156, 161, 163, 172; codes, textbooks, 132, 136, 137; libraries as champions for, 134, 137; to library resources, 8–9, 44, 57, 105, 107–13, 117, 125–27, 156, 172; to post-secondary education, 17, 20, 49, 161. *See also* Open Educational Resources (OER); Textbooks, print reserves

ACRL (Association of College and Research Libraries). *See Framework for Information Literacy for Higher Education* (ACRL); *Information Literacy Competency Standards for Higher Education* (ACRL)

Administration, 2, 10–11, 76, 79, 100, 102, 128, 141, 144; collaboration, 76; impact on retention, 10–11; information literacy integration, 78–79; as stakeholder, 100, 102, 128, 141, 144; transfer experience, 2

Adult Education Theory (andragogy), 159–61

Amarillo College, 151, 167–68; "no excuses," 167–68

American Association of Community Colleges (AACC) (1972), 5, 19, 20, 155, 159, 161; history, 19, 20; student demographics, 155, 159, 161; student enrollment status and employment, 5

American Association of Junior Colleges (1920), 19

Articulation agreements: benefits, 24; defined, 21–22; elements of, 22–23; Florida College System "2+2," 21; Florida University System, 92; UCF "DirectConnect™," 50, 91. *See also* Institutional agreements

Assessment, 34–35, 65–66, 67, 68, 69, 70, 71, 72–73, 78, 80, 81–82, 84, 85, 86, 87, 92–94, 136, 140; assessment project (Nuhn and Kaufmann), 92–94; as "barrier breaker," 68–73; collaboration with discipline faculty, 65–66, 87; *Framework*-based lesson plan, 72–73; informed learning design, 69–70; OER and, 136, 140; real-world, 69; sample online assessment, 70–71; scaffolding and, 81–82; self-referenced *vs.* norm-referenced, 34–45; student learning outcomes, 68; threshold concepts, 68–69, 86; using ACRL *Framework*, 68–69, 84

Associate in Arts (AA) degree, 6, 20–21, 92; retroactive awarding of, 6; "statewide guarantee of transfer," 21–22

Barrier(s), 3, 5, 49, 58, 63–64, 64, 85–87, 100, 106, 107, 109, 113, 121, 144; collaboration to remove, 63–64; leading to "transfer shock," 49, 58; libraries strategic to eliminating, 3, 121; supporting online students, 107, 109, 113; textbook costs as, 144; using information literacy to overcome, 63–64, 64; using transition theory to overcome, 85–87, 106; work-school balance, 5. *See also* "Barrier Breakers"

"Barrier Breakers": assessment, 68–73; building collaborative partnerships, 74–77; information literacy, 65–66; i-Schools training for diversity and inclusion, 77–80; teaching collaborations, 67–68

Bookstore, campus, 132, 135, 137–38, 142, 144; bundled course materials, 132, 137–38; contract, 142; faculty note to students when e-textbook is available, 135; as library partner, 144

Bounded (threshold concept), 45–46, 57

"Celebration of Librarian Collaboration for Transfer Student Success" event, 51, 98–101, 124

Chat reference. *See* Online library tools

Collaboration(s), 8, 10, 18, 22, 24, 33, 34, 35, 36, 38, 42, 48–49, 51, 53–55, 63, 65–66, 67–68, 74, 75, 76, 77, 85–87, 91, 92–96, 103, 109–10, 112, 115, 116, 122, 124, 126–27, 128, 135, 137, 139, 141, 139, 140, 144, 159, 168; faculty, 65–66, 112, 122, 126–27, 135, 137, 139, 141; "feeder" colleges and universities, 8, 24, 33–35, 36, 48–51, 53–55, 91, 92–96, 103, 128; institutional departments, 10, 22, 33, 34, 38, 42, 48–49, 55, 91, 109–10, 115, 116, 124, 137, 139, 141, 159, 168; institutions, 128; junior college resulting from, 18; librarian colleagues, 24, 38, 51, 63; social innovation, 75; successful collaborations, elements of, 74–77; teaching, 66, 67–68, 85–87; textbook affordability initiatives, 140, 144. *See also* "Celebration of Librarian Collaboration for Transfer Student Success" event; Partnership(s)

College Board Advocacy and Policy Center, 7

Communication(s), 8, 11, 31, 32, 33, 38, 49, 50, 51, 65, 75, 83, 91, 92, 98,

100, 106, 107, 108, 112, 113, 115, 116, 123, 127, 137, 140, 158, 170; between two- and four-year institution librarians, 32, 33, 49, 50, 51, 91, 92, 98, 100; clear communication in marketing, 83; email, 11, 38, 106, 117, 123, 158, 170; faculty, 48, 65, 112, 137, 140; gentle and helpful, 52, 158; newsletter(s), 31, 106, 117; online communication, 113, 116, 127; phone, 107, 115, 116–17, 127, 170; relationship with collaboration, 8, 75, 98; touchpoints, 116–17. *See also* Online library tools

Community College Research Center (CCRC), 5, 15

Community colleges, 2, 4–5, 6, 7–8, 15, 16, 17, 18, 19, 21, 29, 30, 32, 33, 34, 35, 36, 49, 85, 135, 140, 155, 156, 159, 158, 159, 161, 162, 164–65, 167; enrollment, 155; historical overview, 18–19; institutional agreements, 15, 21; instructional differences, 29–30, 32, 34, 85; in transition, 17–18; library, 32; reverse transfer partnerships, 6, 49; student demographics, 5, 159, 161, 162, 164–65; tuition cost compared to university, 2; underprepared perception, 158; vertical transfer, 4–5, 7–8, 15–16, 29–30, 135. *See also* Amarillo College; American Association of Community Colleges (AACC) (1972); Articulation agreements; Assessment, self-referenced *vs.* norm-referenced; Associate in Arts (AA) degree

"Credit When It's Due" (CWID) initiative, 6

Critical thinking, 30, 45, 47, 72–73, 81, 96–97, 110, 117, 163, 166; "fake news," 110, 117; student difficulties with, 163, 166; transfer student challenges, 30

Design thinking, 54–55

DirectConnect™, 50, 91–92, 94–95, 96, 124, 169–70; enhanced articulation agreement, 50, 91–92; survey of partner college librarians, 94–95, 124; teaching future transfer students as partner librarian, 169–70. *See also* "Celebration of Librarian Collaboration for Transfer Student Success" event; Partnership(s)

Disciplines, 42, 44–46, 56–57, 63, 66–69, 73–74, 81, 84–87, 96–98, 112–13, 127; metacognition, 44–46; real-world applications, 112–13, 127; threshold concepts, 84–87, 96–98

Distance learners, 106–8

Diversity, equity, inclusion, 77–80, 105, 107, 114–16

"Don't Make Me Feel Dumb": Transfer Students, the Library and Acclimating to a New Campus, 64, 121, 156, 158

Double-dipping transfer, 4, 7

Dual-enrollment (dual credit) transfer, 4, 8, 20, 34, 36, 160

Ecosystem (ecology), 75–76, 110, 128

Education Commission of the States (ECS), 21–22, 24

"Fake News" highlighting critical thinking, 110–11, 117, 122

First Time in College (FTIC), 9, 37

First Year Experience (FYE), 9, 55, 165

Florida College System, 21. *See also* Articulation agreements; Community colleges; DirectConnect™

Florida University System, 10, 92. *See also* Articulation agreements; DirectConnect™

Food insecurity, 152–55; campus food pantries, 153–54; campus food services closures, 153; Canadian universities, 153; food insecurity defined, 152; hunger strike, University of Kentucky, 153; Supplemental Nutrition Assistance Program (SNAP), 152; Warren, Senator Elizabeth, SNAP expansion legislation, 154

Four Ss of transition, 106; 4S model, 41, 54–56, 106. *See also* Transition model

Framework for Information Literacy for Higher Education (ACRL), xv, 44, 45–48, 55, 65, 66, 67, 68, 69, 71, 72, 73, 78, 84, 86, 93–95, 110–11; alignment survey, feeder colleges and university, 93–95; assessment strategies, 68–69, 73; collaboration with discipline faculty, 65–66, 86; *Framework*-based lesson plan, 72–73; *Framework* non-linear, 44; i-School application of, 78; mitigating information literacy "transfer shock," 55, 95; perception challenges, 67–68; threshold concepts, 45–48, 65, 67–69, 72–73, 84, 86; as tool to discern "Fake News," 110–11

Harper, William Rainey, 18–19

Higher education, 1–3, 10, 17, 18, 19, 34, 41, 42, 43, 44, 49, 50, 51, 52, 53, 54, 55, 65, 122, 126, 127, 128, 136–37, 162, 164, 166; graduation and retention, 10; information literacy in, 43–44, 52, 65; institutional transitions, 17–19, 34; Open Educational Resources (OER), 136–37; partnerships, institutional, 49, 126–28; student populations, 162, 164, 166; transfer students, 1–3, 49–51, 52, 122,

127–28; transition model applied to, 41–43, 49, 52–55. *See also* Amarillo College; Collaboration(s); Community colleges; Partnership(s); Performance-based funding; Textbooks, affordability

Holistic approach, 46–47, 54, 69, 72–73, 83, 103, 114; connecting students, 54; incorporating information literacy, 72–73, 83; threshold concepts, 46–47, 69. *See also* Holistic support of transfer students

Holistic support of transfer students, 103, 151, 155, 156, 157, 158, 159, 160, 161, 162, 163, 164, 164, 165, 166, 167, 168; adult students, 159–61; Amarillo College (Texas), 167–68; Asian American students, 161–62; Black students, 162–63; deliberate strategy of support, 155–59; demographics, 159; international students, 163–64; Latina/o students, 164–66; "no excuses," 167–68; student veterans, 166–67. *See also* Food insecurity

Housing, student, 3, 37, 133

Human element, 20, 113–16

Hunger. *See* Food insecurity

Information literacy, 42–43, 44, 45, 46, 47, 48, 51–56, 58, 64–66, 68, 95, 96–99; barriers, 65–66; "five keys to mitigate information literacy transfer shock," 55, 58, 95; *Framework*, 44–47; LIS course, 68; liminality, 45; metacognition, 44; real-world relevance, 55–56; relevance, 96–99; scaffold, 44; scope, 44; tacit knowledge, 42–43; threshold concepts, 45, 47–48; use intention, 44; user experiences, 51–55. *See also* Teaching information literacy

Information Literacy Competency Standards for Higher Education (ACRL), 44, 73

Informed learning, 66, 69–71, 83, 113

Institutional agreements, 15, 23, 92

Instruction and Outreach for Transfer Students: A Colorado Case Study, 8, 32–33, 35–36, 52–54, 77

International students, 106–7, 163–64, 175–76

iSchool(s), 43, 50–51, 68, 77–80, 85, 87, 126; degrees, 43, 50–51, 78–79; Hirsh, Sandy, 68; iSchool curricula, 85, 87

Jack Kent Cooke Foundation, 7, 20

Jacks, Anthony Abraham, 154

Kaufmann, Karen F., 45, 69–70, 96, 98, 126

Knowledge base or knowledge assets, 27, 42–43, 46, 56–57, 66, 81, 85, 96–97, 108

Knowles, Malcolm Shepherd, 160

Learning Management Systems (LMS). *See* Technology

LibGuide(s), 12, 58, 102–3, 106–8, 110, 112, 115, 116–17, 142, 154, 169; event LibGuide, 102–3; textbook affordability LibGuide, 142; transfer student LibGuides, 106–8, 110, 112, 116–17, 169

Librarianship, 30, 52, 78, 80, 84, 113, 128, 161; credit-bearing LIS course, 30, 84, 161; embedded, 113

Liminality, 45, 69, 81, 96, 98

Lowery-Hart, Russell. *See* Amarillo College

Marketing to transfer students, 55, 58, 78, 80–84, 86, 87, 116–17, 125–28; Niche marketing, 125–28; strategies, 87, 116–17

Metacognition, 44–45, 47, 48, 66, 69, 71, 73, 86, 96, 98, 113; defined, 44–45; using *Framework*, 48, 69, 73

Multidisciplinary, 47

National Institute for the Study of Transfer Students, 1

National Student Clearinghouse Research Center, 15

Niche library initiatives, 121, 123–24, 125, 126, 127, 128; boutique personal librarian, 123–24; building transfer student identity in library, 125–26; institutional relationships, 127–28; marketing library to transfer students, 125; pathways to degrees, 126–27; pathways to workplace, 126; transfer services librarian, 124

Niche marketing, 125–28

Northeast Florida Library Network (NEFLIN), 92, 95, 103

Online learners, 106–8, 113, 115–16

Online library tools, 34, 44, 82, 86, 94, 107, 108, 109, 110–11, 112, 115, 116, 117, 127; chat, 94, 108, 115–16, 127; tutorials, 34, 82, 86, 107–8, 111, 115; video, 82, 112, 116, 127; Zoom, 107–8, 117

Open Educational Resources (OER), 135, 136, 137, 138, 139, 140, 141, 148; adoption for introductory courses, 137–38; challenges, 140; "Level 1," 135, 137; "Level 2," 135, 139; OER resources, defined, 136; Open Stax, 137

Organizational theory, 49

Orientations, 9, 12, 23, 32–33, 37, 82, 84, 86, 127, 155, 156, 169; easy handout item, 12; librarian presence at transfer orientations, 33; transfer specific, campus, 155–56; transfer specific, library, 32–33, 37, 82, 84, 86, 127, 156, 169

Partnership(s), 6, 10, 21, 38, 49–51, 55, 57, 58, 63, 66, 67, 68–70, 73, 74–77, 83, 84, 85, 86, 87, 91–92, 94, 98, 100, 103, 106, 110, 112, 121, 122, 124, 126, 127–28, 137, 141, 143, 144, 147, 148, 153, 158, 159, 163, 169, 172; collaborative partnership(s), 55, 74–77, 85, 86, 87, 98, 121; college and university librarians, 10, 49–51, 58, 98, 100, 101, 122; food pantry, 153; institutional partnership, 21, 57, 58, 91–92, 94, 103, 124, 127–28, 172; librarians and discipline faculty, 63, 66, 67, 73, 83, 110, 112, 126; librarians and institutional departments, 10, 38, 84, 106, 121, 127–28, 143, 158, 159, 163, 169, 172; Open Stax Institutional Partner Program, 137, 147; reverse transfer, 6; role of assessment in, 68–70, 73; textbook affordability partnerships, 141, 143, 144, 147, 148. *See also* "Celebration of Librarian Collaboration for Transfer Student Success" event; DirectConnect™
Pathway(s). *See* Transfer student pathways
Pedagogy, 47–48, 73, 81, 93, 160, 172; using *Framework*, 47–48, 73
Performance-based funding, 10, 132, 141
Persistence, student, 11, 16, 17, 20, 23, 34, 76, 126, 137, 155, 171; academic and social engagement, 16–17, 20, 23, 34; impact of negative experience, 23; and retention, student and institutional views (Tinto), 17
Poverty, student, 133, 168
Privileged Poor: How Elite Colleges Are Failing Disadvantaged Students, The, 154

Real World scenarios, 11, 139, 143, 144, 145–46, 169, 171; info lit instruction for future transfers/adult learners, 169; Northwestern University and ILL textbook requests, 145–46; reference, 171; reluctant student, 11; Robert Morris University and textbook reserves, 143; University of Central Florida, OER through collaboration, 139; University of Connecticut and ILL textbook requests, 144
Retention, student, 10–11, 16–17, 23, 49, 56, 98, 126, 137, 141, 143, 155, 158, 166; relationship between retention and persistence, 16–17, 23, 155; relationship to performance-based metrics, 10, 141; role of library, 10–11, 56, 98, 126, 137, 143, 158; transfer receptive culture and, 49; veterans, 166

Satisfactory Academic Progress. *See* Student financial assistance, U.S. Deptartment of Education
Scaffolding, 30, 45, 48, 67–68, 81–83, 85, 96, 170; information literacy instruction, 45, 67–68, 81–83, 87; threshold concepts, 81
Schlossberg, Nancy K., 41–43, 52, 56, 106, 111–12. *See also* Four Ss of Transition; Transition model; Transition theory (Schlossberg)
Social engagement: "emotional and practical support,"157; role of family and colleagues, 156
Staines, Gail M., 29–30, 32, 33–34
Stakeholders, 73, 75–76, 101–2, 128, 141–43, 147–48, 154
Student engagement, 17, 20, 34, 155, 156, 157, 158, 159. *See also* Academic engagement; Social engagement

Student financial assistance, U.S. Department of Education, 2–3, 10, 22, 132, 152, 155; Pell Grant, 132, 152, 155; "Satisfactory Academic Progress," impact on transfer, 2–3

Student retention and persistence, 16–17, 23, 126, 137

Supplemental Nutrition Assistance Program (SNAP). *See* Food insecurity

Surveys, 31, 52, 71, 94, 153

Syllabi/syllabus. *See* Teaching information literacy

Tacit knowledge, 42, 44, 46, 57, 73

Tag, Sylvia, 30–32, 33–34

Tau Sigma, 157

Teaching information literacy, 33, 64, 65, 66, 67, 69, 70, 72–73, 80, 81, 82, 83, 106, 112, 140, 169–71; acknowledging work-school balance, 169–71; active learning, 33, 66, 72–73; faculty, 65; holistic, 83; ILFF (Information Literacy Faculty Fellows), 65; informed learning, 66, 69–70; scaffold, 67, 81–83; scope, 67; syllabus/syllabi, 65, 67, 106, 112, 140; transdisciplinary, 65; transparent, 80–81

Technology, 72, 105, 106, 107, 109–10, 111, 112, 113, 117, 136, 137, 138, 141; Learning Management System (LMS), 112, 113, 117, 136, 138, 141; library, 107, 109; library website, 72, 106, 109–10, 111, 112; OER, 137, 138; single sign-on, 109, 113, 117. *See also* Chat reference; Communication(s), phone

Textbooks, 8, 11, 131, 132, 133–34, 135, 136, 136, 137, 144; affordability, 131–36; bundled with access codes, 132, 137; hierarchy of student educational expenses, **134**; interlibrary loan for, 144; print reserves, 8, 11, 135–36, 144; textbook market advantages, 132. *See also* Open Educational Resources (OER)

Threshold concepts, 45–46, 57, 65, 68–73, 81, 84–86

Townsend, Barbara, 29–30, 68

Transdisciplinary, 42–43, 46, 47, 48, 57, 59, 65, 93, 126; explanation and applications, 42–43, 46; faculty collaboration and, 65, 93; *Framework* and, 48

Transfer fog, 156

"Transfer shock," 9, 27, 28, 34–35, 38, 49, 52, 52–55, 56, 57, 58, 63, 80, 93–95, 122, 135, 163, 166; compared to fever, 28; defined, 9, 27, 38; international students, 163; mitigate, 49, 55, 58, 56, 63, 80, 93–95; self-referenced *vs.* norm-referenced contributing to, 34–35; student veterans, 166; textbook costs and, 135; "transfer shock" or "culture shock," 28, 163, 166; transfer students and the library, 52–55; transfer students and transition theory, 56, 58, 63, 122

Transfer student challenges, 2, 3, 5, 8, 9, 10, 16, 20, 22, 28, 34, 36, 37, 48, 52, 53, 132, 151, 152, 158, 172; credits, 2, 3, 22; fees and deposits, 2; finances, 3, 5, 8, 10, 16, 20, 132, 151; housing, 2, 3, 37, 152; identity, 9, 28; institutional culture, 37; lack of data, 36; lack of social network, 8, 9, 28; outreach, 36, 48; "underprepared," 9, 34, 52, 53, 158, 172. *See also* Articulation agreements; Community colleges; Institutional agreements; Textbooks, affordability; "Transfer shock"; Work-school balance

Transfer student librarian(s), 116, 124.
  See also Niche library initiatives
Transfer student pathways, 4, 5, 6, 7,
  8, 15, 16, 20, 21–22, 23, 36, 43,
  135, 161; double-dipping, 4, 7; dual
  enrolled, 4, 8, 20, 34, 36, 160;
  lateral, 4, 5–6; reverse, 4, 6, 21–22,
  23, 161; swirling, 4, 6; transient, 4,
  7; vertical, 4–5, 7–8, 15–16, 135.
  See also Community colleges
Transformative (threshold concept),
  45–47, 57, 66, 113, 115, 127, 168
Transient transfer students, 7
Transition, 17, 18, 30, 34, 36, 40,
  41–43; community colleges in,
  17–18; instructional goals and
  transition, 30
Transition model, 41, 42, 43, 52, 53,
  54, 55, 56, 57, 58, 63, 64–66,
  74–80, 84, 85, 86, 87, 125–26; 4S
  model, 41, 54–56; self, 41–42,
  52–58, 63, 84–87; situation, 41–42,
  52–56, 64–66, 85, 87; strategies,
  41–42; support, 41, 63, 74–80,
  85–87
Transition theory (Schlossberg),
  42–43, 53–54, 63–64, 74, 107, 122
Troublesome (threshold concept), 46,
  57, 144

Vaughan, George, 18
Virtual transfer students, 1, 5,
  105–6, 119

Website(s), library. *See* Technology
Wood, James M., 19
Work-school balance, 5, 169, 170–71
Workshop(s), 10, 65, 98, 106, 158,
  167, 172; connecting students with
  faculty, 158; faculty and staff
  education on military life, 167;
  transfer specific, 172

Zoom. *See* Online library tools

About the Authors

Peggy L. Nuhn is a "UCF Connect" associate faculty librarian at the University of Central Florida's Sanford/Lake Mary campus, a joint campus with Seminole State College of Florida, where she teaches information literacy for both university and college students, which gives her a unique perspective on content and scope of instruction for these two student populations. Nuhn is a graduate of the Sunshine State Library Leadership Institute, has served on the Board of the Florida Library Association (FLA), and has presented on student information literacy and the importance of librarian collaboration for transfer student success at statewide and national conferences. Nuhn's experience in higher education includes administration of student financial assistance programs. She holds a BS in business management from Franklin University (Ohio) and an MLIS from the University of South Florida. She is a member of FLA, the American Library Association (ALA), and the Association of College & Research Libraries (ACRL).

Karen F. Kaufmann is currently a research and instruction faculty librarian at Seminole State College of Florida. Kaufmann has also served as the postdoctoral research assistant for the Gateway PhD Program School of Information, San José State University. Her research interests include information literacy, information fluency, user relevance, and user information experience. Kaufmann holds a PhD in information science from the Queensland University of Technology and an MLIS from the University of South Florida. Kaufmann is an author and presenter at various conferences and workshops and was a Beta Phi Mu International Library and Information Studies Honor Society recipient of the 2017 Eugene Garfield Doctoral Dissertation Fellowship. She is a member of ASIST, ALA, and ACRL. Kaufmann has served on the Florida Statewide Curriculum Committee and on the Association of College & Research Libraries/Education and Behavioral Sciences Section Online Learning Research Committee (ACRL/EBSS).